THE DAILY DOMINATOR

PERFORM YOUR BEST TODAY, EVERY DAY!

This book is being given to

Cameron High

because I care about you and your success

You've been an incredible friend and I look forward to the years to come!

From, Brock

BRIAN M. CAIN, MS, CMAA

Brian Cain Peak Performance, LLC

What Champions Are Saying About Brian Cain & *The Daily Dominator:*

"Brian Cain has 'IT' - the ability to reduce a lot of important information into manageable 'sound bites.' He provides coaches and athletes with a 'toolbox' of mental/emotional skills to help them perform in competition."

Tom House, PhD
Former Major League Baseball Pitcher
Former Major League Baseball Pitching Coach

"This book is the foundation of our mental conditioning program. Cain keeps simplifying the process and making it easier to train the six inches between the ears that control the six feet below. This book is a must-have for any coach or athlete."

Vann Stuedeman
Head Softball Coach
Mississippi State University

"The Daily Dominator is AWESOME! I read a page a day as part of my routine when I get to the field. I have worked with Cain since my freshman year of college. Every day I read one page and it reinforces his teachings that have helped me to make it to Major League Baseball and play one pitch at a time."

Matt Carpenter
St. Louis Cardinals
Former TCU Horned Frog Baseball Player

"The Daily Dominator is drawn from the simple truth that action speaks louder than words and by doing a little a lot you will far outperform those who do a lot a little. By investing into yourself your green assassin you will win the battle one day at a time."

Mike Bianco
Head Baseball Coach
The University of Mississippi
2009 Southeastern Conference Champions

"Doing a little a lot, not a lot a little, is one of the keys to long-term success. Brian Cain has put a mental conditioning program together in The Daily Dominator that allows you to train your brain one day at a time and build real mental toughness."

Tom Brands
Head Wrestling Coach
The University of Iowa
NCAA National Champions '08, '09, '10
National Wrestling Hall of Fame
1996 Olympic Gold Medalist
Freestyle Wrestling 136.5lbs
4 x NCAA All-American
3 x NCAA National Champion

"What a great follow-up to The Mental Conditioning Manual. This book is an essential part of my training program for each fight."

Vitor Belfort
Former UFC Light Heavyweight Champion
UFC 12 Heavyweight Tournament Winner

"The higher you go in competition the more the mental game becomes important. Training mental toughness is about more than just working hard; you must work smart and understand the process of what it takes to be mentally tough. Cain provides that system for coaches better than anyone else."

Kevin Ozee
Athletic Director
Southlake Carroll, Texas
2011 Texas 5A Football State Champions
2013 National Athletic Director of The Year

"The Daily Dominator is an essential part of our players pre-practice routine."

Kevin Sneddon
Head Men's Ice Hockey Coach
The University of Vermont
2009 NCAA Frozen Four

"You become what you do on a daily basis and Cain has put together the book that will keep you accelerating on your path to excellence."

Andy Shay
Head Men's Lacrosse Coach
Yale University
2012 & 2013 Ivy League Champions

"This book is a critical part of our player development process and playing the game one play at a time. Playing the game one play at a time starts with reading one page a day with Cain."

Dan Nolan
Head Football Coach
Lyndon Institute

If *The Daily Dominator* has had a positive impact on you and you would like to have a testimonial featured in future editions, please e-mail us at **Testimonials@BrianCain.com**.

Please share how *The Daily Dominator* has had a positive impact on you, your game and your life. We look forward to working with you to become a master of the mental game and helping you to DOMINATE The Day.

Brian Cain
Peak Performance Expert
Mental Conditioning Coach
Brian Cain Peak Performance, LLC
Making Masters of the Mental Game

Brian M. Cain, MS, CMAA

THE DAILY DOMINATOR

PERFORM YOUR BEST TODAY, EVERY DAY!

MASTERS OF THE MENTAL GAME SERIES BOOK

BRIAN M. CAIN, MS, CMAA

Brian Cain Peak Performance, LLC

Brian M. Cain, MS, CMAA
Peak Performance Expert
Mental Conditioning Coach
Peak Performance Publishing
Brian Cain Peak Performance, LLC

The Daily Dominator:
Perform Your Best Today, Every Day!

A Masters of the Mental Game Series Book

Printed in the United States of America
Edited by: Mary Lou Schueler
Cover design & book layout: Nu-Image Design
Illustrations: Nicole Ludwig, Noah Stokes and Greg Pajala
Photography: Don Whipple and Paul Lamontangue

Brian M. Cain, MS, CMAA
The Daily Dominator:
Perform Your Best Today, Every Day!

A Masters of the Mental Game Series Book

Library of Congress Control Number: 2013910440
ISBN: 978-0-9830379-8-9

PREFACE

The Daily Dominator: Perform Your Best Today, Every Day! is a proven system for developing mental toughness and giving you the tools needed to consistently perform at your best when it means the most.

This is the fifth book in the Masters of the Mental Game Series. This book is to be read one day at a time and should live in a place that can easily be part of your daily routine. It may live on your desk, in your bathroom on the back of your toilet, in your locker, in your car, or anywhere that you will be able to use it every day.

This is more than just a book to be read. It is designed to help you create the daily routines and processes you need to start living the life of your dreams and to perform at your best today and every day.

The material in the book covers a wide variety of topics necessary to your pursuit of excellence. You are encouraged to share what you learn with others and to create a team of peak performers looking to Dominate The Day. Commitment to excellence and daily domination is a lifestyle, not an event.

Here's to your domination of the day today and every day! Compete in the moment and live in the big picture.

DEDICATION

This book is dedicated to the individual who is in the arena competing and battling one day at a time. To the performers who know they have another level of performance and are looking for the slight edge to get there. To those uncommon people committed to excellence and their personal best.

By signing your name below you are dedicating yourself to reading this book one page a day and to implementing its teachings in your life.

I ____________________________________ (print your name) have been given everything I need to Dominate The Day. I am fully capable of living the life of my dreams and leaving this world a better, more excellent place by going all out, giving everything I have and performing at my best today, every day!

I am devoting myself to the pursuit of excellence, and realize that this journey has no finish line. I am committed to working on myself first and being the best competitor and teammate I can be every day.

I am committing to the creation of a positive legacy. I realize that the legacy I leave will be defined by what I do today, because it is the sum of my todays that constitutes my career and my life.

I realize that my legacy will be further defined by the relationships I develop and how I treat my teammates in life. Thus, I am hereby committed to improving the relationships in my life and my greater community by improving myself.

Every day, I will wake up and make the inspired commitment to improve myself and to take steps closer to my dreams in an attempt to become the person I desire to be.

I realize that each day I will not be as excellent as I want to be and not as excellent as I am going to be, but I will work every day to make progress and to be more excellent than I was the day before.

I hereby sign my name below to certify my commitment to the pursuit of excellence!

____

Your Name Date

ACKNOWLEDGMENTS

It is with sincere and deep appreciation that I acknowledge the support and guidance of the following person who helped make this book possible.

Special thanks to YOU! Without you, this book is nothing more than paper bound together.

Without YOU, this system and my life's teachings die inside of me.

Without YOU, the world will not become a better place.

Without YOU, the teachings contained on these pages will stay on these pages.

I acknowledge you and your commitment to excellence and personal development, and I thank you in advance for teaching these skills to those whom you love and to those who are under your leadership.

YOU are a difference maker and YOU are responsible for working on yourself on a daily basis and performing at your best today, every day.

Thank you for inspiring me to be the best I can be.

BrianCain.com/daily
For BONUS Mental Conditioning Material
& FREE Peak Performance Training Tools.

FOREWORD

This is a book about excellence in performance and excellence in life. If you have this book in your hands, it is my goal that it will become an essential part of your daily routine that you use every day for the rest of your life. A book that gets dominated by YOU!

In my research on success and excellence and in my personal experience in working with some of the most successful performers on the planet, I have found that they all do things a little differently, but they also do a lot of the very same things on a daily basis.

The best performers I have been around in sports, business, school and life all have positive daily habits and routines. Part of their daily routine is to work on themselves every day. They invest into themselves and their personal development a little a lot, not a lot a little. They understand that self-development toward excellence is a daily process and a journey that has no finish line.

In this book I share with you the tips and tactics I teach to the NCAA National Champions, Olympic Medalists, MMA World Champions and top-performing corporate warriors I have been blessed to work with. By implementing what you read on a daily basis you will be creating excellent habits which will yield excellent performance.

Go out and DOMINATE the world one day at a time. Don't count the days - make the days count, TODAY!

CONTENTS

AUTHOR'S NOTE

The intent of the author in writing this book in the Masters of the Mental Game Series was to create a comprehensive daily reader so that you could easily build mental conditioning into your daily training program and routine. Peak performance and personal excellence are achieved by doing a little a lot, not a lot a little, and by establishing sound daily routines and habits.

I hope this book causes you to question the ways that you think and act and takes you on the journey of self-discovery by searching within yourself to see what you are capable of as a performer. When you search within yourself, you learn that all the answers to life's questions and challenges live inside of you. As you work your way through this book, be sure to read with a pencil so that you can answer the questions in the text.

The photo on the next page has lived with me since I first saw it in 2002, and it illustratively captures one's ability to search within oneself. My life's mission is to help you uncover the excellence that lies within you and to coach you so that you can coach yourself to perform at your best when it means the most - today, every day!

The photos contained in this book are to help you visually learn and remember the lesson being taught.

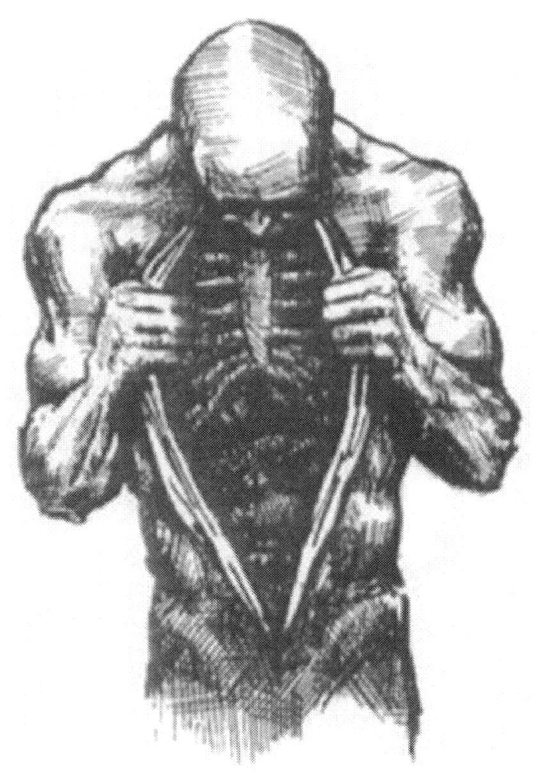

TAKE A LOOK INSIDE OF YOURSELF TO FIND THE ANSWER TO LIFE'S QUESTIONS

INTRODUCTION

The destination is the disease, but the journey is the reward. I know from personal experience and from working with some of the most successful performers on the planet that end-result thinking is a trap. The process, the day-to-day grind, and what you do on a daily basis are really the keys that unlock your performance potential.

In *The Mental Conditioning Manual: Your Blueprint For Excellence* I outlined the Peak Performance System of PRIDE (Personal Responsibility In Daily Excellence) that I teach to my students.

In *Toilets, Bricks, Fish Hooks and PRIDE: The Peak Performance Toolbox EXPOSED;* in *So What, Next Pitch! How To Play Your Best When It Means The Most;* and in *Inexpensive Experience: Champions Tell All*, you learned from many of those students how they applied the system to help them perform at their best on a consistent basis.

The Daily Dominator: Perform Your Best Today, Every Day! contains content previously mentioned in those books and new content that has positive life-changing potential when implemented. Each day has a message and a mission for you to think about and then, more importantly, to act upon.

You are the most valuable asset you own. Make an investment in yourself today, one page at a time.

JANUARY

January is the month for me to dominate...

JANUARY 1

THE CHOICE

Og Mandino, author of *The Choice,* says: *"Happiness has nothing to do with getting. It consists of being satisfied with what I've got and what I haven't got. Few things are necessary to make the wise man happy while no amount of material wealth would satisfy a fool."*

A common mistake is to search outside for success and for happiness. Success and happiness are unique states that depend on each individual. What makes one happy may make another miserable.

British Author James Allen says: *"Man is made or unmade by himself; he holds the key to every situation."*

You have the keys to unlock all doors that are keeping you in and keeping you out. You must simply search inside yourself for the right key to unlock your potential, success and happiness.

JANUARY 2

YOU MUST SEE THE TARGET YOU WANT TO HIT

Moving from goal setting to goal getting is about locking in on your target and shrinking your focus. One of the best archers in the world was Ryan Cameron.

Cameron could split Life Savers® from 50 yards away and then split the first arrow with his second shot. However, if we were to blindfold and point Cameron in the opposite direction of the target, you would come closer to hitting the bull's-eye than he could, even with all of his years of training and preparation.

You would come closer to hitting the bull's-eye because you could see it and Cameron could not. In order to hit your target, you must be clear on what you want to accomplish. If you aren't crystal clear on your goals, you may find yourself hiking up the wrong mountain.

What do you want to accomplish? Starting spot, 4.0 GPA 2.5 ERA, 90 MPH off Mound..

LOCK ON THE TARGET YOU WANT TO HIT
LOCK OFF THE TARGETS YOU DON'T

JANUARY 3

RELEASE YOUR MENTAL BRICKS

Ultimate Fighting Championship superstar Georges St. Pierre was knocked out by Matt Serra in his first title defense at *UFC 69 Shootout*.

Nobody gave Serra a chance in the fight. He was an 11-1 underdog – but that night, April 7, 2007, Serra proved that the best fighter never wins; instead, it is always the guy who fights the best.

That night he fought better than Georges. Since that night, Georges has used that loss, which was the worst thing that ever happened to him, as a springboard to success. He turned the worst thing that had ever happened to him into the best thing that ever happened to him.

When I first met Georges, he was carrying this loss like a brick. If you carry a brick for only a minute, it does not feel that heavy. When you carry the same brick for a long time, it becomes very heavy, weighs you down, exhausts you, zaps you of your strength, and keeps you from making progress and moving forward.

That brick is an analogy for a mental brick. A mental brick is something that has happened to you that you do not forgive yourself for, do not accept and do not learn from - thus it weighs you down and keeps you from moving forward towards the next level.

What are some of the mental bricks you are carrying? ____

No playing time at TC, cheating
____

____

What was the worst thing that ever happened to you that you turned into the best thing?

Turned no playing time to motivation for
____

all aspects of life, turned to God more
____

What is the physical release you use to help you release the mental brick?

The day to day workouts.
____

____

JANUARY 4

FLUSH IT

Adversity is a necessary part of life. Beating yourself up and having stinking thinking (negative self-talk) is not.

When something does not go your way and you recognize yourself carrying a mental brick, you must have a release routine that you can turn to that will help you "Flush" the negativity.

Dr. Ken Ravizza is the top applied sport psychology teacher in the country, a professor at Cal State Fullerton, and my mental conditioning mentor. Dr. Ravizza used to put a flushing toilet bank in the dugouts and locker rooms of the teams he worked with to serve as a visual reminder for the coaches and athletes to "flush" the previous play and move on to the next play.

What can you do to release your negative energy and to flush it? literally imagine it flushing

JANUARY 5

McDONALD's THEORY

Do you think you can make a hamburger as good or better than McDonald's can? If so, why do they make billions in burger sales and you don't?

One reason is that they took massive action and are actually selling burgers. They also advertise so that when you think of a burger you think of the golden arches.

McDonald's Theory is a theory that suggests you should advertise the mentality you want to yourself each and every day, and that by advertising with what I call "Signs of Success" you can create the mindset of a champion.

As we take a journey to excellence together in this book, please stop and take the time to hang up signs of success around your home or office so that you can start to create the mentality you desire, the mentality of the successful.

ADVERTISE THE MINDSET YOU WANT

JANUARY 6

SIGNS OF SUCCESS

Jim Schlossnagle is the head baseball coach at Texas Christian University (TCU) and one of the top college coaches in the country. Schlossnagle led TCU to the 2010 NCAA College World Series and will serve as the TEAM USA Collegiate National Team Head Coach in 2013.

No stranger to success, he has won the conference championship every year from 2004-2012. He is a Master of the Mental Game and utilizes the signs of success around his baseball complex and dugout to help advertise the mentality he wants in his players.

He knows that repetition is the mother of all skill acquisition and that we become what we routinely think about and surround ourselves with.

One sign that he hangs up in his team's dugout says "So What!"

In baseball and in life, adversity will hit. The sooner you can say "So What!" and move on, the better you will compete in the present moment.

What are signs of success that you will hang to help advertise the mindset you want?

So What!
Release The Mental Brick
Flush It
Hit The Target

Please write your signs of success below.

____

____

JANUARY 7

SO WHAT, NEXT _____

Gary Gilmore is the head baseball coach at Coastal Carolina. He has set a standard of success at Coastal by winning 12 conference championships since taking over the program in 1996.

Gilmore hangs a sign in his dugout that encourages his players to get over their failure and success on the last pitch and focus on playing the next one.

He also uses a toilet in the dugout to help his players "Flush" the adversity that is built into baseball and life.

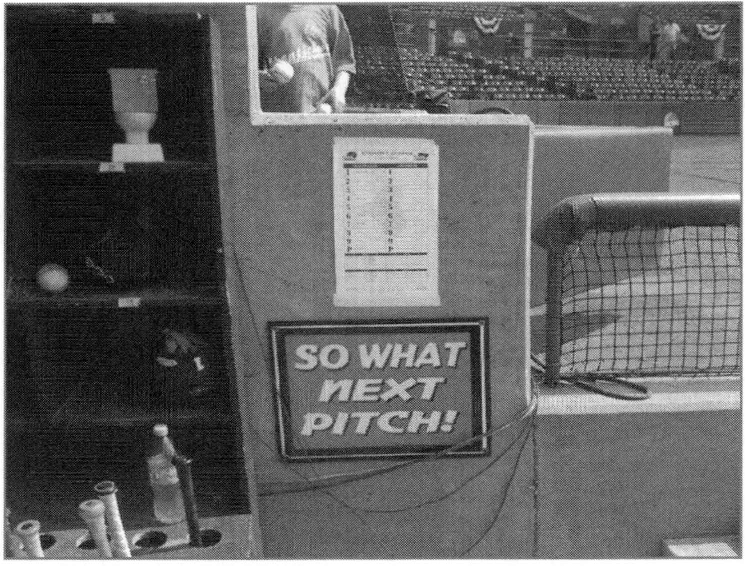

JANUARY 8

THE NEXT 200 FEET

Living in the present moment by focusing all of your time, energy and attention on the process of here and now is essential to success. A great way to reinforce the present moment and the process is to think about focusing on the next 200 feet.

You can drive anywhere you want in the country in complete darkness because your headlights let you see the next 200 feet. By focusing on the next 200 feet, you keep your mind focused on the present and what you can do today to give yourself the best chance for success.

Tina Deese, head softball coach at Auburn University, hung a sign of success in her dugout to remind her team.

The University of Mississippi baseball team and coach Mike Bianco believe in the 200-feet mentality so much that they had it inscribed on their 2009 Southeastern Conference Championship rings. Their rings were designed and provided by Jostens Ring Company.

What will your championship ring for this year say on it?_

THE NEXT
200 FEET

Mississippi
REGIONAL CHAMPIONS
NCAA
44-20
JOHNSON
200 FT
8
Ole Miss
SEC

JANUARY 9

THE MOUNTAIN OF EXCELLENCE

Throughout this book I will refer to our journey together up The Mountain of Excellence. Our journey is to be taken one step at a time. There are essential aspects of performance that you must master to give yourself the best chance to reach the pinnacle of success. It is my mission to teach you these concepts and strategies of success through *The Daily Dominator* and that you will put them into action on a daily basis.

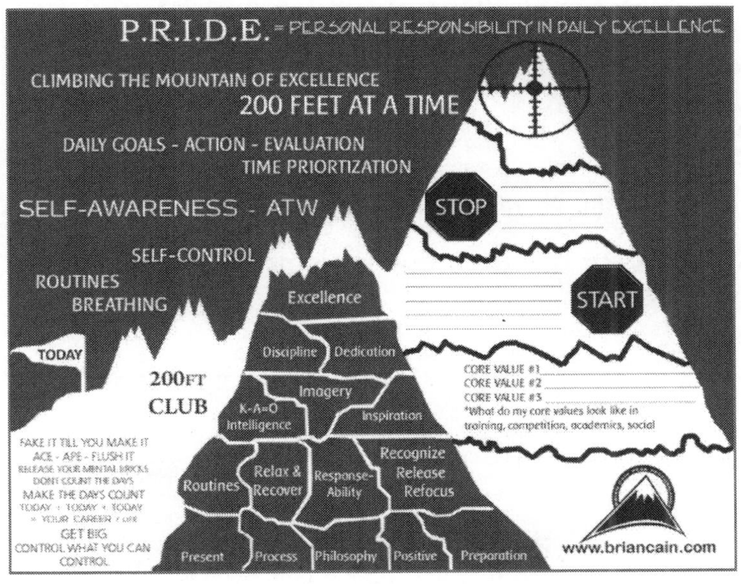

EXCELLENCE IS A LIFESTYLE, NOT AN EVENT

JANUARY 10

LIVE IN THE PRESENT

The time is now, the place is here.

Yesterday is history, tomorrow's a mystery, today is a gift and that is why we call it the present. Yesterday is a canceled check, tomorrow is a promissory note, today is cash - invest it wisely.

Living in the present moment means that you don't count the days, but you make the days count. You are someone that can turn your phone off, then sit face to face and have a conversation while listening and not letting your mind wander to what you need to do after your conversation is over.

Your challenge for today is to be more present in your interactions with others and to start turning your phone off for periods of time during the day when you need to be present.

At practice, at home, in the office, when will you turn your phone off and be present? ______________________________

____

____

THE PRESENT IS A GIFT
DON'T COUNT THE DAYS,
MAKE THE DAYS COUNT

JANUARY 11

DOMINATE THE DAY!

To Dominate The Day, one must be fully present in that day and not stuck with one foot in the past or one in the future while going to the bathroom on the present.

Dominating The Day is about getting totally immersed in what you do and the people you are with as if nothing else matters.

What will you do today to demonstrate a commitment to the present moment?

____

____

____

____

At the end of the day, or tomorrow, come back and write about how you did with accomplishing your goal above.

____

____

____

____

____

____

JANUARY 12

PICK UP PENNIES - DISCIPLINE WINS

My grandfather and I were walking to Space Mountain at Disney World when he stopped and asked if I had seen the penny on the ground that I just stepped over.

I had seen it but was fired up to attack Space Mountain and did not want to waste the time to pick up the penny.

He stopped me dead in my tracks, asked for 30 seconds of totally undivided attention and told me that picking up pennies would make me rich.

I told him that I could spend my whole life picking up pennies and never become rich like a millionaire.

Then, what he said changed my life - the eureka moment that helped paved my path to success.

He said that picking up the monetary value of the penny was not what would make me rich; rather, it was the habit of picking up the penny, the habit of doing what others don't have the time to do, are too busy to do, just don't want to do or don't think is important enough to do.

Next time you see a penny on the ground, discipline yourself to pick it up.

Be reminded that success is about doing what others are not willing to do and is a result of the daily commitment to doing the little things, to picking up the pennies.

What is an example of picking up pennies for you right now? What is the thing that you must do that others are not willing to do?

Constantly improving my health and
always learning and improving myself.

DO WHAT OTHERS ARE NOT WILLING TO DO
PICK UP PENNIES
DEVELOP CHAMIONSHIP HABITS
ON A DAILY BASIS

JANUARY 13

INVEST, NEVER SPEND TIME

Investing time is the opposite of spending time. If you spend money, it is gone; if you invest money, you will get a return on that investment.

If you feel yourself on the rat wheel of life, running in circles and never getting anywhere, it may be your lack of investment into what you are doing. Moving from spending to investing will provide you with the presence necessary to perform at your best today.

JANUARY 14

PROCESS OVER OUTCOME

Focusing on the process over the outcome contains two important factors to lock in on.

1. You must control what you can control and let go of what you cannot control.
2. Focus 80% of your time on today and the steps you must take to arrive at your goal and just 20% on the outcome of where it is you want to be.

What must you let go of in order to gain control today?

____

____

What traps do you fall into that take your focus off of the process and daily domination?

____

____

JANUARY 15

CONTROL WHAT YOU CAN CONTROL

Controlling what you can control and letting go of what you can't is an essential part of success. Take the time to identify what you can control and what you cannot.

CAN'T CONTROL (Red Lights)

1. Officials, umpires, judges
2. Coaches and coaches' decisions
3. Fans
4. Media
5. What others say and think about me
6. Weather, field conditions
7. Politics of the team
8. Scouts, drafts, postseason teams
9. Winning, losing, the outcome
10. Batting average and earned-run average
11. Injuries
12. Parents and their actions
13. The other team
14. How your teammates play
15. ____________________
16. ____________________
17. ____________________
18. ____________________
19. ____________________
20. ____________________

CAN CONTROL (Green Lights)

1. Myself
2. My attitude
3. My appearance, body language
4. My perspective
5. My presence and focus
6. My performance, how I play
7. My process, how I go about my business
8. My preparation
9. My effort, energy, emotions
10. ______________________________
11. ______________________________
12. ______________________________
13. ______________________________
14. ______________________________
15. ______________________________

An easy way to remember what you can control is to think of the acronym APE – Attitude, Perspective, Effort. By focusing on what you can control and letting go of what you cannot, you are increasing your chance for success by locking in on the factors of your performance where you have the most influence.

JANUARY 16

THE STAIRCASE TO SUCCESS

Think about the process as a staircase in which you must go only one step at a time. With the process, you must know what staircase you are climbing and what your outcome goal is. Then you must get immersed in the process of doing all you can today to help you get to where you want to go.

The national championship takes care of itself if you take care of practice today. If you get better today at practice, performance this weekend will take care of itself. Remember, you cannot get to step D without taking steps, A, B and C.

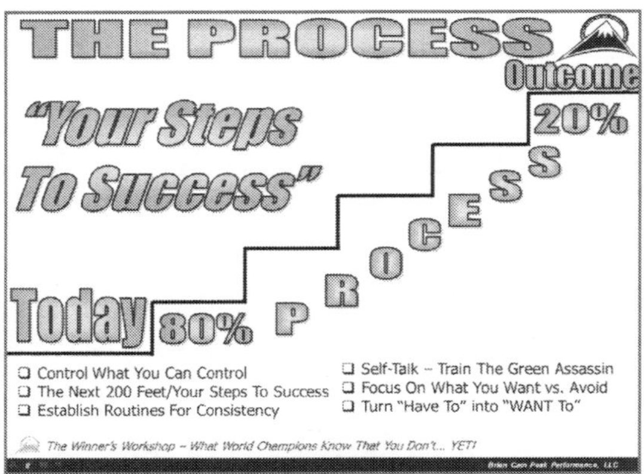

What steps will you take today to get to where you want to be at the top of your staircase?

____

____

JANUARY 17

CONCENTRATION GRIDS: YOUR PROCESS TO THE PRESENT

Concentration grids have long been used in the field of mental conditioning to help performers better understand that they can train their ability to focus on the present moment. The concentration grid is a tool that you can use as a part of your process for developing a present-moment focus.

You are to start a stopwatch and cross off the number 00 and go in succession till you cross off the number 99. What you will experience is that your mind will wander from the present moment and the next number. When that happens, simply bring your focus back to the next number. Resist the urge to judge yourself and don't waste time beating yourself up or getting frustrated, which only slows your progress.

Brian Cain Peak Performance, LLC
Concentration Training Grid - Hit F9 For A New Grid
96 Pinnacle View, Richmond, VT 05477
(802) 999-1096 - brian@briancain.com - www.briancain.com

39	48	59	28	71	26	34	70	95	06
21	91	42	12	30	84	76	97	61	75
58	08	85	32	45	66	36	63	23	29
96	80	00	88	89	11	25	57	02	90
74	33	56	93	52	73	04	10	49	19
87	09	16	81	69	38	64	50	83	41
31	01	40	47	18	77	24	14	13	60
79	72	05	51	82	55	15	17	44	94
54	35	53	68	65	20	03	99	86	27
67	46	07	78	22	92	37	62	98	43

Go to BrianCain.com/grids
For more about concentration grids.

JANUARY 18

STAYING POSITIVE

Developing a positive mentality is one of the simplest yet overlooked aspects of performance enhancement. To be positive means that you:

1. Focus on what you want, not what you are trying to avoid.

2. Turn all of your "Have To's" into "Want To's."

Positive people are energy givers and focus on what they can do, not on what they can't do.

We all have an internal voice that speaks to us in performance. It either speaks positively about what we can do or negatively about why we can't do it.

I refer to this battle royal in your mind as the fight between your mental assassins. The green assassin works for you while the red assassin works against you.

Which of your two assassins do you listen to?

What are some "Have To's" that you are consciously going to turn into "Want To's" today and this week?

____

____

____

JANUARY 19

THE MENTAL ASSASSINS

The battle between your green and red assassins happens all day every day. Mental toughness is one's ability to train the green assassin so that it always wins the battle against the red assassin.

The green assassin tells you what you want to do; it tells you that you can do it and how to do it. The green assassin is your best friend in performance while the red assassin is your toughest opponent.

When you beat yourself in performance it can often be traced back to your inability to recognize your negative attitude, your negative self-talk and your self-defeating beliefs about your chances for success.

The whole goal of mental conditioning is to help you not beat yourself, to get you trained so that your thinking leads to a positive and productive mindset in which you perform your best when it means the most - every single day.

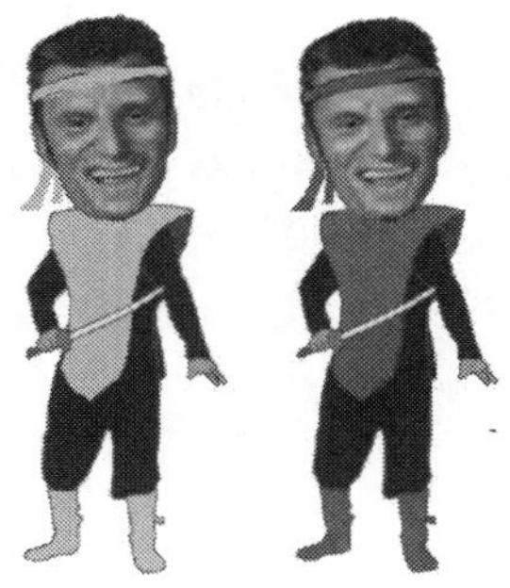

ARE YOU TRAINING YOUR GREEN (+) OR RED (-) MENTAL ASSASSIN?

JANUARY 20

TRAINING YOUR GREEN ASSASSIN

To train your green assassin you must create a list of reasons why you believe in yourself and your chances to perform at your best, resulting in your greatest chance for the desired outcome.

As you look back at the last 10 years of your life, you have had many small wins that you have just swept under the rug as you focused on the next thing. Remember when you first learned to ride a bike? You did not celebrate that you just ditched the training wheels; you focused on going further and faster.

When you graduated from college, did you celebrate that feat and do you still to this day take confidence from that accomplishment, or did you quickly shift your focus to getting that first job?

In that job, if you ever received a promotion, how long did you take confidence from that promotion before you started letting the red assassin show up and win the battle in your mind because you did not feel competent in the new position?

Please write down as many wins as you can remember. No win is too small. Nobody else needs to see this list; it is for your eyes only. Each item that you list is like lifting weights for your mental game and your confidence.

MY LIST OF WINS: ______________________________

____

____

____

____

____

____

____

____

____

____

____

____

____

____

____

____

____

____

CELEBRATE YOUR SUCCESS

JANUARY 21

THE THREE P's OF PEAK PERFORMANCE

The three P's of peak performance are to live in the Present, focus on the Process and stay Positive.

In my live seminars and work with teams I often break the mental conditioning system down into the acronym 4RIP3. If a picture is worth a thousand words, an acronym is worth a thousand pictures in that it has stickiness and is easily remembered.

As you work with the three P's of peak performance, understand that there is overlap and you should think of the three P's as a Venn Diagram in which concepts, strategies and systems are intertwined and not linear.

The performer who takes a deep breath to help get these into the present moment is correct, as is the person who says the deep breath is a part of their process.

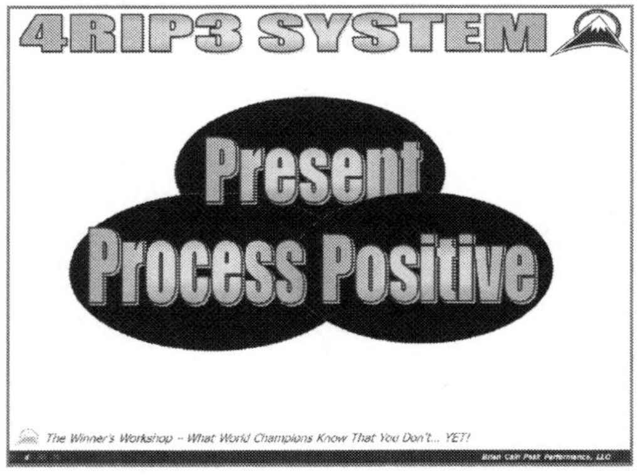

PRESENT – PROCESS – POSITIVE

JANUARY 22

THE FOUR R's OF PEAK PERFORMANCE

There are four essential R's in peak performance that make up the 4RIP3 System.

1. Have performance Routines to keep you consistent.

2. Recognize your signal lights.

3. Release your red assassin and mental bricks.

4. Refocus on the next play, the next pitch and on WIN... What's Important Now.

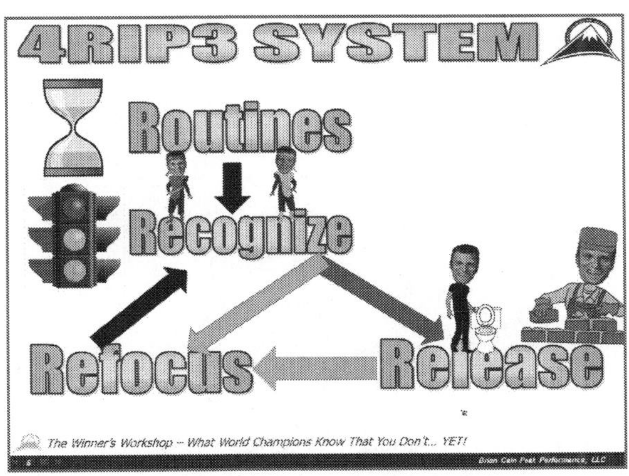

ROUTINES - RECOGNIZE - RELEASE - REFOCUS

JANUARY 23

ROUTINES ARE THE FOUNDATION OF CONSISTENT PERFORMANCE

Routines help you to be consistent in performance. Having a routine that you go through to transition from student to athlete or from coach to parent is necessary in that the routine helps you to create the mindset that you need for success.

The image we use for routines is that of an hourglass. Like the hourglass shape depicts, the routine has a funneling into the performance and then a funneling out.

What is an area of your life where you can build a routine that will help you to be more consistent?

____

____

____

CREATE ROUTINES FOR CONSISTENCY

JANUARY 24

CHANGE YOUR CLOTHES, CHANGE YOUR MENTALITY

Of all the mental conditioning principles I teach, I think having a routine in which you change your clothes and change your mentality is one of the most important.

Just like Clark Kent went into the phone booth as a super nerd and came out as Superman, you want to have a routine in which you change your clothes and put yourself into a mental state of wearing the clothes that get you ready for success.

Putting on your suit to start the day, changing from your street clothes into your practice uniform or simply putting on a whistle are all examples of routines that help you get into the present and a powerful performance mentality.

WHAT IS YOUR PERFORMANCE UNIFORM?

JANUARY 25

RECOGNIZE YOUR INTERNAL TRAFFIC LIGHT

We all have an internal traffic light that tells us whether we should go, slow down, speed up or stop.

Just like driving a car, green means go. If you have green lights, you keep going. Green lights are a powerful positive in the present and are process based.

A yellow light means you are starting to lose it and either need to slow down or pick up your pace and push the accelerator.

A red light means you are out of control physically, emotionally and/or mentally and are beating yourself. If you come to a red light, you better stop or you will crash and burn. If you drive through a red light, you might live to tell about it - but if you make it a habit, you are sure to get killed in competition.

LEARN TO RECOGNIZE YOUR SIGNAL LIGHTS

JANUARY 26

RECOGNIZING YOUR TRAFFIC LIGHTS

Recognizing your traffic lights takes awareness. What you are aware of you can control, but what you are unaware of will control you.

Awareness is the first step to accomplishment. In order to better recognize your signal lights, you must first become aware of how you experience them.

I ask the champions I work with to identify their signal lights in three ways as a starting point to help them learn to recognize their lights.

1. MENTAL: What do you say to yourself when you are in green, yellow and red lights?

____

____

2. PHYSICAL: How do you feel physically when you are in green, yellow and red lights?

____

____

3. SITUATIONAL: What situations in performance trigger green, yellow and red lights for you?

____

JANUARY 27

AWARENESS OF YOUR GREEN LIGHTS

Please answer the following questions below to help develop a better understanding of your green-light mentality and to become more aware of how you experience green lights.

1. MENTAL: What do you say to yourself when you are in green lights?

____

____

____

2. PHYSICAL: How do you feel physically when you are in green lights?

____

____

____

3. SITUATIONAL: What situations in performance trigger green lights for you?

____

____

____

GREEN MEANS GO!
ROUTINES HELP YOU GET GREEN

JANUARY 28

AWARENESS OF YOUR YELLOW LIGHTS

Please answer the following questions below to help develop a better understanding of your yellow-light mentality and to become more aware of how you experience yellow lights.

1. MENTAL: What do you say to yourself when you are in yellow lights?

____

____

____

2. PHYSICAL: How do you feel physically when you are in yellow lights?

____

____

____

3. SITUATIONAL: What situations in performance trigger yellow lights for you?

____

____

____

YELLOW MEANS CHECK IN AND EITHER SLOW DOWN OR SPEED UP!

JANUARY 29

AWARENESS OF YOUR RED LIGHTS

Please answer the following questions below to help develop a better understanding of your red-light mentality and to become more aware of how you experience red lights.

1. MENTAL: What do you say to yourself when you are in red lights?

____

____

____

2. PHYSICAL: How do you feel physically when you are in red lights?

____

____

____

3. SITUATIONAL: What situations in performance trigger red lights for you?

____

____

____

**RED MEANS STOP!
IF YOU PLAY IN RED LIGHTS,
YOU WILL BEAT YOURSELF**

JANUARY 30

PRAYER, PRIMAL, PERFECT

Ken Ravizza discusses the concept of the signal light and the prayer, primal and perfect mentality in his book *Heads-Up Baseball.*

When you get into red lights and start to lose it, champions I work with often can feel themselves becoming either a prayer, primal or perfect competitor.

The prayer players just hope that they get a pitch to hit or hope that they have success.

The primal player takes the caveman approach and tries to do everything HARDER. When you try to do things HARDER, you end up creating tension - and tension is the enemy of peak performance. Try HARDER, lose faster.

The perfect players try to be just that. PERFECT. They try for the perfect pass or the perfect pitch; trying to be perfect is a recipe for disaster.

When you get into red lights, what percentage of the time do you go prayer, primal and perfect?

Prayer___ %, Primal___ %, Perfect___ %

JANUARY 31

UNDERSTANDING 4RIP3

At this point, you should be aware of the 4RIP3 system and have started to notice when you are in the present moment or are stuck in the past or the future.

You should be more aware of when you are trying to control aspects of performance and life that you cannot control and should better recognize when you are living with "Have To's" or "Want To's."

You should have some specific routines and should start recognizing when you are listening to the green or red assassin. If you are listening to the red assassin, you should have some releases you can use to flush him away and bring back the green assassin.

The I of the 4RIP3 system is Mental Imagery. Mental Imagery is another critical piece of the performance pie that you have used without even knowing it

YOU HAVE DONE A LOT OF THIS SYSTEM WITHOUT EVEN KNOWING IT
THE THREE P's OF PEAK PERFORMANCE

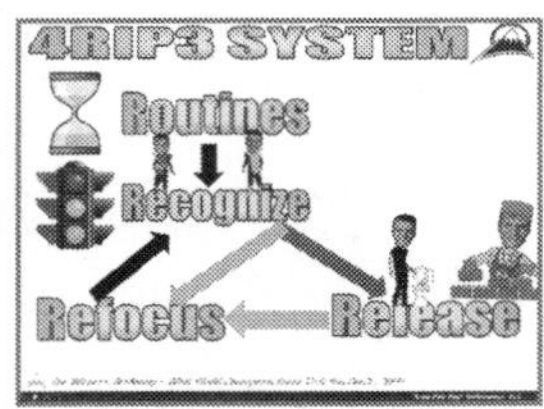

THE FOUR R's OF PEAK PERFORMANCE

FEBRUARY

February is the month for me to dominate...

FEBRUARY 1

MENTAL IMAGERY

The Blue Angels, the United States Navy Fighter Pilots, fly in amazing aerial shows where they pull off maneuvers that take your breath away and show the attention to detail and precision that it takes to be at the highest level.

What you don't see is how they prepare. They will spend about two times as much time briefing and then again debriefing about the show as it actually takes for them to fly the show.

One of the ways they prepare is through mental imagery. Each pilot is given an aerial photograph of the land they will be flying over and they will visualize or get a mental image of themselves flying the show in their minds before they ever go out to fly it with their bodies.

Mental imagery is an effective preparation tool because the brain does not know the difference between what is mentally imagined and what is physically real. The brain processes both sets of information with the same psych-neuromuscular pathways, essentially lubricating your brain and your body's ability to communicate and execute what you want to do in performance.

If you have ever awakened from a scary dream, or that dream where you are falling out of an airplane and you jump out of bed when you hit the ground, you have experienced the physiological (body) response to a psychological (mental) stimulus.

All of the athletes I work with will have a custom mental imagery training track on their iPhones so that they can perform a mental imagery session before going to play or as part of their daily/weekly mental preparation routine.

There are 4 steps to effective mental imagery:

1. Relaxation (5-4-3-2-1 Body scan)

2. Confidence conditioning

3. Mental recall – recalling a previous performance success

4. Mental rehearsal – imagining yourself performing in the future as it is in the present moment.

THE BLUE ANGELS: EXCELLENCE IN ACTION

FEBRUARY 2

GLAD TO BE HERE

The Blue Angels have a statement that they all say when they finish speaking in a debrief after a flight, "Glad to be here."

The Blues say "glad to be here" as a way to remind themselves of the importance of an attitude of gratitude and the importance of appreciating what you have been blessed with.

To whom much is given, much is expected. The Blues are representative of all of the Navy pilots who are executing missions overseas so that the Blues can fly entertaining shows for people to s

The Blues represent the rest of the force in the Navy and the rest of the force in the Navy represents them. The strength of the wolf is in the pack and the strength of the pack is in the wolf.

REPRESENT YOUR TEAMMATES WITH YOUR COMMITMENT TO EXCELLENCE. THE STRENGTH IS IN THE PACK!

FEBRUARY 3

MEMORIZE ANYTHING YOU WANT

Being able to memorize stories, poems, an oral presentation or a grocery list is possible for anyone. You are not born with a good or bad memory; you either have a trained or an untrained memory.

One of the simplest memory techniques is called The Skeleton File System and contains three important aspects:

1. Location
2. Picture
3. Meaning

The brain works in pictures, so by creating a system of organization (location) and creating a picture that has meaning, you can tell your story and memorize anything by going through your Skeleton File System.

In your Skeleton File System you have 10 locations:

1. Top of your head
2. Nose
3. Mouth
4. Ribs
5. Abs
6. Hips
7. Knees
8. Shins
9. Feet
10. Ground

You are to place a picture with meaning on each of those locations to help you tell your story. If you were to tell your team about your mental toughness training system 4RIP3, you could do it by seeing the following images in the locations listed below.

1. Top of your head – Large present

2. Nose – PRO athlete running stairs (Process)

3. Mouth – Remote control (Control what you can control)

4. Ribs – Green + sign tattoo (Positive)

5. Abs – Highlight video (Mental Imagery)

6. Hips – Hourglass (Routine)

7. Knees – Traffic light and car WRECK (Recognize)

8. Shins – Red toilet, "Flush It" (Release)

9. Feet – Green tattoo that says Refocus or Next Play

10. Ground – Dominoes that you are standing on (DOMINATE The Day)

By making your pictures vivid, wild and crazy, you can simply go through your 10 locations and memorize your story.

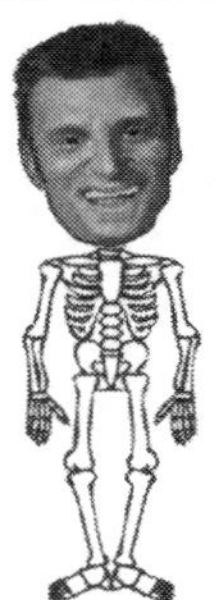

YOU EITHER HAVE A TRAINED OR UNTRAINED MEMORY

FEBRUARY 4

MASTER YOUR SKELETON FILE SYSTEM

Yesterday you read about a simple-to-use memory technique called The Skeleton File System. Your goal for today is to use your Skeleton File System to remember the 4RIP3 System and to teach the 4RIP3 System to someone else.

Please write below your 10 locations and the pictures that create the meaning you want to share in the 10 locations.

1. ______________________________
2. ______________________________
3. ______________________________
4. ______________________________
5. ______________________________
6. ______________________________
7. ______________________________
8. ______________________________
9. ______________________________
10. ______________________________

IF YOU DON'T USE IT, YOU LOSE IT!

FEBRUARY 5

MAKING CHANGE IS MAKING PROGRESS

We cannot become who we want to be by simply staying who we are. We must evolve and we must change. Not just be willing to change, but be working to change.

Do you focus on improving your circumstances or yourself? I believe that looking externally at your circumstances and thinking that if they change you will change is an untrue process - we cannot control the external. Focus on changing yourself and your circumstances will change.

What are some areas that you are working to change to help improve your life and improve your circumstances?

____

____

____

____

____

____

____

____

____

____

FEBRUARY 6

FIVE TIPS ON HOW TO NETWORK

Regardless of your field of endeavor, networking and connecting with others are essential to your growth. It does matter who you know and it does matter what you know. Here are five tips on how to network.

1. **Say something unexpected:**
When someone asks, "What do you do?" be prepared to say something that shows the results you get vs. the standard of what you do. Making your first response something unexpected will often give the conversation momentum and have the other party intrigued to ask for more information.

2. **Have good hand & eye coordination:**
A firm handshake is an important part of a first impression and networking. Lose the fist bump, hug and fraternity brother style handshake that you give to your closest friends. Instead, go with the web-to-web, firm yet gentle squeeze while administering one downward shake that travels about 1 inch.

3. **Be positive:**
A sure way to turn off the person who you are meeting for the first time is to come in with negative energy. Instead of complaining about the traffic or the GPS that got you lost, come in with positive energy and presence.

4. **Ask questions:**
The sooner you can turn the conversation from yourself to them the better. People genuinely like talking about themselves as they are most familiar with that topic. Think TAT - Talk About Them.

5. Tee up the conversation for the future:

You are not trying to close a sale or a deal in the first interaction with someone. You are simply trying to set up another time in the future to talk.

6. Follow up:

Be sure that you follow up on your leads and new contacts. Some people prefer to follow up on LinkedIn or via the handwritten message. Whatever your preferred method, be sure that you follow up and say where you met within 48 hours of your meeting or you are less likely to follow up at all.

TEE UP THE CONVERSATION FOR THE FUTURE

FEBRUARY 7

SYSTEMS & ROUTINES

To be consistent over time, you must be able to describe what you do as a process or a system. A system is a set of actions that you repeat on a consistent basis to get the results you want. You may refer to your process and your system as your routine.

The most successful coaches and athletes I have been around have routines embedded throughout their lives. They have routines for when they wake up in the morning, for when they go to bed at night and throughout their day. They have systems and routines for how they leave a phone message, for how they deal with the hard copy and e-mail they receive, and routines for what times and what food they eat throughout the day.

What is one area in your life where more routine would give you more consistent performance?

FEBRUARY 8

SECRETS OF SUCCESS & ROUTINES

The secrets of success are hidden in the routines of our daily lives. Routines are the foundation for consistency.

At one point in my life, I was about 40lbs over my desired weight. I felt terrible physically and was very inconsistent in my lifestyle that I had no chance to function consistently at my best.

What propelled me to get into a routine was when a good friend said this to me: "Brian, you look terrible physically. How can you work with people at being their best when you physically look your worst?"

His brutal honesty was exactly what I needed. I became a creature of routine and ate the same thing at the same time every day, worked out at the same time every day, went to sleep and woke up at the same time every day - and in about one year I had lost the 35lbs I was looking to lose.

It is the start that stops most people. Whatever your goal - lose weight, gain weight, read more, spend more time with loved ones - the path to your success is paved with routine. Start creating more routines in your life and see how much more consistent you feel and how consistently you live and perform. Routines create habits, and the habits you keep will determine your success and failure in life.

START TO CREATE HOURGLASSES/ROUTINES FOR YOUR LIFE

FEBRUARY 9

THE HABIT POEM

I am your constant companion,
I am your greatest helper or heaviest burden.
I will push you onward or drag
you down to failure.

I am completely at your command.
Half the things you do might
just as well turn over to me
and I will be able to do them
quickly and correctly.

I am easily managed -
you must merely be firm with me.
Show me exactly how
you want something done
and after a few lessons,
I will do it automatically.

I am the servant of all great people;
and alas, of all failures as well.
Those who are great,
I have made great.
Those who are failures,
I have made failures.

I am not a machine,
though I work with all
the precision of a machine
plus the intelligence of a human.

You may run me for a profit
or run me for ruin -
it makes no difference to me.

Take me, train me, be firm with me,
And I will place the world at your feet.
Be easy with me, and I will destroy you.

WHO AM I? I AM HABIT.

(Author Unknown)

FEBRUARY 10

BOOKEND ROUTINES

To be consistent over time you must be able to describe what you do as a process. The best way to DOMINATE your day, every day, is to start and stop with a consistent routine. We call these Bookend Routines.

Your bookend routine starts the moment you wake up and can last anywhere from 15 minutes to 2 hours. Your morning bookend routine is the process you go through to start your day. This may include making your bed, breakfast, vitamins, exercise, reading, writing, time with loved ones and a shower before you start work.

An end-of-the-day routine may be closing your e-mail, moving anything from your today to-do to your tomorrow to-do list, turning off your computer monitors, listening to relaxing music, changing your clothes and letting go of the work day.

What can you do to start and stop your work day on a consistent basis?

START-OF-DAY BOOKEND ROUTINE:

____

____

____

____

____

END-OF-DAY BOOKEND ROUTINE:

____

____

____

____

____

____

____

____

FEBRUARY 11

THE TOUCH IT ONCE FOUR D SYSTEM

To stay organized and on top of your e-mail, phone mail, snail mail, text, Facebook and Twitter, I suggest that you subscribe to "The Touch It Once Four D System."

When you read an e-mail, open snail mail, listen to a voicemail or get into your Facebook and Twitter accounts, you are spending time twice on the same task if you have to check a message more than one time. Invest your time once by:

1. Doing it in that moment
2. Deleting it
3. Delegating it to someone else
4. Dating the material so you can do it at another time when you won't be interrupted or dragging it to a to do later folder so you can do it at a date and time that works for you.

Touching your paperwork and communications once will help declutter your work space and inbox, which is one of the first steps to an organized and excellence work environment.

**EVERYTHING HAS A PLACE
THERE IS A PLACE FOR EVERYTHING**

FEBRUARY 12

THE 4 ESSENTIALS OF VOICEMAIL

Did you know that 7 out of 10 times when you call someone you get their voicemail? Did you know that 20% of the time it takes you longer to listen to the person's message than it does to actually reply to them and give them the information they need? In today's Want It Yesterday information age, speeding up the communication process and being as efficient as possible is a requirement.

To be efficient and consistent you need a system. Here is my 4-step system for leaving a voicemail.

1. State the name of the person you are calling. Often people share phones or have someone else who checks their messages for them.

Ex. "Ken Ravizza"

2. State your first and last names. Don't you feel frustrated when you get the call from Joe and he doesn't leave his phone number? You know 10 Joes and you don't know who to call!

Ex. "This is Brian Cain."

3. Time stamp and contact information.

Ex. "It is December 24, 2012, 9:16am EST (always include the time zone you are in if you travel a lot) and you can reach me at 802-555-5555, that's 802-555-5555, or by e-mail, brian@briancain.com - that's brian@b-r-i-a-n-c-a-i-n.com (I spell out my name because you can never assume that they know how to spell it correctly).

4. This is the critical step that often gets missed. You must leave information to move the conversation forward. Why are you calling? What information do you need? NEVER say, “Hey, it’s Brian, call me back.” That would be just like e-mailing someone and writing “Hey, It’s Brian, e-mail me back.” You want to leave enough information so the person can call or e-mail you with the information you need.

Ex. “I was wondering if you were going to be in Vermont for the holidays? I would love to come and see you. Please let me know if you will be in Vermont and if so, when we might be able to get together. Please call, e-mail me or text me back. DOMINATE The Day!”

Here is what the entire message would sound like, and it would be all under one minute. Any message over one minute means you were not prepared to leave a message and that you are not respecting others’ time. Since we only have 86,400 seconds in a day, I suggest you respect everyone’s time, especially your own.

Full Example:

“Ken Ravizza, this is Brian Cain. It is December 24, 2012, 9:16am EST and you can reach me at 802-555-5555, that’s 802-555-5555 or by e-mail, brian@briancain.com - that’s brian@b-r-i-a-n-c-a-i-n.com. I was wondering if you were going to be in Vermont for the holidays? I would love to come and see you. Please let me know if you will be in Vermont and if so, when we might be able to get together. Please call, e-mail me or text me back. DOMINATE The Day!”

BE CONSISTENT IN ALL OF YOUR COMMUNICATIONS

FEBRUARY 13

THE 5 LOVE LANGUAGES

Legendary basketball coach John Wooden said that love was the most powerful motivator of all. Joe Erhmann in his book *A Season of Life* talks about the importance of his football players knowing that they are loved by their coaches and that their #1 goal is to love each of their teammates.

Marriage counselor and author Dr. Gary Chapman says In *The 5 Love Languages* that there are five primary love languages that people speak and that to fill another's "love tank" you must speak your partner's primary love language even though that is often not your primary love language.

The five love languages are:

1. Words of Affirmation
2. Quality Time
3. Receiving Gifts
4. Acts of Service
5. Physical Touch

Chapman goes on to discuss how, much like speaking languages, each of the five love languages has different dialects and different ways for you to make a quality time deposit to help fill your partner's "love tank."

He writes, *"I am convinced that no single area of marriage affects the rest of marriage as much as meeting the emotional need for love."*

If you are a busy professional, as I anticipate most people reading this will be, you understand that your time together is limited and want to make the most of it. Understand that what speaks loudly and clearly to you may be meaningless to your significant other.

Chapman clearly explains that the key to understanding each other's unique needs is learning to apply the right principles and the right language of love. If you are looking for a better understanding of emotional relationships and how to best express love with the important people in your life, I highly suggest that you read this book.

How would you rank the five love languages for how you wish to receive love?

____

____

____

____

____

How would you rank the five love languages for how you think your significant other would wish to receive love?

____

____

____

____

____

FEBRUARY 14

SHARING YOUR FEELINGS EACH DAY

I have never been one to be in touch with my emotional self. Emotion clouds reality in competition, and you want to focus more on an emotion-free, focused and present performance than you do tapping into your feelings. I am a teacher of focusing on function over feeling and acting differently from how you feel. I also recognize that feelings are important in my personal life and relationships, and that I must better develop that side of my being in order to live a truly fulfilled life.

Based on the reading of *The Five Love Languages* by Dr. Gary Chapman, I have established a routine in which my significant other and I share three things that happened to us each day and how we feel about them. It is our minimum daily requirement to make sure that we communicate and the love tank stays full.

Today speak with a significant other about one thing that happened to you and how it made you feel.

____

____

____

FEBRUARY 15

3 RULES FOR SUCCESSFUL INTERVIEWS

One of the top coaches in college football has a three-step approach for answering all media questions. His approach would be beneficial for anyone to use when answering questions to the media or to the masses.

3 RULES FOR SUCCESSFUL INTERVIEWS

1. Mention another person, a teammate or staff member in a positive way. Deflect praise to others.

2. Mention your program core values with every answer.

3. When giving your answer, look at the camera if you are on TV vs. the person who is asking you the question, so that you can make eye contact with everyone who is watching.

PASS PRAISE WHEN POSSIBLE, AND IT IS ALWAYS POSSIBLE

FEBRUARY 16

ENERGY GIVER OR ENERGY TAKER

There are two types of people in the world: Energy givers and energy takers. Energy givers are like fountains - they are uplifting, fun to look at in action and a joy to be around. Energy takers are like drains - they will suck you down if you let them, as their number one purpose in life is to suck you down into the sewers of negativity.

Today, put your focus on being an energy giver and spend less time letting the drains in your life suck you down to their level.

ARE YOU A FOUNTAIN OR A DRAIN?

FEBRUARY 17

MAKE A COMMITMENT BURN YOUR SHIPS

You can make excuses or you can make it happen, but you cannot do both. One of the essential ingredients to making it happen is to make a commitment.

In the 1500's a Spanish Conquistador landed on the shores of Mexico with only one objective: Seize the great treasures that were hoarded by the Aztecs.

The Conquistador was driven by the need to acquire the riches of the land. He was a great competitor and an excellent motivator, and he convinced more than 500 soldiers and 100 sailors to leave the comfort of their homes in Spain for the riches that awaited in Mexico.

What researchers find fascinating is how the Conquistador and the 11 ships that landed in Mexico were able to arrive on the shores of a strange land and overthrow a large and powerful empire that had been in power for over six centuries.

The answer was simple: COMMITMENT. Commitment and victory or commitment and death, but COMMITMENT. In one of the most brilliant motivational strategies battle has ever seen, the Conquistador rallied his men on the shores of the Yucatán and ordered his men to "Burn the Ships."

Initially met with resistance, he ordered his men again to "BURN THE SHIPS." He said that if we are going home, we are going home in THEIR boats with THEIR riches.

And with that, the ships were set aflame and the next level of commitment was reached. It was victory or death - the highest level of commitment to a task at hand.

With their commitment to success, the Conquistador and his men were able to defeat the much bigger and more talented Aztec armies. They had no escape; their backs were against the wall.

To get what you have never gotten, you must be willing to give what you have never given. Eliminate your escape routes and excuses. If you know your ship is waiting, you will retreat when things get tough; it is human nature.

Make a COMMITMENT like your life depends on success and BURN YOUR SHIPS.

What are the goals you want to accomplish this week?

Beat Brevard, finish HW
____

What are the ships you are going to burn?

____

____

FEBRUARY 18

SERVANT LEADERSHIP

You see it all the time in athletics. The freshmen are the ones who carry the equipment, pick up the locker room and pick up the bus. The seniors and captains are the ones who give orders and can often be the last to follow them.

Many athletes and organizations have a top-down leadership philosophy, which I will diagram here with the coaches on top followed by the captains, seniors, juniors, sophomores and freshmen.

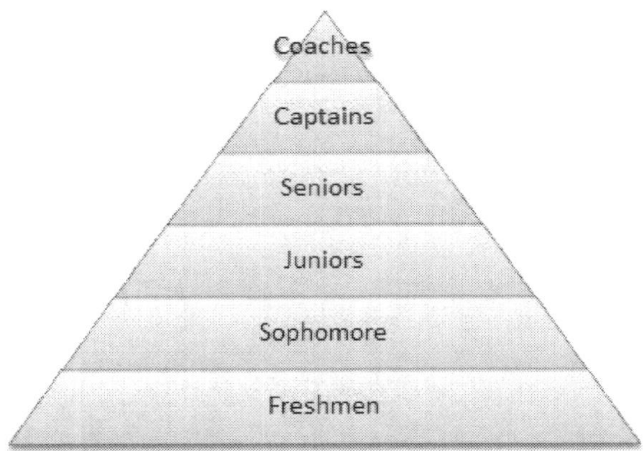

This is the model of leadership I see in most programs. Most programs fall into the category that makes up average. They are part of the best of the worst and the worst of the best. The worst of the worst have zero leadership model and the best of the best have this pyramid turned upside down.

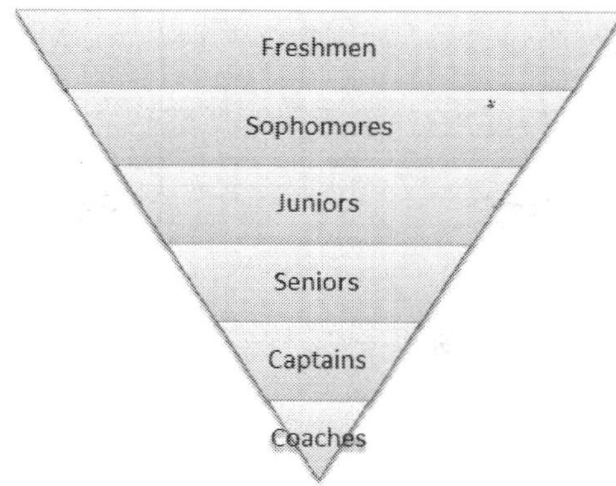

The best programs in the country have a servant leadership model. They put the coaches, captains and seniors at the base of the pyramid with the focus on serving others. The coaches, captains and seniors have been a part of the program for the longest amount of time and know best what the program's standards of excellence are and what needs to be done when

Servant leadership is about actively finding ways to help and serve others. You are not a doormat that gets walked on, used and taken advantage of; you are a foundation that the program is built on and you serve others in their pursuit of excellence.

Steve Smith, head baseball coach at Baylor University and the 2012 Big XII Conference Coach of the Year, told me once that great programs have leaders who are a model to see more then they have a motto to say. Coach Smith understands the importance of leading, building up and serving.

What can you consciously do today to be an active servant leader?

____

____

LEADERSHIP IS SERVICE TO OTHERS

FEBRUARY 19

WATCH OUT FOR WHAT YOU WANT - YOU JUST MIGHT GET IT

Jim Rohn, motivational speaker and author, gave great advice when he said, *"Be careful of what you give up in pursuit of what it is that you want."*

Having worked with some of the most committed, dedicated and disciplined people on the planet, I can assure you that their laser-like focus is an essential part of their success. I can also assure you that, although it may be their greatest strength in the office, it can also be their greatest weakness at home.

I see too many people sacrifice family, love and relationships at home to pursue success at the office. It does not have to be this way. You can be excellent both in the office and at home. You do not want to have sharp knives in your drawer at the office and dull knives in your drawer at home.

What can you do today to help sharpen your professional and personal knife set?

PROFESSIONAL:

____

____

PERSONAL:

____

____

FEBRUARY 20

FIVE TIPS ON HOW TO LISTEN

Listening is an essential part of leadership and success. Listening is a skill that can be developed and improved just like the physical skills of your game. Here are five essentials to listening and enhancing your leadership.

1. Maintain direct eye contact with the person you are speaking with. In today's time of cell phone, text and Facebook, eye contact is more important than it has ever been for your presence in face-to-face communication. Your eyes tell the story, and gaining eye contact (take your sunglasses off, Coach!) is a critical part of the communication process.

2. Be fully present. Resist the urge to do something else while listening. When we multitask and do something else while listening, we are dividing our attention resources and listening with only 50%.

3. Observe your contact's feelings. Communication is approximately 70% physiology. Learn to watch and listen for feelings that come out in communication.

4. Watch for body language. Becoming more aware of the body language and position of those who you communicate with is a critical part of improving your listening skills, as their body language and physiology say more than their words.

5. Refuse to interrupt. As you listen, actually listen. Refuse the mental interruption of thinking about what

you are going to say and refuse to interrupt while the other person is speaking. Listen to listen and then offer your feedback or opinion if it is asked for; if it is not asked for, don't offer it.

What will you do today to become a better listener?

____

____

____

YOU HAVE TWO EYES AND TWO EARS
LISTEN TWICE AS MUCH AS YOU TALK

FEBRUARY 21

THE I OR ME vs. WE & WE or US vs. THEY or THEM RATIO

John Brubaker, a former NCAA lacrosse coach, author of *The Coach Approach* and one of the top peak performance coaches in the country, kept track of the amount of times he would hear himself, his staff or his team use the words “I” or “me” vs. “we” and the amount of time he would hear “us” vs. “they” or “them.”

Brubaker wanted to be sure that the people in his program kept a focus on the team first and on them vs. their opponent.

He says that “the only time you should use the words ‘I’ or ‘me’ is when you are accepting the blame or holding yourself accountable for something. Otherwise you run the risk of being viewed as self-absorbed and not thinking of the team first.”

The most successful coaches and athletes I have worked with are first to accept criticism and first to pass praise on to others. Look for ways today to pass praise on to others.

Where can you pass out praise as a part of your daily routine?

FEBRUARY 22

THE PILLOW TEST

Do you realize the power of the present? Today is ALL you can control. The past is history, the future is a mystery and *today* is the gift - that's why we call it the present.

TODAY is the day you must DOMINATE. All of the championships you want to win will take care of themselves if you take care of today.

Tonight when your head hits the pillow you will take the "Pillow Test." You will ask yourself, *"Did I do everything I could today to get better and take one step closer towards my goals?"*

If the answer is "Yes, I am glad I did," then you won. If your answer is "I wish I had," then you lost, and your competition took a step forward.

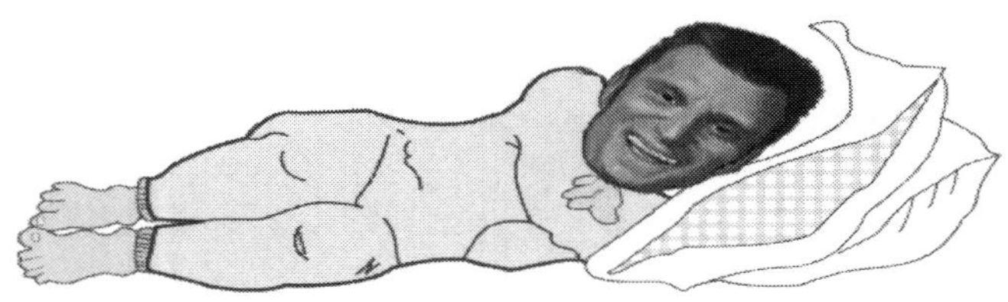

TODAY + TODAY + TODAY = YOUR LIFE

FEBRUARY 23

THE VALUE OF THE DAY

To realize the value of a sister, ask someone who doesn't have one.

To realize the value of ten years, ask a newly divorced couple.

To realize the value of four years, ask a graduate.

To realize the value of one year, ask a student who has failed a final exam.

To realize the value of nine months, ask a mother who gave birth.

To realize the value of one month, ask a mother who has given birth to a premature baby.

To realize the value of one week, ask an editor of a weekly newspaper.

To realize the value of one minute, ask a person who has missed the train, bus or plane.

To realize the value of one second, ask a person who has survived an accident.

To realize the value of an inch, ask the persons who just came up short of their goals in competition and ask them if they could have worked 1% harder?

That 1% makes all the difference. Just 1 degree of extra effort turns hot water at 211 degrees into boiling water and steam that can drive a locomotive at 212 degrees.

Give 1% more to excellence today. Give 1% more at the office, at home, to yourself and to those who are closest to you.

Don't count the days… Make the days count.

What will you give today that will be that extra 1%?

____

____

____

____

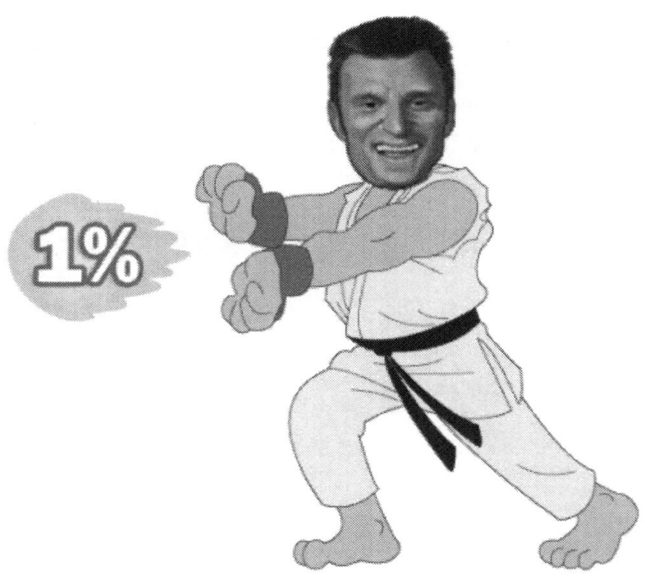

1% OF YOU MIGHT MAKE THE DIFFERENCE BETWEEN CHAMP & CHUMP

FEBRUARY 24

THE COMPOUND EFFECT

One of my goals is to read at least one book each month. Recently I was working with a program and their head coach, one of my favorite people in the world, gave me *The Compound Effect* by Darren Hardy.

Hardy is the founder of *Success Magazine* and has interviewed some of the most successful CEO's, athletes and people on the planet. He shares the simple, yet profound, idea that the PROCESS of your daily decisions is the most important factor in your success or failure in life. The compound effect of your daily decisions adds up over time and ultimately determines your fate. It is the start that stops most people; once you get into a routine and have momentum on your side, you keep building off of your successes and keep moving in the direction of your goals.

Remind yourself of the importance of today and the necessity of DOMINATING THE DAY! Inch by inch, it is a cinch.. Yard by yard it is hard. Stick with the process, focus on the next 200 feet and remember that all of your decisions add up over time. EVERYTHING COUNTS - there are NO LITTLE THINGS. The Compound Effect is ALWAYS in action.

What can you do today that you know you should do and want to do, but don't feel like doing, that will help you create the momentum you need to achieve the goals you have set for yourself? ____

____

____

FEBRUARY 25

CHOICES OR SACRIFICES?

There are tremendous demands on your time. You are pulled in many different directions. You must ask yourself: Am I making choices or sacrifices? Great achievers don't make sacrifices; they make choices.

Many people have made sacrifices to get you where you are, but YOU are not making a sacrifice to be where you are. Rather, you are making a choice – you have a unique opportunity in your life to do something that very few people can ever say they did. Be sure you ENJOY the grind, appreciate what you have and don't count the days - make the days count.

If you were to improve just .003 each day - that's only 3/10 of one percent, a very slight edge - and kept that up for the next five years, here's what would happen to you:

> The first year, you would improve 100 percent; you would already be twice what you are today.
>
> The second year you would improve 200 percent.
>
> The third year, 400 percent.
>
> The fourth year, 800 percent.

By the end of year five, by simply improving 3/10 of one percent each day, you would magnify your value, your skills, and the results you accomplished by 1,600 percent.

That's 22 times more than you are today.

That's a commitment to excellence made with a great ATTITUDE and a PRESENT-MOMENT FOCUS ON DOMINATING THE DAY!

Everything matters – the food you eat, the fluids you drink, the movies you watch, the e-mails you read, the people you hang out with, the attitude you take TODAY!

What decisions will you make today to help you get 3/10 of a % better?

____

____

____

____

____

____

____

____

____

____

____

____

EXCELLENCE IS A LIFESTYLE, NOT AN EVENT

FEBRUARY 26

EVERYTHING HAS A PLACE

Jane Von Bergen wrote in her article *So Many Reasons to Neaten Up, But It's Too Imposing,* featured in the Boston Globe on 03/12/2006, that three out of four workers surveyed worldwide agreed with this statement:

I find myself becoming more stressed when everything is a mess and I can't find important documents when needed.

There is a proper place for everything and everything has a proper place. The most successful coaches I have been around are also the most organized. They know the value of a second and don't waste time looking for their keys, cell phone or wallet - those items are always in a proper place, as is everything else in their life.

Focus + Organization = Greater Productivity. One of the first things you want to do is organize your work space - clear the clutter.

I always felt that I was organized and efficient. Then I met Tim Corbin, the head baseball coach at Vanderbilt University and one of the most well-respected coaches in all of collegiate sports.

Corbin is at the next level of efficiency and organization. He lives the compound effect and knows the value of each second and the value of being organized. One of the tips that he shared with me and that I have used ever since is to put all of the hangers in the closet in one direction, and then after wearing an article of clothing to hang it back up in the opposite direction. After

3, 6, 9 or 12 months, whichever you prefer, any hanger that is in the original direction indicates that you have not worn that article of clothing - it can be given away to Goodwill or another organization where it will get worn.

What clutter in your life can you get rid of to help better organize yourself and improve your efficiency?

____

____

____

____

GET ORGANIZED, STAY ORGANIZED

FEBRUARY 27

SIT IN THE LEARNING T

As a former high school and college coach and teacher, I have found that one of the biggest obstacles student athletes face in achieving consistent levels of academic performance is a lack of organizational and study skills.

I have yet to hear of a school that requires student to take a year-long course in study skills, time management, organization, stress management and life skills that can be used in everyday life.

The next few days will cover more of my top tips and techniques for student athletes and coaches to increase their academic and organizational performance.

One of the easiest ways to improve learning is to sit in what is called the learning T, the front row and the middle row of the classroom. The instructor spends most of the time looking at people who sit there, and that eye contact will subconsciously keep you more locked in and focused on the class.

Research shows that communication is at least 50 percent body language, and if you can keep your eyes on the teacher, you will retain more of the information.

FEBRUARY 28

THE 30-SECOND DRILL

As a former high school administrator, I was always looking to hire boring and monotone teachers.

The reason was that if our athletes could learn to focus, get distracted and refocus for 30 seconds when they were spacing out, that change in attention and focus could develop into what I define as mental toughness.

Mental toughness is your ability to be distracted, lose focus, quickly recognize that you lost focus, and then release and refocus back into the present moment.

Being able to shift your focus to what's important now in the classroom is great practice for being able to do it on the field.

Remember, you don't block out; rather, you lock in on the moment. When you focus so intently on what you are doing that everything else disappears, that is true present-moment focus.

FEBRUARY 29

MAKING A TO-DO LIST

Making a to-do list is essential for staying organized and on top of the things that you need to accomplish.

Keeping a small notepad or an assignment book with you will assure that you write down correctly the assignments you have in school or the items you need to do in the office or at home. It will also give you a sense of accomplishment and motivation when you cross that completed item off the list.

Be sure that you use both a today and a tomorrow to-do list. Tasks that can be done later can be placed on the tomorrow to-do list so that you don't forget about them and won't feel the stress of having to do them today.

Today is also an extra day of domination if this happens to be a leap year? Extra production baby!

TODAY TO DO:

____

____

TOMORROW TO DO:

____

____

MARCH

March is the month for me to dominate...

MARCH 1

ORGANIZE & EAT THAT FROG

Organize homework assignments in the order which they should be done so you have a plan of attack to get started.

There are two schools of thought here.

1. You can attack the smallest assignments and the ones that you can get done the quickest to build some momentum, and then tackle the major projects, much like you would take batting practice and infield practice before a game.

2. Start with the biggest, ugliest task first as this is often when you are most fresh. In the business world this is called "eating a frog." It's an analogy borrowed from the book *Eat That Frog* by Brian Tracy, an excellent introductory book on time management.

The basic idea behind "eating a frog" is that you start your day with your toughest task. It's the task you are most likely to procrastinate on.

Take, for example, exercising. Most people put off exercising in the morning and then later in the day they just don't feel like it. By getting your workout done in the morning, you'll feel a lot better about yourself.

On top of that, for the rest of the day all the other tasks and chores coming your way feel EASY in comparison. You can swap exercise for any other activity you might procrastinate on, such as cleaning your room, starting your homework, running errands or anything you feel like you would delay starting.

Eating a frog is a simple habit but very powerful. Just implementing this one habit will change your life more than you realize.

WHICH FROG DO YOU EAT FIRST?

MARCH 2

DETERMINE A STUDY AREA & TIME

Determine and designate a study area and time as a part of your routine. When you study in the same place at the same time every day, you get into a routine and are more consistent in your performance and production.

Make sure that supplies and materials are close by and clear your place of clutter, debris and distractions. Also make sure your area is well lit. Using the same place to study every time will get you into the mindset that this is where you go to get smarter, much like the weight room is where you go to get stronger.

Set aside designated study time each day to provide you more structure and consistency for academic success. The most opportune time is often a few hours after school is finished. It is recommended that you take an hour or so after school to unwind and decompress from the rigors of everyday academic life.

Where will be your pre-determined study area?

____

What time will you start your study routine?

____

____

____

____

MARCH 3

GET ORGANIZED – STAY ORGANIZED

Keeping a 3-ring binder or organized notebooks for each class is a great way to make sure you know where all your notes, assignments and work are when you need them. Having dividers will also aid in your organization.

Time invested up front on organization will pay off in the long run. The compound effect is felt here as well. You will not lose valuable time hunting for something that you need immediately. You will know where to find it.

Much like the stress you feel when you are looking for your glove when coach calls on you to go play defense and you can't find it because you are unorganized in your dugout, being organized in all aspects of your life will make you more efficient and more successful.

If you were to do one thing today to get more organized, what would that one thing be?

____

____

____

____

**INVEST TIME UP FRONT
TO GET MORE BACK IN THE LONG RUN**

MARCH 4

CONDUCT WEEKLY CLEANUPS

Conduct weekly cleanups by going through your school and gym bags on a weekly basis and purging what you don't need. File old papers. Throw away food wrappers and wash your old socks. School and gym bags are often a place where papers go to die. Doing weekly cleanups will keep you and your bag feeling more confident and light on your feet.

Keeping a detailed calendar and a master schedule of your classes and athletic commitments will allow you to feel more organized and give you the confidence to take on more tasks.

Writing down when your assignments and papers are due and also when you will do them will give you a good visual as to what times of the week or month you will need to spend more time on academics.

Communicating this with coaches and others who are close to you will let them know that you will be under some stress at that time.

When will you conduct your weekly cleanups?

____

____

____

DO A LITTLE A LOT, NOT A LOT A LITTLE

MARCH 5

PREPARE FOR THE DAY AHEAD THE NIGHT BEFORE

Prepare for the day ahead before you go to bed at night by packing your bags for practice and school as well as laying out what you will wear the next day. That will save you valuable time in the morning.

You may be able to sleep a bit later or sneak in a short agility ladder, core or flexibility/yoga workout in the morning to help get you off on the right foot.

You must be sure that you plan on breakfast the next day. As you know, breakfast is the most important meal of the day. When you wake up, you will probably have not eaten for almost 10 hours. Grab a banana or make yourself a protein shake or a PBJ. I personally have the goal to get 40 grams of protein in my system in the first 20 minutes of being out of bed. I accomplish this by having two high-protein shakes waiting for me in the bathroom so I can eat them as soon as I get out of bed, before I brush my teeth.

Just like you would prepare a scouting report for a game, you should do your own scouting report for tomorrow. More often than not, it is the start that stops most people. Get started tomorrow by organizing yourself tonight.

What can you do tonight that will help you get started on the right foot tomorrow? What is one simple thing you can do to improve your morning routine?

MARCH 6

DOMINATE OR PROCRASTINATE #1
LIST POSSIBLE INSTANT TASKS

Procrastination is at the root of all unproductiveness. I want to share with you 15 ways in which you can DOMINATE vs. procrastinate and get started on the path to productiveness.

By listing the instant tasks, you are warming up the mind and starting to funnel yourself into work mode. By knowing how you could start if you wanted to, you are much closer to actually getting starte

By looking over your assignment book, packing your bag for school the next day, cleaning and organizing your room, you are taking instant steps towards improving your academic success.

What are the instant tasks you could take today to beat procrastination?

MARCH 7

DOMINATE OR PROCRASTINATE #2
SET YOUR PRIORITIES

What are the most important tasks you need to accomplish? Listing your tasks as A1, A2, A3, B1, B2, C1, etc., will draw your attention to what needs to be done today, in what order, and what can wait so that you are assured of spending what little time you do have on what needs to be done first. For example:

> A1 - Work on the paper that is due tomorrow for English class.
>
> A2 - E-mail my teachers to let them know I will be out on Friday for a road trip with the team.
>
> B1 – Pack my bags by 12:00 tomorrow for the road trip.

What are three tasks you need to get done today and in what order will you do them?

1. A1 - come pack after meeting
2. lift before going to eat
3. After Eating then.

MARCH 8

DOMINATE OR PROCRASTINATE #3
USE THE FIVE-MINUTE DRILL

Using the five-minute drill is a great way to start into your pile of work. By saying "I will work for five minutes only," you will get started because working for only five minutes is pretty easy and anyone can work for five minutes.

More often than not, you will begin with the intention of only spending five minutes but will end up actually working for a longer period of time.

Again, it is the start that stops most people because they focus on the finish line instead of taking the first step of the race, which is to get started. You don't have to finish if you start, but you do have to get started to finish.

What will you get started today for only five minutes? ____

____

____

____

____

____

____

____

____

MARCH 9

DOMINATE OR PROCRASTINATE #4
USE THE MAGIC "IF"

"If" you were to get started, what would you do? That is the magic "IF."

If you catch yourself saying you cannot get started, say to yourself, "I cannot... but if I could, what would I do?"

By listing and thinking about what you would do, you again are priming the pump to get started. By knowing what you would do, you are one step closer to actually getting started.

IF you were to get started on that project today, what would it be?

____

____

____

____

____

____

____

____

____

____

MARCH 10

DOMINATE OR PROCRASTINATE #5
GET MORE INFORMATION

Getting more information and resources will help you feel more prepared and motivated to get started. Often we are intimidated or unmotivated to get started because we feel unprepared and do not feel knowledgeable about what we are doing.

Having more information about the type of questions that will be on a test or on a topic that you have to give a presentation on will make you feel more confident in tackling your task and more motivated to get started.

What will you get more information on today?

____

____

____

Where will you go to get it?

____

____

____

____

____

____

MARCH 11

DOMINATE OR PROCRASTINATE #6
TRY A LEAD-IN TASK

Try a lead-in task first to help you build momentum. Sharpening your pencil, turning your phone and TV off or removing clutter and organizing your work space are all examples of things that you can do to help you get started on the project at hand.

A lead-in task is a lot like a routine. You will find that the more consistent you are with your lead-in tasks the more consistent you will be in your production.

What are some lead-in tasks you can do?

____

____

____

____

____

____

____

____

____

____

MARCH 12

DOMINATE OR PROCRASTINATE #7
GIVE YOURSELF A PEP TALK

Telling yourself that "I can do it, I will get it done, all I need to do is get started" is often all it takes to get yourself moving to get the job done.

Start talking to yourself about finishing the project and start thinking about how good it will feel when you are done - you will get more excited about starting... and closer to finishing.

You may want to have a working music mix that you play to help you get energized for work or have certain motivational messages posted in your work space that will help get you going. Two of my personal favorites are below.

"IT'S THE START THAT STOPS MOST PEOPLE"

**"YOU DON'T HAVE TO BE GREAT
TO GET STARTED,
YOU DO HAVE TO GET STARTED TO BE GREAT"**

What music would you play to get energized for work?

____

What motivational messages inspire you to get started?

____

____

____

MARCH 13

DOMINATE OR PROCRASTINATE #8
MAKE A COMMITMENT TO SOMEONE ELSE

Make a commitment to someone else. By verbalizing your goals and making a commitment to someone that you will be there for them either at study hall, the weight room or at the office, you are enhancing your level of commitment. It is a lot harder to let someone else down. It is human nature to take the easy road and avoid work if you are on your own.

If you say you will work out at 6am or will have a rough draft done by a certain time, you are increasing your commitment to the task; and commitment is the key that can unlock the door to beating procrastination.

Who is a person you could make a commitment to and what commitment are you willing to make?

____

____

____

____

____

____

____

____

MARCH 14

DOMINATE OR PROCRASTINATE #9
SET A DEADLINE FOR YOURSELF

Setting a deadline for yourself and giving yourself an end point can give you the hour you need and the exit time to force you into getting started.

Deadlines have a funny way about getting you to make decisions. We often don't get started because we use the excuse of "I will do it tomorrow." Tomorrow never comes. So set a deadline and mini-deadlines or checkpoints along the way to put more structure on yourself and the task at hand.

What are examples of deadlines you could set for yourself?

MARCH 15

DOMINATE OR PROCRASTINATE #10
DON'T LET FEAR GET IN THE WAY

Fear is nothing more than false evidence appearing real. We often put unneeded pressure and stress on ourselves because we magnify the importance of the outcome and lose sight of the process we must take to get there.

First, recognize and admit what your fears may be and then ask yourself, "What is the worst thing that can happen to me? How bad or difficult could it really be to have to go and talk to my supervisor?"

I am sure that once you identify the worst thing that could happen you will find that you are placing too much emotional stress on the outcome and that you need to get on with it. Sitting around will get you nowhere. Get going.

What are some fears that may be holding you back?

____

____

____

____

____

____

____

MARCH 16

DOMINATE OR PROCRASTINATE #11
ASK YOURSELF THE QUESTION, WHAT IS THE PRICE OF DELAY?

We often spend a lot of time beating ourselves up because we know we should have gotten started already, but just can't get going. If you are in that situation, ask yourself, "What is the price of delay?" By thinking about all of the other stuff you could be doing with your time after you finish what needs to be done, you will often find the motivation to get started.

Is the price of delay in the office time away from your family? Is it time away from starting an exercise routine or time away from doing charitable work to help make the world a better place?

Whatever your price of delay, every second that you waste in getting started is one second closer to death. It is one more second you waste and will wish you had back in the end.

If you have not started yet, ask yourself if you like being average and wasting your life away, because that is exactly what you are doing when you procrastinate.

What is the price of delay? ____________________________

____

____

____

____

MARCH 17

DOMINATE OR PROCRASTINATE #12
STRESS THE BENEFITS OF GETTING STARTED & FINISHED

Stress the benefits of getting started and getting finished. Reward yourself if you can get started and get done on time. Work for a specific period of time.

For example, if you work for two hours on your budget report or presentation, you can go to the gym when you are done. If you get that English paper done, you can go and hang out with your girlfriend.

By rewarding yourself you will be energized to finish, thus more eager to begin.

What are the benefits of getting started?

____

____

What are the benefits of getting finished?

____

____

____

____

____

MARCH 18

DOMINATE OR PROCRASTINATE #13
ADMIT WHEN YOU ARE WASTING TIME

Taking an honest look at yourself and admitting when you are wasting time is not easy, but is necessary to defeat procrastination.

If you can admit to wasting time, you will then come to grips that you are not being productive and need to get started on what is most important right now. By not admitting that you are wasting time, you will continue to put off what needs to be done and will avoid getting started.

How do you recognize when you are wasting time? What are the things you do that can help you to recognize you are wasting time?

MARCH 19

DOMINATE OR PROCRASTINATE #14
CUT OFF ESCAPE ROUTES

If you are the type of person that has a hard time focusing on your academic work or paperwork at home due to the many distractions, you must cut off all your escape routes.

An easy way to do this is to have a friend drop you off at a local library, book store, coffee shop or quiet place where you won't be bothered by distractions. Also, be sure to give your friend your cell phone so that you cut yourself off from outside communications.

Where would you go to cut off your escape routes?

____

____

____

____

Who would you have bring you?

____

____

____

____

MARCH 20

DOMINATE OR PROCRASTINATE #15
DRESS FOR SUCCESS

Much like you go to your locker to dress for a successful practice, and you would dress first class for that big job interview, having the correct attire is essential for you to get into the right frame of mind to get started.

I encourage students to have a homework uniform, a set of clothes or article of clothing that they wear when getting ready to hit the books. It may be a certain pair of jeans or a cozy pair of sweats. Whatever it is, make it special and significant to you being the best student you can be in that moment.

I also encourage athletes not to wear their practice gear to school and to class, as those articles of clothing are special to you as an athlete and should only be worn when you are dressing up for competition and the bounty hunter mentality.

What clothes do you wear to help you get into a state of mind for performance?

____

____

USE YOUR CLOTHES AS A WAY TO GET INTO THE MENTALITY YOU NEED FOR SUCCESS

MARCH 21

YOU ARE STRONGER THAN YOUR HABITS

You are stronger than your habits. You can change your habits anytime you wish. You form your habits and then your habits form you.

Whatever change you want to make, you can make in an instant. For it to hold, try it over time - you must condition it by doing a little a lot, not a lot a little.

Right now, as you read this, fold your arms. Now fold them in the opposite direction. Feels weird, doesn't it? However, if you folded them this way for 21-28 days, you would most likely start to fold them this way all the time. You would have formed a new habit.

What habits do you have that need changing?

____

____

What habits do you have that are worth keeping?

____

____

____

____

____

MARCH 22

YOU FIND WHAT YOU ARE LOOKING FOR

A man sat on a park bench when a traveler stopped by and asked:

"What are the people like in this city?"

The man on the bench then asked:

"What are the people like where you came from?"

The traveler said, "They were a horrible bunch - mean, backstabbing and rude."

The man sat up on the bench, looked the traveler in the eye and said, "You will find the same people here in this city."

About an hour later, a second traveler approached the man on the bench and asked:

"What are the people like in this city?"

The man on the bench then asked:

"What are the people like where you came from?"

The second traveler said: "They were wonderful - the nicest warm and welcoming bunch you would ever find. It is so hard to leave, but my job takes me here."

The man sat up on the bench, looked the traveler in the eye and said, "You will find the same people here in this city."

The moral of the story is that you will find what you are looking for. If you are looking for negativity, you will find it; if you are looking for positivity, you will find it.

Your perspective is often a reflection of yourself. Start by changing the person you see in the mirror and the rest of the world will change with you.

PERSPECTIVE IS REALITY

**CHANGE IN THE WORLD
AND CHANGE IN OTHERS
STARTS WITH CHANGE IN YOU!**

MARCH 23

BREAK THE ROCK

The University of Iowa has a rock in their weight room that has the words "Break the Rock" inscribed into it.

When you hit a rock with a hammer, eventually the rock will break. You do not know when it will break. It may not show any signs of breaking or giving in - and then all of a sudden, with one more swing of the hammer, BOOM! The rock breaks in half.

Break the Rock is analogous to life. You keep hammering away at the process, not knowing when the rock will break; and eventually you break through, get over the hump, get momentum on your side and reap the rewards of your efforts.

SWING ONE MORE TIME, BREAK THE ROCK

MARCH 24

THEORY AND APPLICATION

In theory, all theory and application are the same. In application, they are totally different.

What separates a theorist and a true application artist? What separates the theorist and the successful practitioner who applies and helps elicit positive change in the real world setting? The answer lies in the character qualities of the individual person.

To be successful at application, I believe you must know the theory behind what you teach. Your audience may not want to know the theory; they just want the to-do application steps, but you must be able to deliver on both fronts if you are going to excel.

Be leery of the theorist that has spent years in the ivory tower but has not come down long enough to live in the trenches of the battlefield of which they are an expert.

When in your life have you experienced a difference in what theory says is true and what actually worked in application?

MARCH 25

25 GUYS, ONE COMMON GOAL

The San Francisco Giants franchise is one of the most successful organizations in Major League Baseball and all of professional sports, in recent years winning the 2010 and 2012 World Series.

The formula for their success was documented in the Showtime series *The Franchise,* in which you were able to see the relentless positive energy and synergy that existed among the club.

There is a sign hanging in their facility that says it all about the foundation of a successful organization. A great definition of what it means to be a team.

MARCH 26

WHAT DOES SUCCESS HAVE IN COMMON?

What did Michael Jordan have when he was the best basketball player in the world and also when he was trying to play professional baseball? It is the same thing that every athlete who participates in the Olympic Games and every fighter in the UFC has...

A Coach

The most successful people on the planet all have coaches. You are a seed and the coach is the sun and water that help you to grow. Finding the right coach for you is critical to your success.

Not all coaches are right for you. There may be some that overwater you with negativity and cause you to drown. And there may be others that give you only sunshine, causing you to burn out and die because you have a false sense of reality.

A balance of sunshine (praise) and water (constructive feedback) is necessary for your optimal growth and development.

Do you have a coach that you work with on a regular basis?

Write that person's name here: ___________________

If you don't have a coach, write some ideas of who could be your coach or where you could get one:

____

____

____

MARCH 27

THE PERSPECTIVE PRESCRIPTION

What does a pair of glasses have to do with your perspective?

Everything.

If you wear glasses and your prescription is off, it changes the way you see the world. The world is the same, but to you it looks blurry, out of focus and gives you a headache.

If your perspective is off, your world has the same effect. What you see is what you get. Have a negative perspective and you get a negative world. Have a perspective of scarcity and that is what you get. If you have a perspective of positivity and abundance, that is what you get.

Check in on yours today and ask yourself: Do I have a complete perspective and see things as they truly are, or am I making a mountain out of a molehill?

PERSPECTIVE IS REALITY

MARCH 28

ACT AS IF IT WERE IMPOSSIBLE TO FAIL

There was a second grade teacher who had a student that everyone knew was going to be the senior class president in ten years. She had it all, she had belief.

One day her teacher asked the class to draw anything they wanted. Most kids drew dogs, cats or other animals; but when the teacher approached this girl, she had not drawn anything yet.

The teacher asked her, "Why have you not drawn anything yet?" The girl replied, "I am visualizing just exactly what my picture is going to be, and I want get it exactly right."

"What do you want to draw?" asked the teacher.

"I want to draw God," answered the girl.

"Nobody knows what God really looks like," said the teacher.

"Oh, they will when I am done," said the girl.

The girl had the secret to success: Believe in your abilitity to do anything to make the impossible possible.

What have you done in your life that at one time you thought was impossible, but after you did it, you were amazed at how easy it was?

____

____

____

In what areas of your life do you need to develop a stronger belief in yourself?

____

____

Confidence is a choice made more easily by celebrating small wins every day. What are three wins that you have had in the last 24 hours?

WIN 1 ______________________________________

WIN 2 ______________________________________

WIN 3 ______________________________________

MARCH 29

PICK UP ON STRENGTHS

Did you know that you are one of the best in the world at something? That you are an expert?

According to research, you are better at one thing or more than at least 10,000 other people. You have an ability inside of you that is truly great and offers tremendous value to others. Do you know what that ability is?

Many coaches and teachers will spend their time focused on getting you to see what's wrong with you, where you are deficient. The best of the best help you to see your strengths. They help you to see that limitless potential that resides inside of you and get you to find your passion.

Once you discover this ability, you are on your way to a life of fulfillment. Imagine if you could be the person whose ability is to help others find the ability that resides in them? Today, help someone else find greatness inside of them.

What are your strengths?

____

____

____

____

____

____

MARCH 30

DO YOU MAJOR IN MINOR THINGS?

Do you ever lose sight of the big picture because of the small challenges? Are you somebody who gets hooked on the small challenges of everyday life and is so busy doing what is urgent that you can never get to what is important? Are you someone that is majoring in minor things?

If you have a lot of drama in your life, you are majoring in minor things and have lost sight of the big picture. What may seem like a mountain today will be a molehill in the future.

Focus your time and energy on what is truly most important. Throughout your day, routinely ask yourself: Is what I am doing right now taking me one step closer to, or further away, from my ultimate goal? If you are going in the opposite direction of your intended target, you are most likely majoring in minor things.

KEEP THE MAIN THING, THE MAIN THING

MARCH 31

ARE YOU STEERING THE SHIP OR CHARTING THE COURSE?

Do you spend more time steering the ship or charting the course? Do you spend more time planning out your work or mindlessly working? Investing time up front each day into preparing a plan and process to help you get where you want to go is time gained back in the long run.

One of the best coaches in college football spends time each year meeting with his staff about how they are going to meet. He invests the time to go over the routine of meetings - how they are to be run as efficiently and effectively as possible to get the most return on investment

Most anyone can steer the ship and do the work. It takes a visionary leader to chart the course and make sure that you end up where it is you want to be at the end of the season. Today, chart your course for tomorrow and have a plan of attack so you maximize your time.

APRIL

April is the month for me to dominate...

APRIL 1

STAKE TOGETHER

There once lived a tribe whose warriors, before a battle, would give away all of their prized possessions to friends, relatives and family. When these soldiers went into battle, they knew only one of two things would happen: Victory or death.

This elite group of warriors would arrive at the battlefield and drive a stake into the ground, then tie a rope from the stake to their ankles. They would then stand in a circle shoulder to shoulder, back to back, and focus on fighting their one battle.

They knew that the other warriors in their tribe had been trained, and they fought with a controlled rage and focus that allowed them to fight one battle at a time.

Staking together was an exhibition of trust in their fellow warriors, and that trust allowed them to focus with full intent on the task at hand knowing that their teammates had their back. Today, stake together with your team.

APRIL 2

KEEP THE WORMS WARM

Brian and Ron were ice fishing in holes less than two feet away. Brian pulled in fish after fish after fish and Ron caught nothing.

Ron was convinced that the fish must have been migrating around Brian's hole and asked if they could switch. When they did, Brian continued to catch fish in the hole where Ron had previously been fishing and Ron continued to catch nothing.

When Ron asked Brian what his secret of success was, Brian mumbled, "You must keep the worms warm." Ron did not understand what Brian had said and asked again what his secret of success was.

This time Brian put down his pole, reached into his mouth, took out 5 worms and said, "You must keep the worms warm."

Are you trying to capture the hearts of others with cold worms or warm ones? A compliment catches more than criticism.

APRIL 3

EMBRACE THE COMING CHANGES

Many people are content to live their lives by playing it safe. Change is hard work; and if I take inventory of my current situation and where I have to go to change and if fear, pain, and hard work are prerequisites of that change, it's easier to understand why some people are so dedicated to resisting it.

They might be good at giving all the best-sounding excuses why this particular change is not right for them or their team. However, their underlying concern may be their fear about how the change will affect them and their social status, their position on the team or their view of themselves.

If you've been reacting negatively to change, it's important to modify your attitude and your behavior before it's too late. Think about what you really want. To be comfortable or to be excellent? If you embrace challenge and welcome change, you will be on the right path to success.

When in your life have you embraced change and after initial resistance you found the change beneficial?

____

____

____

____

____

APRIL 4

SYNERGY (2 + 2 = 5 OR MORE)

Henry Ford once said, *"Coming together is a beginning, staying together is progress, and working together is success."*

Working together is harder than working by yourself. To be independent places a ceiling on your potential and production. The most successful people on the planet are great team players. They know that the only way to reach the top is to synergize with others so that your collective sum will exceed the output of both individuals independently.

My friend Brad owned a farm. He had one mule that could pull 1000lbs and another that could pull 1200lbs. When hooked together, math would tell you they could pull 2200lbs. Synergy tells why they could pull over 2500.

When a team outgrows individual performance and learns team cooperation and confidence, excellence and peak performance become a reality.

APRIL 5

STAND FOR NOTHING, FALL FOR ANYTHING

What are your core values? What are the character traits that define you and how you live your life?

Most people stop what they are doing, get a checkup from neck up, and ask themselves if they are living their life the way they intended.

None of us make it out of the game called life alive. Let's begin today with the end in mind.

What 3-4 words would you want engraved on your tombstone to describe the values that you lived in your life? Would integrity be inscribed?

Are you a person of integrity who does the right thing at all times even though doing what's right is not always popular and doing what is popular is not always right?

What words would you want to be inscribed?

____

____

____

____

____

____

____

APRIL 6

ANTICIPATE ADRENALINE

When you compete, you must anticipate adrenaline. You must be aware of how you respond mentally and emotionally when the pressure is on and the game is on the line.

Adrenaline, if harnessed, can help take your performance to another level. If left unchecked, adrenaline released too early can leave you with nothing left in the tank to fight the championship rounds.

The Ultimate Fighting Championship warriors I work with know all about anticipating adrenaline.

We will actually go to the locker room the morning of the fight and practice the warm-up and the walk-in to the arena and the cage to help deal with the butterflies that they will have later that night when it is time to compete.

Anticipate adrenaline and know that the #1 skill you can use to calm yourself down is only one deep breath away.

GET YOUR BUTTERFLIES TO FLY IN FORMATION

APRIL 7

BITE IT NOW OR SWALLOW IT LATER

As a peak performance coach who works with some of the top athletes and corporate professionals on the planet, I have found one common characteristic that consistent performers possess that flash-in-the-pan, good-once-in-a-while performers do not.

The consistent performers in any arena know the importance of putting off what they want in the moment for what they want most.

They know that today's efforts are tomorrow's results. They know that as competitors they are always staring down the barrel of a gun, and they choose to bite the bullet now and do what needs to be done TODAY!

The inconsistent have success early and then get away from the processes and day-to-day attention to detail that made them successful.

They believe that they don't need to do what they used to do because of their success.

They are the ones who will swallow the bullet of regret later because they were not willing to bite the bullet today, every day.

TODAY'S EFFORTS ARE TOMORROW'S RESULTS

APRIL 8

THE WORLD'S GREATEST AUTHOR IS...

You are the world's greatest author. You just may not be writing. Today is the first blank page of a 365-page book called The Year.

If you were to write one page a day by investing 5-10 minutes, you might end up having a best seller at the end of the year.

My first book and first best seller, *Toilets, Bricks, Fish Hooks and PRIDE,* was written one page at a time. The book you have in your hands right now was written one page a day for an entire year.

As I type this, I am sitting on a United Airlines flight from Birmingham, Alabama to Chicago, Illinois.

Writing is not hard; you do it every day. Having the discipline to create the habit to do it every day is what can be intimidating because you look at doing it every day for a year and don't know if you can do anything for 365 straight days.

Start writing your story today. If you miss a day, so what - next page. Be flexible with yourself and you will never be bent out of shape.

APRIL 9

DO IT OR TOSS IT ASIDE?

You are the person who has to decide whether you'd do it or toss it aside. You are the person who makes up your mind whether you'll lead or will linger behind – whether you'll try for the goal that's afar, or just be contented to stay where you are.

Edgar Guest

What is it that you really want? What can you do today to help you get what you really want?

APRIL 10

GOLD MEDALS

Dan Gable, former wrestling coach at The University of Iowa, is one of the NCAA's greatest coaches of all time. He won 16 NCAA National Championships as their head coach. As a wrestler himself, Gable was 181-1 while in college, won two NCAA National Championships himself and was a gold medalist in the 1972 Munich Olympics.

Gable said: *"Gold medals are not really made of gold. They are made of blood, sweat, tears and a rare-to-find alloy called guts."*

Gable knows that champions are not crowned when they win a match, but in the hours, weeks, months, and years spent preparing to battle. He knows that the victorious performance itself was merely demonstration of their championship efforts, commitment, character and discipline compounded over time.

GOLD MEDALS ARE NOT MADE OF GOLD

APRIL 11

COMPETE WITH YOURSELF

Arguably the greatest athlete in snow sports history, two-time Olympic Snowboarding Gold Medalist and thirteen-time X-Games Gold Medalist Shaun White knows the value of competing against yourself and the game.

If I try to beat someone, then I can only get as good as they are. If I try to be as good as I can be, there's no telling where that might lead.

Shaun White

What are you competing with yourself for to be the best version of you that you have ever been?

I want to throw harder and get in the best shape of my life. I really want to help this team win.

APRIL 12

HOW TO FIX ALL OF YOUR PROBLEMS

You cannot fix your problems with the same approach that you used to create them. If you do not change, why would you anticipate your problems changing?

Albert Einstein said, *"Insanity is doing the same thing over and over again and expecting a different result."*

You are accountable for behavioral change first if you want to see situational change in your life.

You will be the same person 10 years from now that you are today and probably have the same problems unless you change. You will be the same person except for the books you read, the experiences you have and the people you meet.

WORK AT YOURSELF FIRST

APRIL 13

YOU DON'T HAVE TO BE SICK TO GET BETTER

A common mistake people make is that they wait till they get sick before they go to a doctor. They wait until they are overweight before they get on a nutritional plan.

Why wait till you fall short of the goal to get started? What are your strengths? What do you do well? Can you enhance your strengths and keep working on yourself without letting any aspect of your life get too far out of balance?

To win a championship, you must first become a champion. Champions know that their greatest strength is themselves and that iron sharpens iron.

What are you working on today to make yourself better?

APRIL 14

DON'T CONFUSE ACTIVITY WITH ACCOMPLISHMENT

Another common mistake people make is that they think just because they are busy, they are accomplishing something. If you are majoring in minor things and are busy doing something that does not need to be done on your priority list or are doing something that can be delegated, you are not accomplishing. You are simply spending time.

Activity is not always accomplishment. The best leaders I have worked with are able to delegate. Their formula: Delegate that which can be done 80% as well as you can do it so that you can focus your time, energy and talent into what only you can do. There is a 3R test that you must ask to see if what you are about to do will pass.

1. Reward – Do you personally enjoy the task?

2. Return – What will be the return on your time investment?

3. Requirement – Are you required to do this task because there is nobody else who can?

APRIL 15

PUT YOURSELF IN OTHERS' SHOES

Andrew was always the popular kid who never knew why the new kids who moved into his school always sat alone and had a hard time adjusting.

He would roll his eyes and laugh when a new kid moved in and his teacher encouraged everyone to take the time to get to know the new student.

Andrew had his group of friends. He was perfectly content with his inner circle. Then his mother changed jobs and the family moved.

Andrew was now the new kid. He finally realized why his teachers had said what they had said and why the new kids ate alone, because that was what he was doing.

All the looks, the stares and the snickering were now about him.

What can you do to welcome others who are new to your area?

Can you expand your inner circle today to include those who have no circle or are looking for a new one?

APRIL 16

E-MAIL – PROPER SIGNATURE

We live in a time where e-mail can be a tremendous time saver or a tremendous time sucker. The choice is yours.

There are some key things to know about e-mail.

1. Your email must have a signature: your name; job position; phone number identified as mobile, office or home; shipping address; and e-mail address.

2. Most people fill their contact database, aka digital rolodex, with the information from people's e-mail signatures.

3. Often people forget to put their e-mail address in their e-mail signature. When others go to cut and paste your contact information into their contact database, they have to go back and forth to get your e-mail signature and a second time to get your e-mail address.

PUT YOUR E-MAIL ADDRESS IN YOUR SIGNATURE

APRIL 17

E-MAIL – TOUCH IT ONCE

As common as it is for everyone to have e-mail, most people still do not know how to properly manage their inboxes.

Although many people see the inbox as a place where e-mails are stored, you should view your inbox as a temporary holding place. Once you open and read an e-mail, you have touched it once; you must then either reply, delete, or move it to a folder.

Each time you process e-mail, the goal is to get your inbox to zero by using folders to file your messages.

The key is to touch it once. If you read it twice, you are wasting time, especially if you deal with dozens or hundreds of e-mails a day.

Using the touch-it-once rule allows you to go through your inbox very fast and initially process only what is necessary.

If someone needs a quick response, you take care of it; if an e-mail needs more attention, you can work on that later and prioritize which gets the most attention.

APRIL 18

E-MAIL – FOLDER STRUCTURE

If you are an e-mail grazer who processes messages one by one as they hit your inbox, you may need a more effective way to manage your e-mail. Applying a folder structure to your e-mail will keep you organized and more efficient.

There is a folder for each of my clients. Folders within those folders help me stay organized around various projects; I call these archive folders. I archive almost all of my e-mails so that I can refer back to them if needed. I also have two folders that I use to help me clean my inbox upon checking messages.

1. Reply-2-Min Folder: Use this folder to file e-mails from your inbox that will take more than 2 minutes for a reply. For example: an e-mail request from a client to go to Maui and speak at their annual retreat in December.

2. Waiting for Action Folder: This folder is for e-mails that need a response. For example, I ordered a book on Amazon and am waiting for it to arrive. I will file the e-mail here and when the book arrives, I will archive the e-mail in my Amazon, Book Orders folder.

APRIL 19

E-MAIL – CHECK IT SECOND

A big source of distraction comes from e-mail. It's common to read an e-mail, click on a link, read something interesting, then click on something else - and before you know it, you've wasted an hour surfing the web.

You must develop the awareness to recognize when you are wasting time on e-mail and the internet if you are going to be able to refocus on your priorities for the day and get them done.

I process my e-mail only twice a day and at fixed times: once in the morning after I've done my most important tasks and once in the evening as I close down my work day and get my plan ready for the next day.

I learned early in my career to never check e-mail first thing in the morning, as it will pull you into the vortex and will kill your productivity for the day.

My daily routine is to do my highest-priority tasks first and then, and only then, get into e-mail.

APRIL 20

HYDRATION EQUATION

Did you know that approximately 70% of the planet Earth is made up of water? Did you know that approximately 55-65% of the human body is water?

A hydration equation that I follow each day is to drink two thirds (2/3) of my body weight in fluid ounces of water.

The times when I am able to consume two thirds of my body weight in water I feel like I have more energy and greater focus than I do when I am unable to consume my daily hydration goal.

Research shows that when you are dehydrated you decrease reaction time and will experience a change in mood that will negatively affect performance.

Make sure that you carry a water bottle today and fully hydrate yourself for peak performance.

APRIL 21

CONFIDENCE CONDITIONING

Confidence is a choice. That choice is easier to make when you have conditioned yourself for confidence.

One of the best ways to condition your confidence each morning is to write five confidence conditioning statements that you can read, picture and feel. Writing them will help imprint them on your subconscious mind and rewire your confidence and self-talk. Confidence conditioning is a great way to train your subconscious mind to help you make changes to your current mentality and self-talk.

When writing your confidence conditioning statements, be sure to write them in the first person and present tense. Keep them positive by indicating achievement, and make them vivid so you can see and feel the image you are creating.

Some common confidence conditioning samples are:

> It is easy for me to firmly and politely say "no." I safeguard and prioritize my time.
>
> I limit alcohol consumption to 0-2 drinks when I go out; alcohol is a poison that slows down my progress.
>
> I remain calm and rational when others are upset, frustrated and emotional.
>
> I am an energy giver. I make it about others every day and in turn make myself better.
>
> I feel fit, functional and in shape at my ideal weight of 195-200 and at 10% body fat.

I listen attentively when others speak with me and I stay in the present moment.

I make bonds with others that last a lifetime; friendship is a fine art.

I live with integrity and honesty, and I do the right thing at all times.

I am a model of discipline in all I do. Discipline is my key to unlocking my potential.

I am 100% responsible and accountable for my career and life success.

I bring a natural and relentless positive energy and enthusiasm with me to work each day. My relentless positive energy is contagious and lifts others to another level.

I am constantly evolving and learning each day; every day in every way I am getting better and better.

I make the best use of my time and am always looking for ways to be more efficient and effective.

I am well organized, detail oriented and systematic in my approach to life and daily domination.

I welcome constructive criticism and coaching and use it to get better every day.

APRIL 22

CONTEXT AND CONTENT RELATIONSHIP

I attend a lot of coaches' clinics, close to ten a year. While I am there to present, I will set up shop in the front row for all other speakers as I am a learner first.

Speakers often discuss content more than context:

How to do what they do vs. how to best connect with whom they are teaching.

Content is what you teach; context is the relationship you have with the persons you are teaching.

The best coaches I have heard speak, worked with and played for had the balance between content and context.

Without the context, your content will not be received; and without the content, you will not be able to get the people you lead to reach their maximum potential.

People don't care what you know until they know that you care. Start today by investing into others and start strengthening your context.

INVEST IN OTHERS TODAY

APRIL 23

WHY ASK WHY?

There are leaders and there are people who lead. Leaders hold a position of power or authority while those who lead inspire others into action.

One of the greatest ways for you to lead is to know why you do what you do.

Most people will talk about what they do and how they do it, but they fail to hit us on the emotional level of why they do what they do.

You must ask yourself why you do what you do, and be clear in your communications of why you do what you do, if you are ever going to get others to do what you want them to do.

Help answer your why.

What is your purpose? ______________________________

____

Why do you exist? __________________________________

____

Why do you get out of bed in the morning? _____________

____

Why should anyone care? ____________________________

____

APRIL 24

HIRE FOR ATTITUDE, TRAIN FOR SKILL

When you hire someone to work with you, be sure that you hire for attitude and train for skill.

Be sure that you hire for belief and then train for talent.

If you hire someone who can perform a job, they will come and work for money; but if you hire someone for belief and attitude, they will come and work for a bigger purpose and will invest in your company with blood, sweat and tears.

Why is it that some full-time employees give a part-time effort while some part-time employees give an overtime effort?

Belief.

What can you do today to inspire those around you to make a difference in the lives of those you lead and inspire them to greatness?

Who will you help reconnect with their why today and how will you do it?

Just be a positive influence and if there is something they need to do, motivate them.

APRIL 25

MAKE TODAY YOUR BANQUET

Imagine that you are attending a banquet in honor of your retirement from the profession of your choice.

All of your friends, family, colleagues, teammates and competitors are there to send you their well wishes and help you celebrate in style. After a meal of grilled chicken and soggy salad, someone who you choose will come to the stage and speak about your legacy.

After a few humorous putdowns - ok, many humorous putdowns - that person will get serious and talk about your legacy, how you treated others, how you went about your daily business and how you will be remembered. What do you want them to say at your banquet?

That I was always the hardest worker and brought the best out in others not just myself.

APRIL 26

LAND THE PLANE AND FLY AGAIN

In life there are going to be storms. You must land the plane and fly again.

Storms come in the form of relationships, jobs, athletic contests and periods of life where you must navigate the challenges presented to you and safely land your plane so that you can fly again.

The reality is that there will be days and periods in your life of transition where you get dominated. These times are not to be ignored but to be embraced. There are times to take a deep breath, land your plane and fly again.

When the weather of life is so challenging that you cannot fly safely any longer, may your air traffic control (internal voice of intuition) guide you to land the plane and fly again.

APRIL 27

ASK THE RIGHT THREE QUESTIONS

Asking the right question is a key component of coaching others to peak performance. When in the heat of the moment and in the competitive arena, you want to ask the right question of those you lead during performance to get the information you need while not putting your team on the defensive.

Rather than ask the players why they did what they did, which indicates that they may have done something wrong, ask them to explain what actually happened and get them to learn in the process. Three questions to ask.

1. What just happened?

2. What would be preferable?

3. How would you correct that next time?

These three questions will help bring out the information you need to refine your process and keep moving to the next level.

APRIL 28

TAPE ACRONYM USED BY SUCCESSFUL COACH

Paul Niggebrugge is the athletic director and head baseball coach at Caravel Academy in Bear, Delaware. He is one of the nation's top high school coaches and builds his program's championship culture around the acronym TAPE.

Trust

Team

Authenticity

Accountability

Presence

Preparation

Energy

Enthusiasm

He uses the TAPE acronym as the foundation of his program and uses it to create a team culture that allows for accountability and risk-taking without the fear of retribution.

Niggebrugge teaches the young men he leads that *"The privilege of a lifetime is to be who you are."*

His advice for coaches:

People need to know that you are authentic and genuine and that you have their best interest at heart, that you want to see them succeed and you are providing them with an opportunity for them to become the best they are capable of becoming.

He also suggests that you work with people together as partners and not as servants in your grand scheme for the group.

What could be an acronym that describes the philosophy of your team or in your office?

APRIL 29

4TH QUARTER TOUGHNESS

I had the great opportunity to work with The University of Maryland Men's Lacrosse program and their head coach Dave Cottle, a true Master of The Mental Game. Coach Cottle developed a 4th quarter toughness in the Terps through a daily commitment to teaching the five core covenants of Maryland Lacrosse.

1. Discipline
2. Commitment
3. Toughness
4. Effort
5. Pride

Cottle brought this same 4th quarter toughness into his role as head coach with the Chesapeake Bayhawks of Major League Lacrosse and led them to the 2012 World Championship.

What are your personal core covenants?

____

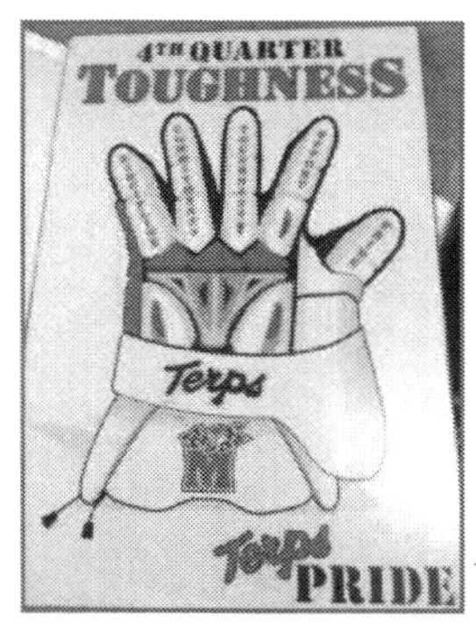

APRIL 30

DROP THE GUILLOTINE ON PERFORMANCE

In the old days, they used the guillotine to get people to stop thinking so much. It was used for other reasons as well, but this was the sole purpose for its use in performance.

As a performer, if you think too much, you lose. You must be in a trusting, not thinking, mentality when you compete. As a part of your routine, you must have a guillotine that you use to cut off thought process.

Athletes that I have worked with have used a deep breath, a final thought or a number of other physical cues to signify dropping the guillotine and cutting off thought process from performance.

What part of your routine signifies the time when you drop the guillotine and shift from thinking to trusting?

MAY

May is the month for me to dominate...

Workouts, yoga, diet, Quit drinking when I get back from the beach, start summer classes, internship and training off on a good note. Study hard to finish semester off strong!

MAY 1

MAKE, THEN MANAGE YOUR DECISION

When you wake up in the morning, have you already made the decision that you are going to Dominate The Day because you have a plan of what to do, or more importantly a plan as to how to live?

When you wake up, you must make the decision to live the way you want to live.

To be an energy giver who moves from *me* to *we* and is constantly working to help others and share their vision for the team's success.

Once your decision is made, get ready for adversity and the challenge of life. Get ready for its mission to throw you a continual stream of challenging events and issues to get you to act differently from that early-morning decision about how you would carry yourself and how you would act.

Make your decision, and then manage your decision to live the way you intend to live today.

How do you want to live today?

____

____

____

____

____

MAY 2

A LEGEND'S LESSON

There once was a young woman who wanted to be successful.

When she met a legend in her field and wanted to be his apprentice, he told her to meet him at the beach at 4am the next day for a run as a test of her commitment.

After the run, where they spoke about her wants and wishes, the legend asked her to walk out shoulder deep into the ocean with him.

When they got shoulder deep, the legend stopped and asked her how badly she wanted to be successful?

She said that it was her #1 goal in life.

The legend then dunked her head under the water and held her there as she began to fight, scratch and claw to get back to the surface.

When she finally popped her head up, gasping for air, the legend looked her in the eye and said, "When you want to be successful as badly as you want to breathe right now, that is when you will be successful."

MAY 3

THE NUMBER 52

There are 52 cards in a playing deck, and one NFL linebacker wears number 52 with Pride.

While growing up, he saw his mother get abused by her boyfriend and he vowed not to let her ever feel that pain again.

He knew as a child that if he got bigger and stronger he could protect her from the abuse.

He asked his mother for a deck of playing cards. She told him that he was not to gamble with his friends, and he told her that it was for something much more important than that.

When she handed him that deck of cards, he went right to his room and started doing push-ups according to the number that was on the card.

If it was a face card, he did 25. An ace was 50 and a joker was 100. Over time he was able to complete the entire deck and his upper-body strength, confidence and discipline improved.

Now he trains with 2 and 3 decks.

This player put the compound effect into action and benefited from his daily decisions adding up over time and resulting in a Hall of Fame NFL Career.

MAY 4

THE POSITION & THE LEADER

The title of leader is just that, a title.

Whether you are a coach, teacher, athletic team captain or have the title of leader in your position, that does not make you a leader.

Titles do not make a leader. Positions don't make a leader. Selfless service is what makes you a leader.

Thinking *we* instead of *me* is a critical part of solving the leadership puzzle.

Being able to put the wants and needs of the group over your own is a demonstration of leadership.

The best leaders I have been around have been able to walk the walk and talk the talk.

They not only lead by example - they also communicate clearly, effectively and efficiently with the people who they lead.

What is one aspect of your leadership self that you can improve to enhance your credibility and effectiveness?

PUT OTHERS FIRST – LEADERSHIP IS SELFLESS SERVICE TO OTHERS

MAY 5

TURN A DREAM INTO REALITY

How do you turn a dream into a reality? When you know what your dream is, find someone who has made that dream a reality and ask them how they were able to do what they did. Success leaves clues; if you do what they did, you will most likely get a similar result.

Your dream must motivate you to do what most others are not willing to do. Sir Edmund Hillary had a dream of climbing Mount Everest. He had a dream, made a plan and prepared relentlessly to put that plan into action. He did not wake up one day and decide to go for a walk and end up on the top of the mountain. Neither will you reach the summit you seek by just going for a walk.

You must work till you are in pain; and when you are in pain, keep going - get a reward from it.

YOU DON'T DECIDE TO GO FOR A WALK AND REACH THE SUMMIT. PLAN YOUR SUCCESS.

MAY 6

BUILD IT BIG, ALL THE TIME

There once lived a master carpenter who built custom homes for a real estate tycoon for the better part of his career.

The master carpenter had been paid well and had made a lot of money due to his excellent craftsmanship and attention to detail. He was a carpenter of excellence; he never cut corners and always double-checked his work.

He used only the best materials and built homes that would stand the test of time.

When the master carpenter decided it was time to retire, the real estate tycoon begged him to build just one more.

Reluctantly the master carpenter agreed and spent the next half-year building a mansion with a HAVE-to mentality, the opposite of the WANT-to and GET-to mentality he had carried his entire career.

With his have-to mentality the master carpenter purchased the cheapest lumber that was available so he did have to wait for the lumber to be shipped in, and he used materials that he would otherwise have not used because they did not meet his standard of excellence.

He just wanted to get done with this house. It was a HAVE-to and the last home he would ever build. Instead of doing all the work himself or carefully supervising a team of excellence-seeking workers, he hired contractors and went to play golf - something that he had said he would never do earlier in his career. He just wanted to get the job done and was not focused on getting it done right.

When he finished the job, it looked awesome on the outside; but the house was built as a HAVE-to and the infrastructure where it mattered most, the skeleton of the house, was weak.

The master carpenter had a different feeling when finishing this house. He was happy it was done, but he was disappointed in his efforts and knew the home was not built to the standard of excellence that he had exemplified throughout his career.

When the real estate tycoon showed up to see the final product, he was impressed.

He thanked the master carpenter for his years of selfless service, dedication and commitment to excellence.

He then handed the keys to the carpenter and said that he hoped he would enjoy retirement in his new home. The house the carpenter had built was his own.

MAY 7

MEASUREMENTS OF SUCCESS

You treasure what you measure. Measurement leads to motivation. However, not everything that counts can be measured and not everything that can be measured counts.

A crude measure of the right thing beats a precise measure of the wrong thing any day.

What is it that you are measuring in your life?

Is there anything that you need more of? Time with loved ones? Time invested into your personal health, exercise, sleep or continuing education?

Is there anything that you need to stop by measuring? Alcohol consumption, gambling, empty calories?

What is one aspect of your life that you will start measuring for improvement and one aspect you will try to eliminate by measuring?

IMPROVE:

____

____

ELIMINATE:

____

____

MAY 8

LIVE UNDER YOUR MEANS

When you are in college or enjoying the opportunity to earn a paycheck in your first job, be careful that your lifestyle does not hang on your income.

One of the biggest mistakes I made in my mid-twenties that I see repeated often by the professional athletes and young entrepreneurs I coach is that as their salary goes up, so do their living expenses.

This common mistake causes you to live paycheck to paycheck and keeps you from getting ahead financially.

If you can keep a humble lifestyle below your means and pay yourself first (put the first 10-30% of your paycheck to work for you in a retirement account, IRA, ROTH IRA, investment) you will set yourself up for financial freedom in the long term.

Put off what you want in the moment for what you want most.

Don't spend money you don't have on what you don't need to impress people you don't care about.

MAY 9

CHOOSE TO BE EXCITED

We often think that we will get enthusiastic about our life or our career when we have a life or a career that is exciting.

I have learned that the opposite is true. When you get excited and enthusiastic about your life and your career, then your life and career will become exciting.

When you get excited about going to your career each day, your career becomes exciting.

When you get excited about going home each day after work to invest time with your family, your family time becomes more exciting.

Be excited first, and then the excitement will follow. What in your life have you wanted to become exciting? Get excited about it now - and it will thus become exciting.

I will be enthusiastic about:

____

____

____

____

____

____

____

MAY 10

CARRY YOUR GOALS WITH YOU

I recently spoke at a seminar in Las Vegas and asked my audience to answer three important questions.

#1. I asked them to raise a hand if they had goals. Every hand went up.

#2. I then asked them to raise their hands if they had their goals written down on paper and posted where they could see them each day. Only about half of the hands went up.

#3. I then asked them to raise a hand if they had their goals physically written down and in their possession at the conference.

Only 3 people pulled out their goals from their pocket; two of them had been to one of my seminars before and knew that I would be asking this of my audience.

That meant there was only one person there who was not tipped on the importance of writing their goals and was carrying them on a daily basis.

Carry your goals on you at all times and you dramatically increase your chances at success.

MAY 11

ATTITUDE IS AN ASSET

When you make the decision that you and only you are 100% responsible for your attitude and effort at all times, you will have the key to unlocking your success.

Attitude in life is the most important controllable asset you possess.

It is your attitude that will determine your altitude, and the attitude you take is a decision you make. Make sure that your attitude is your greatest asset and not your greatest liability.

Attitudes are contagious. Is yours worth catching?

What about your attitude is your greatest asset?

____

____

____

What about your attitude is your greatest liability? ______

____

____

____

____

____

____

MAY 12

WHAT'S IN YOU?

Former UCLA basketball coach John Wooden is one of the greatest coaches and greatest winners who ever lived. He encouraged his players to *"not let what you cannot do interfere with what you can do."*

Wooden was known for teaching excellence over winning in his program and encouraging his players to work toward their personal potential and personal best vs. trying to beat the opposition.

Wooden never made winning a championship his goal because he knew that winning an NCAA title was a by-product of working the process and doing things the right way on a daily basis.

Similar to Steve Jobs, the former CEO of Apple, Wooden is quoted as saying: *"The journey is the reward and the destination is the disease. Focus on the journey and the destination takes care of itself."*

Wooden had a singular focus for the aspects of performance that he could control. That singular focus helped earn his UCLA teams four undefeated seasons, an eighty-eight game winning streak and an amazing ten national championships.

As you move forward this week and this month, remember that what happens inside of you is more important than what happens to you or around you. You CAN control your attitude on the journey, and you have no control over the actions and attitudes of others. You need to keep your focus on what you can control - yourself and your performance within the framework of the team.

You can control what you put on your calendar; however, you can't control today's circumstances. The majority of fear and stress that people experience in life is most often from things they can do nothing about. Don't let that happen to you. Control what's in you!

**CONTROL WHAT'S INSIDE OF YOU,
LET GO OF WHAT YOU CAN'T CONTROL**

MAY 13

THREE STAGES OF DEPENDENCE

When I first read Stephen Covey's *Seven Habits of Highly Effective People,* one of his teachings stuck out to me more than any other.

His comments about the three stages of dependence caught my attention, as I see many people who are never able to move out of the first stage and subsequently are enabled for their entire lives.

Stage One: Dependent

Stage Two: Independent

Stage Three: Interdependent

When we are first born, we are dependent on our parents for food, shelter, love and just about everything.

As we reach our teenage years, we thirst for independence where we start to make our own decisions about how we live our lives and have a very inward perspective of the world.

Interdependence is the synergy that comes from knowing that together you are better than if you are on your own.

Interdependence is what makes great teams, marriages and families work.

Together we are better than alone.

MAY 14

CAN YOU HELP ME?

When you hear someone ask you for help, what is most often your initial response? My guess is that it is usually "Yes, I can."

If you are the first person willing to help, you may unfortunately be the last person willing to ask for help.

Asking for help is a sign of strength, a sign that you know you cannot get to where you want to go by yourself.

When you request help, the persons you ask are immediately put on the side of care and giving vs. on the defensive of having to give something up to help you.

When you ask for help, they have the opportunity to feel as if they are providing you with value and support, and in turn they receive an intrinsic feeling of giving and empowerment that they might not otherwise feel.

Who can you ask for help today?

____

What is a situation where asking for help vs. demanding help is more likely to get you what you want?

____

____

____

____

MAY 15

HIRE FOR ATTITUDE, TRAIN FOR SKILL, AGAIN

One of the best pieces of advice I ever heard as a high school administrator who had responsibilities for staff hiring was to hire for attitude and train for skill.

With the right attitude you can learn to do anything, and as a supervisor you can train people with the right attitude to perform the way you want them to perform.

When you hire someone with the wrong attitude who may be a better performer initially, you are destined to regret that decision. And the time it takes to clean up after someone with the wrong attitude is much greater over time than training the person with the right attitude.

Those with the right attitude are not focused on *their* way; they focus on the *best* way.

They do not do what they do because that is always how it has been done; they do what they do because it is the best way to do it.

Anything can be accomplished with the right attitude, but very little can be accomplished with the wrong one.

MAY 16

THE IMPORTANCE OF THOUGHT

Leadership guru John C. Maxwell offers four tips for successful thinking in his book *How Successful People Think.*

1. Everything begins with a thought. *"Life consists of what a man is thinking about all day."* – Ralph Waldo Emerson

2. What we think determines who we are. Who we are determines what we do. *"The actions of men are the best interpreters of their thoughts."* – John Locke

3. Our thoughts determine our destiny. Our destiny determines our legacy. *"You are today where your thoughts have brought you. You will be tomorrow where your thoughts take you."* – James Allen

4. People who get to the top think differently than others. *"Nothing limits achievement like small thinking; nothing expands possibilities like unleashing thinking."* – William A. Ward

AS YOU THINK, SO SHALL YOU BECOME

MAY 17

SETBACK SETS UP A COMEBACK

Setbacks are a necessary exit on the road to success. Setbacks are nothing more than a setup for a comeback.

Failure is never final and failure is never fatal. It is how you bounce back from adversity that will determine the impact of your setback.

Failure is positive feedback for learning from each and every situation and circumstance, both good and bad.

Thomas Edison saw each failed attempt at the light bulb as a successful attempt at what did not work. He saw himself as a learner, not a loser.

Edison found valuable information in each setback and used that information as motivation for a comeback.

What setback have you experienced recently where you can learn from the loss and use it as motivation and information to make you stronger in the future?

____

____

____

____

____

____

MAY 18

HAVING A VISION FOR YOUR PROGRAM

A brick in the foundation of any successful organization is that the leaders possess a vision of who they want to be and how they want to act.

Once you have your vision, you must then have a plan to implement and teach your vision to get people to share that vision.

As a leader, you must set the example that you want others to follow by living the principles and values that are important.

Leaders focus on the process of what it takes to be successful. They spend less than 20% of their time talking about what they want to accomplish and 80% or more on how they are going to do it.

They don't talk about winning championships; instead, they talk about being champions.

Seeing your vision come to fruition doesn't come from pie-in-the-sky thinking.

It's the result of consciously doing something each day that will add to your overall excellence.

Each day has a life and a history of its own.

What history are you making today?

MAY 19

THE FOUR LEVELS OF CHANGE

People can be resistant to change because they often think they are living the best life they can in that moment or common sense would tell them to do something else.

Unfortunately, common sense is not common practice.

As a leader, you are a change artist who gets others to change their ideas or perspectives because they want to do so.

Understanding the four levels of change will help you to better understand where you are on the change continuum with others.

4 LEVELS OF CHANGE

1. Resistance to change
2. Good idea for others to try
3. Are willing to try it out themselves
4. Can't believe they lived without the change

When making changes, you will meet resistance. Keep showing the benefits of change and eventually people will not believe they lived any other way.

MAY 20

THOUGHTS ON EFFORT

You must go ALL OUT today to give yourself the best chance for success tomorrow.

Ultimate Effort = Ultimate Victory.

You can make excuses or you can make it happen - you can never do both.

Extra effort is the expected effort of the excellent.

If people have to coach your effort, you will not be able to get past the level of average.

Successful people in any field are driven by an intrinsic motivation.

Failure is always an option.

It is the most readily available option there is in any situation. All you need to do to fail is to show up. Failure is a choice. So is success.

When you are faced with the fork in the road, which path are you going to choose?

Always remember that there are no traffic jams on the extra mile.

EFFORT IS THE #1 SEPARATOR AMONG THE SUCCESSFUL AND UNSUCCESSFUL

MAY 21

THE POWER OF DAILY ROUTINES

Establishing daily routines is an essential part of the success process.

Having a set ritual that you go through in the morning and evening as well as throughout your day will compound over time and either bring you closer or further from your goals.

What are your routines?

Do you text when you drive, or are you opposed to this life-threatening activity? Do you realize that if you send one text message and look at your screen for 4-5 seconds while driving 55MPH you essentially are driving your car around the bases of a major league baseball stadium blind?

Bad routines like smoking, drinking or spending too much time in front of the TV will add up over time and keep you from your goals and dreams. Successful routines of daily exercise and reading inspirational or educational material will propel you to the top.

My routines worth keeping:

Yoga, working out, reading, eating right

My routines worth losing:

Texting too much, drinking too much, staying up late, eating late at night

MAY 22

SETTING DAILY, WEEKLY, MONTHLY AND YEARLY GOALS

You will never hit the target that you can't see, and going through a day of life without goals is like going to the firing range that has no targets to shoot at.

You will throw a lot of ammo down range but will have no idea if you are anywhere near your target. Creating targets/goals for each day, week, month and year is a fundamental of the successful.

They wake up each day on a mission to accomplish their goals. They have also broken down their yearly goals into a more manageable monthly, weekly and daily process that will assure that they arrive at their destination.

What is one of your yearly goals?

____

What is one of your monthly goals?

____

What is one of your weekly goals?

____

What is a goal for today?

____

MAY 23

DAILY WORK ON YOURSELF

The most successful people I have been around have some commonalities regardless of their chosen field. One of those commonalities is daily work at themselves.

Whether it is a subscription to a trade journal or periodical in your field, listening to a free podcast, watching a motivational video on YouTube or reading a page of this book, the strongest investment you can make is the investment you make into yourself and your personal development.

All great leaders are learners first.

What are you doing to work at yourself today?

I am or could be reading:

____

I could do this:

____

WORK AT BEING THE BEST THAT YOU CAN BE TODAY

MAY 24

DAILY EXERCISE

The greatest invention on the plant is you. Your human body is as fine a machine as there has ever been or ever will be.

This machine is self-correcting in that it repairs itself each and every night while you sleep.

It tells you when it likes things by flooding you with positive emotion and when it does not like something by the experience of negative feelings.

Your human body must be maintained through daily exercise. A minimum of 20 minutes of cardio activity and some simple body weight strength training such as push-ups or sit-ups can get you started.

Having a personal trainer or coach you use is ideal, as it takes the guesswork out for you so you can keep your focus and research on what you do best - your career.

What will you do for exercise today?

___

Start tracking what you do on a daily basis for exercise.

DO A LITTLE A LOT, NOT A LOT A LITTLE

MAY 25

DAILY RELATIONSHIP INVESTMENT

Whatever field you are in, you are always in the field of relationships.

The relationships you keep and the relationships you don't will have a tremendous impact on your success.

The most important word in a person's world is his or her name.

Being someone who prides yourself on remembering people's names and important dates such as birthdays or anniversaries will help you to strengthen those relationships you keep with people.

Few people are able to remember important dates, but you can use a calendar on your computer or with paper and pencil to help you remember who was born when.

Start with creating a system to remember birthdays by setting them up as yearly reoccurring appointments on your calendar, and take just a few minutes each day to call those people whose birthday it is.

This will help you to make at least one annual deposit into all of your relationship accounts.

INVEST IN OTHERS TODAY

MAY 26

DOMINATE YOUR DAY IN MODERATION

Anything in excess will become excessive. Moderation is a sign of maturity.

Exercise is important for your physical and mental health. Too much exercise can kill you.

Gambling, consuming alcohol or enjoying a dessert, chocolate or other sweets on occasion and in moderation are aspects of life that can give you pleasure.

Too much and you will be broke, obese and on the highway to Unsuccessful University.

To employ moderation in your life is to have discipline over yourself in all areas.

You control what you put in your mouth, where and when you spend your money, and what you do or don't do on a daily basis.

In what parts of your life do you demonstrate moderation?

____

____

Where in your life can you better demonstrate moderation?

____

____

____

MAY 27

DEVELOP A DO IT NOW MENTALITY

Procrastination is a sure way to put off what needs to be done today so you can enjoy what opportunities arise tomorrow.

Nike made the "Just Do It" slogan famous because it is the truth. Having the mentality to Do It Now and get it done is key to your success.

Putting the pressure or eustress (positive stress) on yourself to meet a deadline will help you get done what needs to be done, when it needs to be finished.

What are you putting off that you can get started on and finish today?

____

____

____

What is keeping you from having the Do It Now mentality?

____

____

____

Who do you know who has the Do It Now mentality? ____

____

____

MAY 28

DAILY CONFIDENCE CONDITIONING

You will be where you are one year from now because of the books you read, the people you meet and the experience you have in this coming year.

You can supercharge your progress by doing daily confidence conditioning. Confidence conditioning is simply writing out who you are going to become, your new way of thinking and acting. By simply writing that you currently are that way, you are turbocharging your subconscious mind to put you in that position so that you can experience success.

Examples of confidence conditioning statements are:

> I live with discipline in all areas of my life.
>
> I exercise each and every day; it fuels my energy tanks for success.
>
> I have a Do It Now mentality and invest my time into getting things done effectively and efficiently.

When writing your confidence conditioning statements, please write them in the present moment as if they are happening now.

Please write one confidence conditioning statement below and then start each day with writing all of your statements in your notes app on your iPhone or in a peak performance journal.

1. ____

____

MAY 29

PAY YOURSELF FIRST

One of the best pieces of financial advice I ever received was from my financial planner, one of the best in the business, Phil Spillane of Bell Wealth Management. He advised me to "*pay yourself first.*"

I did not know what that meant and frankly felt a little strange meeting with a financial planner at the time because I had no finances to plan with.

Meeting with Phil gave me a plan and helped me to understand the power of compound interest and the critical financial importance of paying yourself first: taking at least 10% of what you get every paycheck and putting it towards retirement as early in life as you can so that the 9th wonder of the world, compound interest, can go to work for you.

Begin with the end in mind. Pay yourself first and get with a financial planner to create a plan for your future. It is never too early or too late to do this. Make your appointment today.

PAY YOURSELF FIRST
PUT THE COMPOUND EFFECT TO WORK
ADD A FINANCIAL PLANNER TO YOUR TEAM

MAY 30

HAVE SELF-CONTROL AT ALL TIMES

My mentor in mental conditioning is Dr. Ken Ravizza, and I have his two rules of peak performance cemented into my core values.

1. You must be in control of yourself before you can control your performance.

2. You have very little control of what goes on around you, but total control of how you choose to respond to it.

Maintaining control of yourself physically, mentally and emotionally under stress and pressure when everyone else is losing theirs is an essential part of your growth and maturity as a performer and as a person.

The best way to gain and maintain self-control in any situation is to take a deep breath.

The deep breath pulls you into the present moment and brings oxygen into your system to help you relax, think more clearly and perform at your best.

SELF-CONTROL IS ONLY A BREATH AWAY

MAY 31

MOOMBA DISEASE

One of the best motivational speakers on the planet and a mentor of mine is Ed Agresta. Ed taught me about the most deadly disease on the planet.

Moomba Disease.

Moomba stands for My Only Obstacle May Be Attitude.

The attitude you take is a decision you make, and you must choose wisely. Attitude is the strongest and weakest muscle in your body. Like all other muscles, if you don't use it, you lose it.

You must do a little a lot, not a lot a little, and you must do strength training for your attitude. How? By continuing to read one of these pages each day and by remembering that you have the personal power to choose your attitude each day.

How will others describe your attitude today?

____

____

____

____

____

____

____

JUNE

June is the month for me to dominate...

JUNE 1

BROKEN WINDOWS

We all have broken windows in our lives that need to be replaced, and replaced quickly.

We need to fix problems when they are small. If you have a broken window and fix it within a short period of time, mental vandals are much less likely to break more windows or do further damage.

Clean up your sidewalk every day, and the tendency is for litter not to accumulate (or for the rate of littering to be much less).

If you supervise others and they have broken windows or dirty sidewalks (metaphorically speaking), that is a great sign that they don't have a strong investment or sense of ownership. The negligence of your team towards any form of a "broken window" signifies a lack of concern for the organization and community.

Remember this today: If you see it, you own it. If you see something out of order, take ownership and fix it.

IF YOU SEE IT, YOU OWN IT

JUNE 2

THE SCOREBOARD VS. THE PROCESS

The scoreboard has nothing to do with the process. In each play you look across at the opponent and commit yourself to dominating that person.

Success as a team in competition comes when you have individuals dominating the individuals they're playing against.

If you get your team to focus on executing their individual jobs and playing the game one play at a time and eliminating the distractions, you give yourself the best chance for success.

I'm tired of hearing all this talk from people who don't understand the process of hard work. They remind me of children in the back seat asking, "Are we there yet?"

You will get where you're going 200 feet at a time. Enjoy the journey.

What is a part of the journey that you are not enjoying as much as you could until today?

____

____

____

____

____

____

JUNE 3

GRIND

George Horton, head baseball coach at The University of Oregon, talks about enjoying the grind.

As a member of his staff for two seasons, I used to hear him say "the grind" a lot.

The grind is about doing the little things you might not want to do so that you can do what you want to do - like play for the national championship, get drafted or have the type of season that you desire.

If you love it, is it a grind?

Get

Ready

It's a

New

Day

GET YOUR MIND RIGHT TO GRIND RIGHT

What do you consider to be part of the grind?

____

____

JUNE 4

DANGEROUS TIME OF YEAR

This is a dangerous time of year in college baseball and softball. With the NCAA postseason in full swing, there will be some teams playing with 40-50 wins and some who have in the high twenties or low thirties. Why is it a dangerous time of year?

Because the teams with the fewer amount of wins who make it into the postseason have most likely been playing with a purpose and have been in playoff mode for the last few weeks of the season, while the teams with more wins knew that they would make it and have been in cruise control.

Run your race today like you are in playoff mode. Have an attitude of excellence and make extra effort your expected effort.

If you give what everyone else gives, you will get what everyone else gets.

Average.

There can only be one champion at the end of the season. What are you doing to position yourself to win today?

____

____

____

____

____

JUNE 5

THE BEST TEAM NEVER WINS

This is one of my very favorite times of the year. The college softball World Series is at its peak and a champion will be soon be crowned.

The college baseball Road to Omaha is underway, and there are 64 teams living the dream.

The team who will win the national championship in both college baseball and softball will not be the best team in the country; they will be the team who plays their best when it means the most.

There may be teams who were the best by far in the regular season's 56-game schedule and don't go home with the national championship because they don't play their best when it means the most.

Postseason success is all about playing your best.

What do you need to do to be at your best today?

____

____

____

____

____

____

____

JUNE 6

CONVERSATIONS AND FEELINGS

The events that happen to you are not as important as how you interpret those events.

When an event happens, good or bad, you start a conversation with yourself.

Understand that the event doesn't cause the way you feel about the situation. The conversation you have with yourself causes the way you feel about the situation.

Although it may appear at times that you don't have control over your thoughts, remember that you do have control over what thoughts you hold on to and what ones you let pass.

Much like watching ESPN and seeing the score ticker on the bottom of the screen, you don't have to pay attention to all of the scores or all of your thoughts - only the scores you are interested in and the thoughts that will help your performance.

**THOUGHTS BECOME THINGS
CHOOSE THEM WISELY**

JUNE 7

HIGH WATERS RAISE ALL BOATS

Competition with yourself and with others is what makes athletics exciting.

Competition is finding out who you match up against with others who have dedicated their efforts to the same craft.

I see too many athletes that try to "step up" in games yet coast through practice and pickup games with their friends.

If you want to take your game to the next level, you must remember that high waters raise all boats.

Competition on a daily basis in practice will make you and your teammates better.

The best athletes I have worked with are fierce competitors in everything they do.

They want to get to the field before you, beat you in every drill and competition, and then stay longer than you do.

What can you do today to raise your competitive metabolism with yourself and your teammates?

____

____

____

____

____

JUNE 8

MAKE THE BIG TIME WHERE YOU ARE

Today, challenge yourself to get totally immersed into the present moment and make the big time where you are.

I see too many coaches who are always job hunting and wondering what the next opening is going to be at that big-time school where they might have a chance to go.

I see too many athletes wondering how they are going to get to the next level and who will draft them or what school will offer them a scholarship.

The best way to get that dream job or to get to the next level as an athlete is to make the big time where you are.

Get lost in your daily pursuit of excellence. Treat today and your current position like it is your dream position and you will perform better than you have in the past.

Increased performance leads to increased results, which lead to promotions.

What can you do today to make the big time where you are?

JUNE 9

BE A TEAMMATE, NOT A FRIEND

The difference between a teammate and a friend is that a friend will most often tell you what you want to hear so that you feel better about yourself. A good teammate will tell you the truth.

We need to have those friends that we go to when we are in need of justifying our decisions and actions or lack thereof.

We also need to have teammates and accountability partners that tell us the truth and tell us when we are wrong, being stubborn, slacking or letting them down.

A coach friend of mine once said that he had only one rule in his programs.

Don't let your teammates down. This meant that you did what you said you were going to do and that you were always going to live and tell the truth, because your teammates' success was dependent on the decisions you made.

Who are your teammates that tell you the truth and will hold you accountable to a high standard of excellence?

____

____

____

____

____

JUNE 10

EFFECTIVENESS vs. EFFICIENCY

Who is winning the battle in your life? Effectiveness or Efficiency?

There is a balance that must be made between working hard and working smart, between being efficient and effective.

I once saw a mail carrier who put his mail in grass vs. in people's mailboxes.

He was very efficient at delivering mail and was always the first carrier back to the office and on his way home for the day.

His colleagues applauded his efficiency, but his effectiveness was terrible.

Where in your life do you need to slow down and focus on being more effective and a little less efficient?

____

____

How will you demonstrate a commitment to effectiveness over efficiency today?

____

____

____

____

JUNE 11

ORGANIZATION & SUCCESS

Having worked in professional baseball as a mental conditioning coach and having spent time in the major and minor league clubhouses at spring training, I made an observation that I want to share with you about organization and success.

I clearly saw a difference in the locker organization of the major league players compared to the minor league players.

Some of that may be attributed to the clubhouse personnel, but I also noticed that the better minor league players had more organized lockers than the players who were identified as players falling short of their potential.

The point here is simple.

There is a peace of mind that comes with organization.

The more organized you are, the less stress you have and the more efficient you can be, resulting in more productive time on the field.

TODAY – GET MORE ORGANIZED IN YOUR WORKPLACE AND YOUR LIFE

What will you do?

____

JUNE 12

THE ATTITUDE MUSCLE

How do you get bigger and stronger muscles? You exercise.

How do you get a bigger and stronger attitude? You exercise.

Attitude is a muscle that you lose if you don't use.

Remember that the attitude you take is a decision you make.

You are always 100% responsible for your attitude. Choose what you say, what you do and what you think wisely today.

Keep your thoughts positive because your thoughts become your words. Keep your words positive because your words become your behavior. Keep your behavior positive because your behavior becomes your habits. Keep your habits positive because your habits become your values. Keep your values positive because your values become your destiny.

Mahatma Gandhi

JUNE 13

THE TWO PAINS WE ALL EXPERIENCE

There are many pains in life. Life is not easy and nowhere does it say that life will be fair or give you what you think you deserve.

Of the many pains in life, there are two that stick out the most.

The pain of regret and the pain of discipline.

Pushing through pain when conditioning or staying up late to get a project done and the pain of regret for not pushing through in conditioning or staying up late both suck.

Here is the difference between those who succeed and those who fall short.

The ones who succeed are able to push through the pain.

They feel the same as the person who quits, but they just keep going.

The unsuccessful and the successful both experience the same pain; the successful choose to endure more pain to get what they want.

What pain will you push through today to get it done? ____

____

____

____

____

JUNE 14

LIFE & DEATH, GOOD & BAD / PERFECT

There is a recipe I have uncovered for indigestion and death. It is the recipe of trying to be perfect.

There never has been and never will be any human being that is perfect.

If you focus on perfection you may not kill yourself, but you are destined to kill your performance.

Champions know that results in competition will be both good *and* bad, not good *or* bad.

Both in victory and defeat there is always good and bad.

Eliminate perfection and strive for excellence.

LIFE = GOOD & BAD PERSPECTIVE
DEATH = PERFECTION PERSPECTIVE

Do you have a life or death perspective? Where can you benefit from evaluating as good and bad vs. good or bad and perfection?

____

____

____

____

JUNE 15

NATURAL DISASTERS

When natural disasters strike like Hurricane Irene, which tore up Vermont in August of 2011, we are reminded of what is truly important.

We are reminded that if we are to WIN, we must remember WIN means What's Important Now. What's important now is that you realize the power of perspective.

When tragedies like 9/11, Hurricane Irene or the mass shooting at the Batman Premier July 2012 in Aurora, Colorado happen, we are reminded of what's truly important to us, and we are grounded for a short period of time with our perspective.

Unfortunately, before too long, many of us get back on the treadmill or doing what's urgent and forget what's truly most important.

I hope there are no tragedies or natural disasters in your world today or ever.

I hope that you challenge yourself to focus on what's important now in your life.

JUNE 16

THREE VERY POWERFUL WORDS

Three of the most powerful words in your mental assassin toolbox are *"Compared to what?"*

Compared to what other people are going through right now in their lives, your insignificant troubles do not seem so big, do they?

The parking ticket, the overdraft on the credit card or the jerk in the media who is slamming you don't seem so big when people have lost their homes and loved ones and cities have billions of dollars of rebuilding to do.

Remember the "Compared to What" mentality and keep yourself grounded. The problems we face are not the problem; how we respond to them is really the problem.

Choose your response and your perspective wisely today.

DEVELOP A "COMPARED TO WHAT?" PERSPECTIVE

JUNE 17

PROBLEMS COME TO PASS

The problems you face will all come to pass.

Know that the problems you face can be minimized or maximized by your attitude and how YOU HANDLE the problem.

Check to make sure that you are not making a mountain out of a molehill by making the problem bigger than it really is. Break the problem down into process-based steps that you can follow so you have a good game plan as to how to address the problem.

Remember that E + R = O (Events + Your Response = The Outcome). Focus more on your response and less on the events and the outcome of what MIGHT happen.

When in your life have you chosen a response to an event that you wish you could redo?

____

____

When did you choose a response you were proud of?

____

____

____

____

____

JUNE 18

FIVE TIPS ON EMBRACING ADVERSITY

Here are five important tips to remember on embracing adversity.

1. Adversity is an unavoidable part of the PURSUIT OF EXCELLENCE.

2. COMPARED TO WHAT others are dealing with, your situation is not that bad. Get over it.

3. The problem is not the problem. HOW YOU HANDLE THE PROBLEM IS THE PROBLEM.

4. The grass is always greener where you water it. BE SURE YOU ARE WATERING POSITIVE GRASS AND POSITIVE THOUGHTS.

5. FAILURE IS POSITIVE FEEDBACK to make you stronger and better at what you do.

Which of these five tips on embracing adversity will help you the most to Dominate The Day?

____

____

WHY? ____________________________________

____

TODAY, EMBRACE ADVERSITY

JUNE 19

WORRYING IS A WASTE OF TIME

Worrying about what might happen or about aspects of life that are out of your control is a tremendous source of stress and a waste of time.

Worrying will make even the smallest troubles seem huge.

When you worry, you focus on the "what ifs" and the potential outcomes and not on "what is," the actual, matter-of-fact way that life is in the present moment.

Today, worry less about what you cannot control and focus more on what you can control.

Focus more on what is and less on what if.

"Worry is an old man with bent head, carrying a load of feathers he thinks is lead."

Billy Graham

JUNE 20

THE PRECIOUS PRESENT & LISTENING

Listening is a lost art.

With cell phones and other technologies today all fighting for your attention, face-to-face interaction has become ever important.

Go to any restaurant anywhere in the world and you are likely to see more people at dinner flipping through their phones than you see interacting with each other.

Learning to be a great listener will separate you from the competition.

Today, really listen to the person who is with you right now, whoever that may be - a client, a friend, a customer.

He or she is the most important person in your world at this precise moment.

If you listen, really listen, with all of your soul, that person may say something YOU really need to hear.

Listen with your ears, your eyes, your heart and your soul.

Be totally present and engaged in each conversation.

The cell phone will store other people's agendas for you to address when convenient.

JUNE 21

PRACTICE AND THEORY

In theory, theory and practice are the same. In practice, they are not.

Albert Einstein

Albert Einstein said it best.

What you learn in school and what happens in the real world unfortunately are not always consistent.

Be aware of those who quote research but themselves have not been in the battle implementing what they know through research in practical and applied settings.

The greatest education I have ever received was not in the classroom but in the field.

The classroom prepares you for success in the field, but you must go to battle and DO THE WORK.

Be your own researcher.

Be the one out there leading the charge; be willing to try new things and fail.

Be the one who does the work and gets into the trenches with other warriors to know more about what they go through on a daily basis.

BE A RESEARCHER, REPORTER AND RESULTS-GETTER

JUNE 22

TEN TOUGH LOVE LESSONS

The Ultimate Fighter Season 17 Jon Jones vs. Chael Sonnen reality show featured two masters of the mental game and mixed martial arts warriors as the head coaches of their respective teams. In season 17 these two great coaches shared mental game wisdom with their fighters that can benefit all of us.

1. Don't count the days; make them count.

2. Turn your have-to's into want-to's.

3. Every opponent is just another human. In competition, anyone can win and the best fighter never wins. The winner is the guy who fights the best.

4. FAILURE IS ALWAYS AN OPTION. Failure is the most readily available option at all times for all people. Failure and quitting is a choice. So is success. Make the choice to do whatever it takes to be successful. Failure is always an option - the easiest one of all - but it is never the right option.

5. Enjoy the suffering that comes with training, and when tired, carry yourself with GET BIG posture. Act differently than how you feel. Walk with confidence and swagger.

6. We live in a cold world that will give you nothing; you have to go out and fight for what you want. You can accomplish anything if you are willing to fight for it.

7. Be aggressive in all you do. The best defense is a great

offense. You can only control your offense and how aggressively you work and push the pace of competition.

8. Good fighters find openings; great fighters make them. Make your own momentum.

9. Confidence is a choice. Everyone has self-doubt and that negative voice in the head. The great ones embrace it, realize it will always be there, recognize it, release it and focus back on the process and what they need to do in that moment to be successful.

10. Do not think about the outcome - focus on the process, step by step, moment by moment.

There are so many awesome mental conditioning lessons to be learned from the most competitive and combative sport on the planet, mixed martial arts. This is a sport where you must absolutely be at your best when it means the most: each and every time you step in the cage if you are going to become a champion.

JUNE 23

MASTER OF THE MENTAL GAME
TODD WHITTING

Todd Whitting is the head baseball coach at The University of Houston and one of the top coaches in all of college baseball.

Whitting shared some thoughts on his team's performance and approach that we all can benefit from:

What we try to do in our program is not worry about momentum, but just keep playing. We make our own momentum pitch to pitch. The term 'so what' is a huge saying in our program; we yell it in our dugout all the time. Anytime something bad happens, 'so what.' We make our momentum on the next pitch with our effort, focus and our routines. Baseball is a long game, and sometimes it's a cruel game. You just have to keep playing, one pitch at a time.

No matter what happens today, keep playing one pitch at a time and make your own momentum with your effort, focus and routines.

SO WHAT!

JUNE 24

CRITICS, VAMPIRES AND FANS

The day you start to have critics and people who pick you apart and try to pull you down, you have started to achieve success.

As your success increases, you will find that you will attract three types of people.

1. Critics
2. Vampires
3. Fans

My experience tells me that there are far more in the #3 category than 1 or 2, but we make the mistake of giving 1 & 2 most of our attention.

There are 2 ways to have the biggest house on the block.

1. Build a bigger house.
2. Knock down all the ones bigger than yours.

Critics can't build their own big houses, so the only way for them to feel any kind of significance is to knock down everyone else's.

The vampires want to feast and suck off of your success.

They don't have what it takes on the inside to go out and make it happen for themselves, so they create a dark and shady life sucking off of others.

Fans are more positive than the critics and the vampires, and they will pat you on the back and beat the drum for you when things are going well.

Be careful! Fans are fickle and will turn on you in a hurry when things go south.

When the critics, vampires and fans show up, you have started to achieve success. You must keep on keeping on or you will be passed up by the next person.

Ultimate success cannot be measured in fans, money, homes or material things.

Ultimate success comes from knowing that you did everything you could to be the best you can be. When you do that, critics, vampires and fans just don't matter.

Find the balance between being your own worst critic and your biggest fan.

NAME ONE CRITIC:

____

NAME ONE VAMPIRE:

____

NAME ONE FAN:

____

JUNE 25

LEADERS AND TEACHERS

There have been many great leaders and teachers in college athletics.

Maybe none is greater than legendary UCLA Basketball coach John Wooden.

Wooden never called himself a coach; he was always a teacher.

A leader, particularly a teacher or coach, has a most powerful influence on those he or she leads, perhaps more than anyone outside the family. Therefore, it is the obligation of that leader, teacher, or coach to treat such responsibility as a grave concern. I consider it a sacred trust: helping to mold character, instill productive principles and values, and provide a positive example to those under my supervision. I like to think the players I coached, however they came to UCLA, left as men of character.

John Wooden, 1910 – 2010

We are all somebody's coach and teacher.

What will your students learn by your example today?

____

____

JUNE 26

THE CURSE OF EXPERIENCE

Thinking like a rookie can help you to sustain your success more than thinking like a veteran.

Experience is often a good thing. If you use it, experience can help you to better prepare for future success.

Experience can also be a curse.

When your experience causes you to focus on the past or the good ol' days and the way things were and causes you to complain about the way things are, you are likely to become resistant to change.

Remember that change is inevitable and growth is optional.

Rookies don't have experience, don't know about the way things were and have no knowledge of the good ol' days, but instead they create their own good ol' days right now in the present.

Make today one of your good ol' days.

RESIST THE TEMPTATION TO STAY IN A MAINTENANCE MINDSET AND GET INTO A GROWTH MINDSET

JUNE 27

EXCUSE EXTERMINATION

Today, eliminate excuses from your life, for just one day. You can do anything for just one day. You don't need to eliminate excuses for your entire life - just do it today.

Exterminate your excuses and start your day by saying: "This is my time, my life and my destiny. I make my own momentum and I will not stop today till I achieve my goal. I will attack today with a relentless positive energy and DOMINATE The Day!"

Being unstoppable and successful is a decision that you make every day - every hour, every minute and every second of the day.

Have the awareness that success is a choice.

Every time you choose to lock in your focus and stay on task, you are strengthening your self-discipline muscle.

With each refocus and excuse elimination, that muscle will grow stronger and stronger, making it easier to bring about the positive changes you seek in your performance and in your life.

JUNE 28

LIVE LIKE YOU WERE DYING

Tim McGraw's song *Live Like You Were Dying* is one of my favorite songs because it reminds me to live today to the fullest.

TO ACTUALLY LIVE TODAY TO THE FULLEST.

If I were dying I don't think I would be going to the airport and getting on a plane, but I would absolutely attack the day and everything I did that day with a relentless positive energy, giving as much of myself to others as I could.

I would have a heightened awareness and enjoy the simple things that are there every day.

Guess what? I am dying. So are you. We are both thirty seconds closer to death than we were when you started reading this page.

WHAT ARE YOU DOING WITH YOUR LIFE TODAY? IF YOU WERE DYING, WOULD YOU TAKE OR GIVE? TODAY, GIVE TO OTHERS, AT YOUR OFFICE, IN YOUR FAMILY, ON YOUR TEAM.

Attack today with an attitude of gratitude and dominate TODAY. Then do it again tomorrow like you were dying today.

JUNE 29

LIVE LIKE YOU WERE DYING, PART TWO

Do you live your life like you will be around forever? Do you take the simple things in life for granted?

Would your perspective change if you believed you were living your last week or last day?

A mentor of mine wakes up every morning surprised that he is still here.

He said his first thought each morning is, "Man, I can't believe I am still here.

"How lucky am I? I have another opportunity to make a difference in the lives of others today.

"Today may be my last, so let me go out by giving as much as I can to others."

Each day you choose your perspective. Live like it is your last, and bring a different sense of purpose and appreciation to everything you do today.

PREPARE, PRACTICE AND COMPETE LIKE THIS IS THE LAST GAME YOU WILL EVER PLAY

JUNE 30

BE WHERE YOU NEED TO BE, WHEN YOU NEED TO BE THERE

Ken Ravizza used to always remind us as his students to be where we need to be when we need to be there. He reminded of the importance of being present and focused during the course of the day.

All too common is the person who, when at home, is still consumed with mentally being at the office and when at the office is mentally home with the family.

Many of us go through the day without really being present. When we listen to others we may be hearing the words, but are we really absorbing the message?

If you go through the day and recognize your thoughts drifting to the past or future, remind yourself to be where you need to be when you need to be there.

Don't be so involved in yesterday or tomorrow that you don't notice that today is slipping by.

MAKE TODAY YOUR MASTERPIECE
SIGN YOUR NAME WITH EXCELLENCE

JULY

July is the month for me to dominate...

JULY 1

CHARACTER

My high school football coach John Allen used to tell us that it was more important to have character than to be a character. At 18 years old, I did not fully grasp what he meant. I must have been a character.

Character is determined in the presence of temptation, and the absence of an audience.

Alexandra Larsen

What you do when nobody is watching shows your character to yourself like looking in the mirror.

When you are walking down the hall and see trash on the floor, do you stop and pick it up or just keep walking?

This reveals your character to the person who matters most, YOU!

You can fool everyone else by putting on a show, but ultimately it is what you do when nobody is watching that counts.

Today, hunt for opportunities to demonstrate your character to yourself.

JULY 2

TIPS FROM *SUCCESS MAGAZINE*

The only magazine I subscribe to is *SUCCESS Magazine.* Its pages are full of great tips and insight from the most successful entrepreneurs on the planet. The following quotes came from the March 2013 issue. They remind me of the importance of doing what you love because you will make a difference over a buck. And that extra effort should be your expected effort.

ON HARD WORK

We romanticize entrepreneurship so much that people don't do the work.... It's not just a dream, not just a goal; it's a lot of hard work. A lot of people are wantrepreneurs, not entrepreneurs.

Mark Cuban
Owner of The Dallas Mavericks

ON MONEY

Make sure you're doing something that you love, that you're willing to do for the rest of your life. If you're doing it for money, that's the only thing you won't make.

Daymond John
CEO of FUBU

JULY 3

A BIG TUNA PHILOSOPHY

One of the greatest football coaches of all time, Bill Parcels, led NFL's New York Giants to victories in Super Bowls XXI and XXV.

Nicknamed "The Big Tuna," Parcels had a unique philosophy he shared with his teams that included three key beliefs.

1. Blame nobody.
2. Expect nothing.
3. Do something.

If you go to work today and blame nobody for your struggles, expect nothing in return for your services and efforts, and are constantly doing something to help your team, you will have a successful day.

Having worked with thousands of high school and college athletes, I can say that too many of them blame others before themselves, expect their coaches or parents to do things for them, and are slow to be proactive and do something to help their situation.

Today, blame nobody, expect nothing and by all means, DO SOMETHING!

JULY 4

THE USA NATIONAL ANTHEM

We play the National Anthem at almost every sporting event in the United States. Have you ever wondered how to stand for the anthem the correct way?

I mean, you don't want to be one of THOSE people who everyone's looking at and saying, "Wow, look at how he's (or she's) standing..."

Even worse, you don't want YOUR TEAM to be the one causing people to shake their heads.

To be honest, I WAS one of those people.

It wasn't until I was 28 years old that I met a college baseball coach, one of the most detailed and excellent human beings I have ever known, who actually practiced standing for the National Anthem with his team.

Here's the correct way to stand for *The Star-Spangled Banner...*

Remove your hat if you are wearing one, and place it in your right hand with the palm of your hand on the brim and the area between your thumb and pointer finger holding the front of your hat where the logo would be. Put your hat over your left chest.

If you are not wearing a hat, put your right hand over your left chest with your fingers and thumb touching, palm flat and open with the tip of your middle finger in line with where you left pectoral muscle and deltoid come together.

Stand at attention, heels together at 45 degrees, left arm straight to your side with your left fist in a position as if you were holding a roll of quarters.

Face the American flag. If there is not a flag present, face the general area of the music instead.

Stay at attention for three seconds after the last piece of sound in the anthem. If there is a color guard on the field, wait until they have lowered the flag.

You can either sing along with the words to the National Anthem, or remain silent. Do not eat, drink, make the noise of cymbals, talk, or use your phone at this time.

I realized I didn't really know much about the history of the National Anthem, so I did some research. After all, winners know WHY they do what they do, and can describe what they do as a process so that their performance will be consistent over time.

The tradition of performing the National Anthem before every baseball game began during World War II, but the song was sung at games before that.

Professional and amateur singers have been known to forget the words, which is one reason the song is sometimes pre-recorded and lip-synched.

One of the greatest leadership demonstrations in history happened on April 25, 2003, when Maurice Cheeks, coaching with the Portland Trail Blazers, gave Natalie Gilbert, a 13-year-old 8th grader, a little help singing the National Anthem before 20,000 fans.

I know you are making a difference in people's lives like Maurice Cheeks did for all those in attendance at that game when he came to the aid of Gilbert, who had forgotten the words to the song.

Today, what can you do to help others live a day with a little more Commitment to excellence?

JULY 5

IRON SHARPENS IRON

I recently spoke with one of the premier managers in all of Major League Baseball and our conversation quickly turned to leadership, continued education and the books that we each read.

The manager told me that he, his staff and the organization's leadership group select three books a year that ALL their staff will read.

They also assign "Battle Buddies" so each man has an accountability partner to read through the book with and to answer questions that are e-mailed to all during the reading.

What a wonderful way to help develop the leadership qualities of your staff.

Books contain a lifetime's worth of wisdom. Find the books by the people who are in the top of your field and invest into your development with "Battle Buddies."

Iron sharpens iron. The stronger you and your staff become together, the stronger your organization becomes and the more you win games.

Who could be your "Battle Buddies" in reading this book?

____

____

____

JULY 6

IT IS OK TO SEND FLOWERS

It is ok to send flowers to others, but do not let the flowers do all of the talking.

They don't say much.

Flowers have a very limited vocabulary.

The words you use do two very powerful things.

They provide light for understanding and food for the mind.

Your vocabulary will largely determine your ability to communicate, your ability to communicate will largely determine your relationships and relationships determine success.

A high school teacher I worked with turned me on to the Word of the Day challenge.

A challenge in which you learn a new word and use it each day.

If you do an internet search for Word of the Day, you can actually have a word and definition delivered to your inbox each day.

Add this to your To Dominate List with your accountability partners or "Battle Buddies" and keep working at yourself today.

JULY 7

SIGN YOUR NAME WITH EXCELLENCE

A man once lived to be 97 years old at a time when the average life span was 40-45.

He was a self-made man who taught himself his trade and often worked alone with primitive tools. His greatest tool was the laser-like focus he put into this work each day.

He made musical instruments and labored over each and every process and step to ensure that he had "signed" them all with excellence.

Today, some three hundred years later, the name of this craftsman who was committed to excellence is the benchmark for the best in musical instruments.

His instruments sell for hundreds of thousands of dollars because they simply are excellent.

When this man labored, he did not know of the legacy he was creating. He was doing his best, day in and day out, to reach his standard of excellence.

He didn't spend the extra time and pay extra attention to detail because he wanted to receive praise for his work or to stand out in the crowd. He did it because excellence was part of his focus, mission, and obsession.

It is easy to do world-class work when you are part of a world-class team or have someone who is looking over your shoulder at all times. The true test of excellence is what you do when no one is looking.

Peak performers have the ability to stay locked in when they are alone and working by themselves.

Does your quality or performance fluctuate based on who is in the office or which customer you are serving?

Excellence is a lifestyle, not an event. Excellence is not something that you can just turn on and off whenever you feel you need it.

It is a habit rooted in your attitude about your life, your career and how you sign your name on everything that you do.

Sign your name with excellence below:

____

Your Name Here, Signed With Excellence

JULY 8

THE 20-MINUTE RULE

One of the greatest high school basketball coaches of all time had what he called the magic 20-minute rule he used to start every practice.

The coach made a daily commitment to compliment each player individually within the first 20 minutes of practice.

As simple of a rule as that may seem, if you are a college baseball coach with 40 players, that leaves you with only thirty seconds per player to start passing out the praise.

Having a sense of urgency as a leader to find something praiseworthy early in your interactions with each person may seem simple, but simple is not always easy.

Make sure that your comment is also positive and specific.

What people want to hear most is their name attached to a positive specific coming out of the coach's mouth.

Use the 20-minute rule today in your pursuit of excellence.

JULY 9

ATTACK THE DAY WITH AN ENTHUSIASM UNKNOWN TO MANKIND

The story line of Super Bowl XLVII was that two brothers, Jim and John Harbaugh, were squaring off as head coaches of their respective teams for what could be the biggest prize in all of professional sport: the Vince Lombardi Trophy and NFL World Championship.

What I find most impressive is what their father Jack Harbaugh, a former collegiate coach, would say to them every day when dropping them off at school:

Attack today with an enthusiasm unknown to mankind.

Can you imagine hearing those words every day from your father when you got dropped off at school?

Can you imagine the powerful impact that those words would have on your approach to dominating the day?

Jack Harbaugh may not be your father, but I do suggest that you heed his advice and attack every day with an enthusiasm unknown to mankind.

Living with enthusiasm is essential to your success and reaching your full potential.

I had the chance to meet Jim Harbaugh at the 2009 Heisman Trophy Ceremony, where his prized running back Toby Gerhart was a finalist representing Stanford University.

I asked Jim what characteristic he found common among the best players he had ever coached or played with. His answer....

Enthusiasm, energy and mental toughness!

JULY 10

MOST BATTLES ARE WON BEFORE THEY ARE FOUGHT

Win Every Battle Leading up to the Game

Win the Battle of Preparation

Win the Battle of Focus

Win the Battle of Nutrition

Win the Battle of Conditioning

Win the Battle of Listening

Win the Battle of Decisions Off the Field

Win the Battle of Mental Toughness

Win the Battle of Selflessness

Win the Battle of Brotherhood

Win the Battle of TEAM

Win the Battle of Taking The Field

Win the Battle of Warm-ups

Win the Battle of YOURSELF

Win the Battle of the Game

JULY 11

COFFEE BEANS, CARROTS & EGGS

An athlete once told me about how college was so difficult for her. She wanted to quit the team and drop out. She was tired of fighting and struggling.

As one problem was solved a new one arose. Luckily for us, we were meeting in the dining hall. I had made friends with the chef and asked if I could use three pots with water to teach a lesson.

In the first pot we placed carrots, in the second eggs and in the last, ground coffee beans.

We then went back to the table where we were eating and let the carrots, eggs and coffee sit and boil for about twenty minutes as she continued to talk about her challenges.

The chef then brought us the carrots, eggs and a cup of coffee and put them on the table. I asked the athlete what she saw.

"Carrots, eggs, and coffee," she replied. I asked her to feel the carrots. She did and noted that they felt soft. I asked her to take an egg and break it.

After pulling off the shell, she observed the hard-boiled egg. Finally, I asked her to sip the coffee. She smiled as she tasted its rich aroma.

The athlete then asked, "Cain, What's the point of all this?"

I explained that each of these objects had faced the same adversity - boiling water - but each reacted differently. The carrot went in strong, hard and unrelenting; and after being subjected to the boiling water, it softened and became weak.

The egg had been fragile. Its thin outer shell had protected its liquid interior. After sitting through the boiling water, its inside became hardened.

The ground coffee beans were unique and excellent. After they were in the boiling water, they had changed the water.

Which are you? When adversity knocks on your door, how do you respond? Are you a carrot, an egg, or a coffee bean?

Are you the carrot that seems strong, but with pain and adversity, you wilt and become soft and lose strength?

Are you the egg that starts with a malleable heart, but changes with the heat and pressure?

Do you have a fluid spirit, but after a loss, getting injured or getting benched you become hardened and stiff?

Does your exterior shell look the same, but on the inside you are bitter with a stiff spirit and a hardened heart?

Or are you the coffee bean?

The bean actually changes the hot water, the very circumstance that brings the pain. When the water gets hot, it releases the fragrance and flavor.

If you are like the bean, when things are at their worst you are at your best. When the heat is on, you get better, not bitter, and change the situation around you.

Who do you know that is a carrot? ____________________

Who do you know that is an egg? ____________________

Who do you know that is a coffee bean? ______________

JULY 12

ANTICIPATE ADVERSITY, EXPECT THE UNEXPECTED, MAKE YOUR OWN MOMENTUM

Jacoby Jones of the Baltimore Ravens set an NFL record for the longest plan in history by returning the 2nd half kickoff 108 yards to put the Ravens up 28-6 and essentially put the lights out on the 49ers in Super Bowl XLVII.

Then the lights actually went out on both teams.

The stadium lights inside of the New Orleans Superdome went out and caused a 34-minute delay.

From that moment forward it was all San Francisco as the 49ers scored 17 points in a span of 4 minutes and 10 seconds after the lights went back on and mounted a comeback for the ages.

The announcers spoke about how the momentum was with the Ravens and that the power outage was the best thing that could have happened for the 49ers.

I totally disagree.

A power outage affects both teams exactly the same: the only difference is how they manage the adversity, how they respond to the unexpected.

YOU make your own momentum.

Just like a coin being flipped has a 50/50 chance of coming up heads or tails, each play in football, each pitch in baseball and softball has a life and a history of its own.

Momentum lies within you. Each play can go either way, success or failure, every time.

Your success or failure will be determined by how you handle the adversity thrown your way.

Today, anticipate adversity, expect the unexpected and make your own momentum by living with an enthusiasm unknown to mankind, having a purpose bigger than yourself, doing a little a lot, visualizing and predicting your future, and by playing one play at a time.

YOU CAN LEARN A LOT ABOUT LIFE BY WATCHING SPORTS IF YOU WATCH AS A LEARNER, NOT AS A FAN

JULY 13

THE BUMBLE BEE BEATS THE ODDS

Scientists have been baffled by the bumble bee for decades.

Physicists have deemed it physically impossible for the bumble bee to fly because its delicate wings cannot support the weight of its body.

Bumble bees could care less about science. They have plants to dominate and pollen to gather for their hives.

The next time you see a bumble bee, instead of being afraid to get stung (if you have allergies, carry an epi-pen) be mesmerized by its ability to defy the odds and prove people wrong.

Who do you listen to?

Do you believe what others say or what you do every day?

Be like the bumble bee and defeat all odds.

JULY 14

THE STINGRAY AND THE GLASS WALL

There once was a baby stingray, born in a tank at an aquarium.

The stingray grew up inside of a tank separated from another by a glass wall.

The glass wall was temporarily in place because at the time of the sting ray's birth, the other side of the tank was having repairs made.

The stingray was born with a great energy and a spirit to venture out and seek new places in the world.

However, after swimming head first into the glass wall many times in his first few weeks of life, the stingray never ventured past that spot in the aquarium, even when the temporary glass wall was removedWhat temporary glass walls have you run into in the past that may no longer be there but are still holding you from venturing out into other places in the world?

JULY 15

LEARNING OPPORTUNITY, STAY STRONG

Did you know that the greatest of the great all faced adversity in their lives?

Albert Einstein could not speak until he was four years old. He did not read until he was 7. His parents thought he was mentally challenged.

Beethoven's early music teacher said that as a composer he was hopeless.

Muhammad Ali had a teacher who told him he wouldn't amount to anything. He showed her and the world that he was the greatest after all.

Google tried to sell their business to Yahoo for a few million dollars and were told to come back when they were finished with their little school project.

Steve Jobs was once fired from Apple.

Walt Disney was told his ideas were stupid.

Michael Jordan was cut from his high school basketball team.

Georges St. Pierre was bullied as a child and worked for years as a garbage man before becoming the icon and UFC World Champion he is today.

Every day we face negativity, challenges, fears and obstacles that hit us with left jabs and right hooks. We get caught up in the details of our day-to-day lives, paying the bills, pressure to perform on the job, raising our own and others' kids, fixing the house and a hundred other to-dos.

Failure is a necessary stop on the road to success. Failure provides you with feedback about what you must do to improve and what is not working for you.

Thomas Edison tried over 1,000 different filaments for the light bulb and with each failed attempt he believed he was one step closer to letting there be light.

What is a LOSS (Learning Opportunity, Stand Strong) in your life that will become a springboard to your success?

What is a LOSS you have experienced that has been a springboard to your future success?

JULY 16

LESSONS LEARNED FROM GEESE

Did you know that geese fly in a certain formation for a reason?

In the fall when you see geese heading south for the winter, flying along in the "V" formation, you might be interested in knowing what science has discovered about why they fly that way.

Is has been learned that as each bird flaps its wings, it creates an uplift for the bird immediately following. By flying in a "V" formation, the whole flock adds at least 71% greater flying range than if each bird flew on its own.

People who are part of a team and share a common direction get where they are going more quickly and easily, because they are traveling on the trust of one another.

Whenever a goose falls out of formation, it suddenly feels the drag and resistance of trying to go through it alone and quickly gets back into formation to take advantage of the power of the flock.

If we have as much sense as a goose, we will share information with those who are headed the same way we are going.

When the lead goose gets tired, he rotates back in the "V" and another goose takes over.

It pays to share leadership and to take turns doing hard jobs.

The geese honk from behind to encourage those up front to keep their speed.

Words of support and inspiration help energize those on the front line, helping them to keep pace in spite of the day-to-day pressures and fatigue.

Finally, when a goose gets sick or is wounded by a gunshot and falls out, two geese fall out of the formation and follow the injured one down to help and protect him.

They stay with him until he is either able to fly or until he is dead, and then they launch out with another formation to catch up with their group.

If we have the sense of a goose, we will stand by each other when things get rough.

The next time you see a formation of geese, think of the many important roles on a team.

FLY IN FORMATION LIKE THE GEESE

JULY 17

TO BE GREAT IS TO BE GRATEFUL

Nothing new can come into your life until you are grateful for what you already have.

One of my professors at The University of Vermont challenged us as her students to think of three things we were grateful for each day before we got out of bed and three things each night that we were grateful for before we went to sleep.

Having an attitude of gratitude helps you to stay positive and appreciate what you do have instead of focusing on what you don't have.

When was the last time you were thankful for the eyesight to see these words, the ability to know what these words mean and the opportunity to have the means to have this book in your hands?

What will you appreciate today?

____

____

____

____

HAVE AN ATTITUDE OF GRATITUDE

JULY 18

WORK AT YOURSELF FIRST

Working at yourself first is one of the key success principles most commonly discussed in the books I enjoy reading the most.

Kaizen is the Japanese word for improvement. Self-help guru Tony Robbins coined the term "CANI" – Constant And Never-ending Improvement.

The pursuit of excellence is more about constant and never-ending improvement than it is about achievement and accomplishment.

To work at myself I listen to audio books in the car and when I am on planes.

You can find almost any book on audio in iTunes and can access the greatest minds of all times.

Your challenge this week is to purchase one audio book. You can start with picking up *Toilets, Bricks, Fish Hooks and PRIDE* or *So What, Next Pitch!* or any other book and start trading your satellite radio for audio books.

JULY 19

MY DOG BEA & COMMUNICATION

My dog's name is Bea. Short for Beatrice and an acronym for Bring Energy All the time.

BEA is also an acronym for one of the greatest communication activities around.

Get your team seated in a circle and have an empty seat.

That seat is the feedback seat.

By sitting there you are welcoming your team to give you feedback, both positive and constructive.

Your teammates are to say what your behavior is, how it affects the team and what action you want them to take.

An example would be, "Brian, when you bring a relentless positive energy to practice (B) it has a positive effect on us as your teammates because it makes us want to play harder (E). I want you to keep bringing that relentless positive energy to practice every day (A)."

I would then reply by saying: "[Your name], thank you for your feedback.

"What I heard you say was that you want me to continue to bring a relentless positive energy to practice every day because it has a positive effect on you as my team. I will commit to bringing a relentless positive energy to practice every day."

By restating what you heard them say, you are confirming that you heard their feedback clearly and accurately.

When doing this activity, most of the comments will be positive to begin with and eventually the elephant in the room will be called out and addressed.

You can also call someone to the feedback chair, but they must be willing to go when called upon. If they are not willing, they are not required to go.

Feedback is the breakfast of champions. If they are not willing to go, you must set a train 'em or trade 'em deadline and address the elephant in the room or it will destroy everything in its path.

COMMUNICATION IS AN ESSENTIAL INGREDIENT INSIDE ANY EXCELLENT ORGANIZATION

JULY 20

TRAIN 'EM OR TRADE 'EM

My friend and mentor Bruce Brown talks in his book *Teaching Character Through Sport: Developing a Positive Coaching Legacy* about setting a train 'em or trade 'em deadline.

No individual can be bigger or more important than the program.

The core values of your organization must drive the behavior inside the organization if you are going to deliver a consistent performance and consistent product over time.

I have worked with coaches who have different standards for different players - and you should.

Some players have more stock invested in the company than others.

They should have different standards. But no individual should come before the program.

When individuals are not acting in line with your program standards, you must set a train 'em or trade 'em deadline: They must either meet your agreed-upon standards by a certain date or you must trade them to someone else or send them down the river.

JULY 21

LITTLE STREAMS = BIG RIVERS

My friend Ryan Cameron and I once went hiking in the Colorado Rockies when he was playing for their professional baseball organization.

As we were hiking, I pointed out a small stream rolling down the side of a cliff. The stream was so small and moved so slowly that you had to really focus to see it or you might miss it.

When I pointed this out to Ryan, he told me that the stream was actually a part of the Colorado River that flows through the Rockies and that all of the little streams we passed by would turn into the big river.

What an analogy for life.

Little streams make big rivers.

The small daily decisions you make add up over time to become the bigger you.

What you put into your body nutritionally, what you listen to for music, what you read, who you associate with and how much sleep you get at night all add up to make you the person who you are in this moment.

JULY 22

TWINS IN LIFE, NOT IN ATTITUDE

The Bayliss twins looked identical physically, but were strangers from each other mentally.

When their mother brought them to see a sport psychologist to try and find out why one was so positive while the other was so negative, the psychologist quickly decided to give them the attitude test and perspective challenge.

The sport psychologist led the pessimistic brother into a room where most kids would be in heaven: A large-screen TV with a 3D video game system with every game ever made.

The room also had a candy stand full of anything you would want and a trampoline that you could jump off into a 100-degree swimming pool.

The psychologist then led the optimistic brother down a long flight of steps into the basement of the old farmhouse on Lake Champlain that he called an office.

When they opened the door to the basement, there was a pile of manure in the center of a room and the smell was terrible.

After leaving the optimistic bother in the basement, the sport psychologist went back upstairs to check on the pessimistic brother.

He was sitting in the corner of the room with his arms folded and a scowl on his face.

When the two of them went to the basement to check on the optimistic brother, he was nowhere to be seen.

Then all of a sudden he popped out of the top of the manure pile and said: "Hey guys, with all this manure there must be a pony in here somewhere. Have you seen him?"

The point of the story is that you will find what you are looking for and that a positive, optimistic attitude in any situation is always better than a negative, pessimistic one.

Attitude is a decision and today you are to choose what attitude you will take.

Make your decision wisely and check in on your decision every half hour.

The constant checkup from the neck up will help you to stay positive and optimistic today.

JULY 23

THE BALANCE BETWEEN HUMILITY AND CONFIDENCE

When I go in to work with a team and start teaching about confidence, much of my audience thinks that the great athletes I get to work with are always confident and that is a large reason why they are great.

I have learned that nobody is confident all the time.

The best out there have learned that they must act confident all the time even if they don't feel confident.

The greatest coaches and athletes I have been around have a balance between humility and confidence.

Their humility reminds them that on any given day anyone can beat anyone.

Their confidence reminds them that they can beat anyone in the world if they perform at their competitive best.

Today, know that you can beat anyone and do anything, and you can also get beat and fail.

This will keep you confident and also keep you humble.

This is a place of great strength.

JULY 24

COOKED ONE DEGREE AT A TIME

There once lived a great chef who made the greatest frog legs in the world.

His secret was to use live frogs so that the meat was as fresh and tender as it could possibly be.

The chef knew that if he put the frogs in a pot of room-temperature water and slowly turned up the heat, he could leave the lid off the pot because the frogs would try to adjust to the slowly increasing heat in the water, would not jump out and would allow themselves to be cooked to death.

The habits you keep in your life are like the pot that boils the frog.

Day by day the decisions you make will either help you get to where you want to be or will keep you from getting there.

Nobody ever has or ever will escape the ramifications of their daily decisions and the habits they keep.

What are some habits you would be better off getting rid of now so that you don't cook yourself to death?

____

____

____

One may be texting and driving?

JULY 25

QUICK-LIST GOALS

Make sure you have a pen or pencil ready for this reading.

I want you to write down three to five things you want to accomplish without giving it much thought.

I call these your quick-list goals.

Writing these down in less than one minute and not taking the time to think about them makes you get to it quickly and helps you to see where your focus and priorities lie.

READY!

GO!

1. ____
2. ____
3. ____
4. ____
5. ____

JULY 26

THE TORTOISE ALWAYS WINS

You know the story. The Tortoise and the Hare go out for a race and the Hare is much faster, in better shape and should win the race every time. It shouldn't even be close. But who always wins? The Tortoise. Why? The Hare beats himself.

Are you your own worst enemy? Do you have all of the physical talent of the metaphorical Hare in your arena but keep losing the race to the Tortoise who is not as talented as you are and doesn't deserve the success that you do?

Talent is overrated. I have worked with a lot of Hares that thought that their talent would get them to the top and failed to invest into their mental game and evaluate their daily decisions.

Slow and steady will win the race, fast and steady will win the championship. Work hard and work smart. Make sure that your daily decisions and daily actions are leading you to where you want to be at the end of your race. Talent alone won't get you there.

JULY 27

WORK/LIFE BALANCE AWARENESS

My friend John Brubaker is one of the leading experts in the field of work/life balance for coaches and athletic administrators.

This is a topic that I find of critical importance for the coaches I work with.

As a person in the pursuit of excellence, balance is something to strive for and is relative to the individual.

Your definition of work/life balance may be completely different than mine and we are both right.

The key to achieving work/life balance is having awareness that such balance is important and can be accomplished if defined, communicated and committed to.

Striving for balance keeps everything rotating around the center of our lives and helps us to live with a heightened awareness as to whether we are moving towards our definition or away from it.

How can you demonstrate work/life balance today?

____

____

____

____

____

JULY 28

IF 99% EFFORT WERE GOOD ENOUGH

If 99% effort were good enough then...

5.5 million cases of soft drinks produced would be produced flat.

2.5 million books would be shipped with the wrong covers.

2 million documents would be lost by the IRS.

880,000 credit cards in circulation would turn out to have incorrect cardholder information on their magnetic strips.

114,500 mismatched pairs of shoes would be shipped.

103,260 income tax returns would be processed incorrectly.

20,000 incorrect drug prescriptions would be written this year.

18,322 pieces of mail would be mishandled per hour.

3,056 copies of tomorrow's *Wall Street Journal* would be missing one of the three sections.

315 entries in Webster's dictionary would be misspelled.

291 pacemaker operations would be performed incorrectly.

12 newborns would be given to the wrong parents daily.

2 planes landing at Chicago's O'Hare airport would be unsafe every day.

If you want to make it to the top, 99% effort and focus is never good enough.

You must fully commit to and focus on the task at hand while you are doing it, understanding that your results will not likely be 100%.

Understand the difference between 100% effort and perfection.

Perfection is unattainable; extra effort must become expected effort if you are to get to the top.

Learn from your mistakes and get better with each day.

What can you give a little more effort to today that will help increase your results?

JULY 29

THE STUDENT & THE SENSEI

A young mixed martial arts student travels to meet a renowned sensei...

The student tells the sensei that he wants to train under him to become a world champion and asks, "How long will it take"?

The sensei tells him it will take 10 years of dedicated training.

Unsatisfied, the student says that he will work harder than any student, to which the sensei replies that it will take 20 years in that case.

Still unsatisfied, the student says he will train harder day and night and never take a day off.

This time the sensei replies that it will take 30 years.

The confused student asks the sensei why it will take longer the harder he works.

The sensei responds, "When one eye is fixed upon your destination, there is only one eye left with which to focus on the present."

What is the destination you are focusing on that is pulling you from DOMINATING the Day and the present moment?

____

____

____

JULY 30

ASK SPECIFICALLY AND YOU SHALL RECEIVE

There was a study done around goal setting and motivation in financial giving.

The corporate donors were divided into two groups. The donors in group one were thanked for their generosity the prior year and asked to "do the best they could" in donating toward the upcoming campaign.

The donors in group two were thanked for their generosity the prior year and asked specifically to "do 10 percent better than last year."

The donors that were specifically asked to "do 10 percent better than last year," on an average, did 24 percent better.

The donors that were told to do the best they could actually did worse than the year before.

Start asking more specifically for what it is you want.

Identifying what you really want provides clarity and direction in your life.

What do you really want?

____

____

____

____

JULY 31

WHICH ASSASSIN DO YOU LISTEN TO?

The battle between your green and red mental assassins is being fought as you read this.

Which assassin are you listening to?

The red assassin is always wrong.

The red assassin's strongest weapon is to lie to you so convincingly that in moments of discomfort you listen.

Turn a deaf ear to the red assassin and start listening to the green assassin, the voice of reason that speaks to you in positive tone and specific process-based actions that you can take to ease the discomfort.

The red assassin wants you to carry mental bricks; the green assassin wants you to turn those mental bricks into stepping stones on your journey to excellence.

The biggest battle you fight is not the economy, the other team or politics. It is the battle going on in the six inches between your ears.

Win the internal battle and the externals ones will take care of themselves.

AUGUST

August is the month for me to dominate...

AUGUST 1

SURVIVE OR THRIVE?

A difference I have seen between the athletes I have worked with who have gotten the most out of their abilities and those who have fallen short is that those who get the most thrive and those who don't survive.

Next time you are in the weight room you will notice that some people are there for exercise while others are there for conditioning and training.

The exercise group is there for fun, to survive the workout, while the conditioning group is there pushing themselves beyond what most normal people are willing to do.

They thrive in that environment known as the wall.

They push themselves to the point where they want to quit, the same point where you want to quit. The difference is that instead of hitting the brake, they hit the gas.

They attack and thrive vs. try to survive.

Today, make the conscious decision to move from survive to thrive and attack your day!

AUGUST 2

PAIN IS A PERSONAL CREATION

What do you do when you hear someone is stabbing you in the back or throwing you under the bus?

If you react to this negative knowledge with a feeling of anger or sadness, you are destroying your own peace of mind.

The pain you feel is a personal creation.

My suggestion in this situation is to let the negative knowledge pass you by as if it were the wind blowing through the trees on a cool fall day in Vermont.

Nowhere does it say that you must feel a certain way when you hear the negativity of others pass your way.

You will not be able to avoid negative and difficult situations, but you can control the extent to which you suffer from these events by choosing your response to the situations.

You are always 100% in control of your response. We call it response-ability, your ability to choose your own response.

Choose wisely today when negativity comes your way.

AUGUST 3

TURN A DEAF EAR TO NEGATIVITY

Every year in Vermont there is a race between frogs up Mount Mansfield, a mountain so large that most frogs quit before they get to the top.

One year, a frog was so determined to make it to the top that, despite all of the screaming from the people in the crowd lining the course to stop and turn back before he died, the frog made it across the finish line miles up Mount Mansfield.

When he crossed the finish line, there were reporters wanting to know how he was able to push himself through the pain and discomfort and through the negativity of the crowd telling him to turn back or he was sure to have a heart attack and die.

The frog looked at the lips of the reporter and said: *"Oh, they were telling me to turn back? I am deaf, and all I could see was them jumping up and down and I thought they were telling me to keep going in encouragement."*

Today, turn a deaf ear to the negativity and the naysayers who are telling you that your goal is stupid, that you are not big enough, strong enough or good enough to get where you want to go.

Run your race, turn a deaf ear to the negativity of others, and turn their presence and words into fuel to burn your fire.

Who do you need to stop listening to in order to achieve your goals and dreams?

____

____

____

____

____

____

AUGUST 4

GET BIGGER

Confidence is a choice that you make each and every day to wake up and attack the day. Confidence comes from preparing physically and mentally to be at your best.

There will be days when you don't feel good, don't have your best stuff and have your red assassin or red bull screaming at you to stop, to quit and not go any further. This is when you must GET BIGGER.

Remember, it is easier to act yourself into feeling than feel yourself into action. If you don't feel confident, act as if you are and you will soon get the confident feelings you are looking for. The alternative is to act how you feel and if you feel like garbage, here comes a garbage performance. GET BIGGER TODAY!

AUGUST 5

MEASUREMENT AND MOTIVATION

What you measure gets done.

What you treasure you measure and measurement equals motivation.

What are you measuring in your life to make sure you are improving?

A friend of mine who is a marriage and family counselor says one of the best ways to improve your relationship at home with your significant other is to measure the amount of positive comments, acts of service and physical touches you give your partner each day.

By simply measuring these three things, she said that you are increasing your awareness of the importance of doing these things on a daily basis, and what you measure gets done.

What are you measuring today in your life? When you run drills in practice, are you using a stopwatch to make sure that you are moving quickly and efficiently?

Are you using a stopwatch to keep track of your time on the computer and every time you get distracted and start browsing the internet or checking e-mail? Are you keeping track of your time on task and then trying to beat your time-on-task record every time you sit down and lock in at command central? (For many people that is the desk and computer in today's computer and e-mail driven world.)

Work fast, work hard and finish.

Today, what are you going to keep track of to make sure you are staying on task and working as effectively and efficiently as possible?

____

____

____

WHAT YOU MEASURE GETS DONE

AUGUST 6

CONDITION YOURSELF LIKE A DOG

Russian physiologist Ivan Pavlov is most known for his "conditioning reflex" research, in which he proved that a dog's mouth would salivate when it heard a bell and was then given food. Over time the dog's mouth would salivate when it heard the bell ring.

What are your conditioning responses? How do you respond when confronted with adversity or negativity? Are you conditioned to take a breath and gather control of yourself before you speak or do you wait till you put your foot in your mouth before you take a breath?

Start to condition your responses by having awareness and taking a breath to gather self-control before you speak and before you act.

AUGUST 7

WATCH OUT FOR FISH HOOKS

When a fish hunts for a worm with awareness, it will stop and nibble your worm off the hook because it can see the hook. If a fish is out of control mentally or emotionally because it has not eaten in a while or is overly excited to crush a dangling worm, it will get hooked.

There are fish hooks around you at all times. They are factors outside of your control looking to rip you out of the waters of excellence and into the boat of failure. What other people say, what other people think, the media, parents, the competition - they can all be fish hooks. Trust your training, stay in control of yourself and eat around the fish hooks that are there to rip you away from your goal.

What are the fish hooks in your life that rip you out of the present moment that you will be more aware of today?

FISH HOOKS IN MY LIFE:

____

____

____

____

____

____

____

BE AWARE OF FISH HOOKS TODAY!
DON'T GET HOOKED

AUGUST 8

HOW TO CATCH CRABS

Have you ever been to the beach and tried to catch crabs and put them in a bucket?

If you only catch one crab, you had better put a cover on the bucket, because the lone crab will likely escape. If you catch multiple crabs, however, no cover is necessary.

The crabs actually keep each other in the bucket. When one tries to climb to freedom, the others grab at his legs and pull him down, ensuring the collective demise of all.

This detrimental behavior has spawned an analogy to human behavior reflective of the saying, "If I can't have it, neither can you."

This "crab mentality" is evident when the group or team will attempt to "pull down" a member who achieves success beyond his peers out of envious emotions and competitive feelings.

In athletics, the term "crab" is thus applied to an individual with short-sighted, non-constructive thinking rather than a unified, long-term, constructive perspective.

Unfortunately, these crabs are everywhere in life, and you need to be consciously aware that those who are unwilling to help themselves are not worth your time if you are in pursuit of excellence. Stick to what you do and don't let their negative perspectives pull you down.

Right now, I want you to reflect on some of the crabs in your life. Who are some of the people that pull you down and tell you that you can't accomplish your goals?

Who are some of the people that tell you that you are never going to make it? Who are the people you hang out with that hold you back? Brainstorm your list below.

____

____

____

____

____

____

AUGUST 9

ATHLETIC ADVERTISING

During practice or competition, a great method of self-advertising is to write inspirational messages on athletic tape or clothing such as wrist bands or batting gloves.

When you consistently see the messages in front of yourself, you are reminded of what your mentality must be to give yourself the best chance for success.

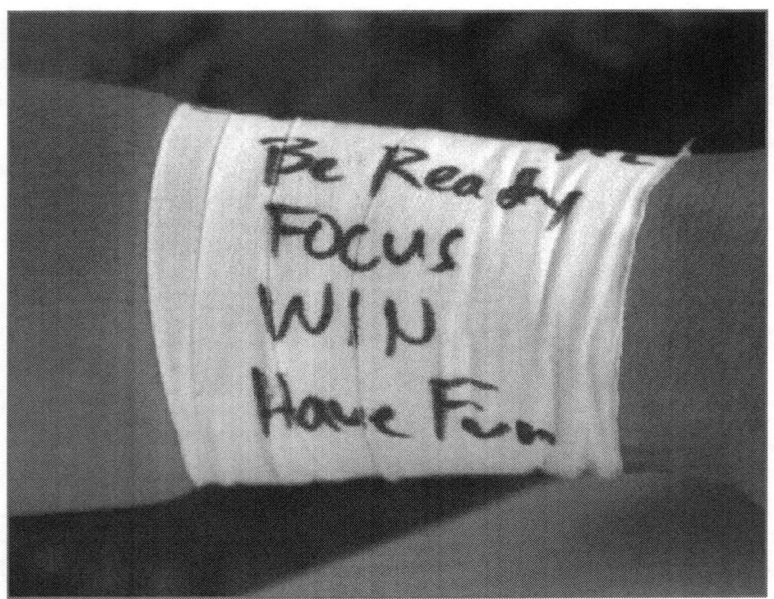

AUGUST 10

THE INVERTED U

Sports Psychology 101 is about understanding the Inverted U. On the North-South axis, we have performance; on the East-West axis, there is arousal or energy, aka how fired up or excited are you?

When your energy is not high enough, performance is low. Conversely, when you are over-adrenalized, performance is still low. This is why it's important for peak performers to maintain a consistent mental state through the use of routines.

Having routines allows you to be more consistent mentally and emotionally and increases your chances of getting out of the optimal energy zone. Having routines gives you the best chance of performing your best.

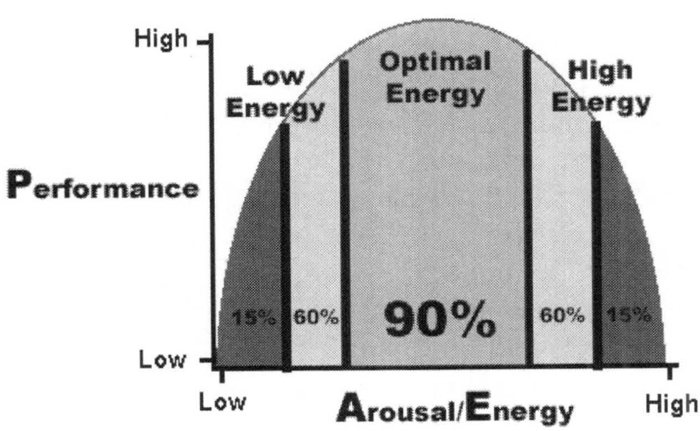

AUGUST 11

DON'T FREEZE TO DEATH

In the February 1978 issue of *Success Unlimited*, psychologist Dr. Dudley Calvert tells the story of a railway employee in Russia who accidentally locked himself in a refrigerator car.

Inside the car, he could not unlock the door nor could he attract the attention of those outside. Unable to escape, he resigned himself to his fate.

As he felt his body becoming numb, he documented his story and his approaching death in sentences scribbled on the wall of the car.

"I'm becoming colder now," he wrote, "still colder, now. I can hardly write..." and finally, "these may be my last words." And they were.

When the car was opened upon arrival at its destination, other railway employees found him dead. Yet, the temperature of the car was 56 DEGREES!

The freezing apparatus had been out of order in the car.

There was no physical reason for his death. There was plenty of air – he hadn't suffocated.

What had happened was he had given away his personal power and defeated himself by not responding appropriately to the challenges in front of him.

He let the power of his mind negatively affect his reality. Remember, perspective is reality and you are response-able for choosing any attitude and any perspective you want in any given situation.

His own lack of response-ability led to his demise, a victim of his own illusion.

What illusions are you holding that may be leading to your own demise?

____

____

____

DON'T FREEZE TO DEATH IN THE HEAT
A VICTIM OF YOUR OWN ILLUSION

AUGUST 12

E + R = O

There's a simple math equation that I want you to learn and, more importantly, want you to put in to action.

E [Event] + R [Response] = O [Outcome]

In life, it's not what happens to you; it's what you do with what happens to you.

It's your ability to respond (response-ability) that's going to determine your outcome when life's adversity is thrown your way.

As a human being, YOU have the ability to respond to an event in the manner you deem appropriate. The response is your choice.

Humans have the unique ability to choose their innate responses to events with the three steps of performance change.

1. Awareness

2. Strategy

3. Action

We often have little control over the events in our lives but we can always control our response in any situation.

This is an empowering notion, because once you realize that you control half the equation, you recognize that you control half the outcome.

If a negative event occurs and you keep a positive present-moment focus with a big-picture mentality and a "compared to what?" perspective in a response to counteract that event, then the outcome will be a result of your perception.

This is the process of mental conditioning that you prepare for through the establishment of mental routines.

The practice of mental conditioning will teach you how to be responsible by accepting the events, formulating responses and, therefore, best influencing the outcomes.

We are all capable of using this process to our benefit in life because we all have the ability to control our responses.

Choose your responses carefully today!

AUGUST 13

TIPS FOR IMPROVED SLEEPING

Want to improve your energy and performance? Try improving the quality of your sleep and prioritizing your recovery.

1. Relax Before Retiring – Take some time for a pre-sleep ritual to break the connection between stress and bedtime. Try listening to the 5-4-3-2-1 relaxation session or listening to relaxation music, do light stretching or take a hot shower.

2. Watch the Caffeine – Caffeine is the stimulant present in coffee (100-200 mg), soda (50-75 mg), tea (50-75 mg) and various over-the-counter medications. Caffeine should be discontinued at least four to six hours before bedtime.

3. Watch the Alcohol – Although alcohol is a depressant and may help you fall asleep, the subsequent metabolism that clears it from your body when you are sleeping causes a withdrawal syndrome. This withdrawal causes awakenings and is often associated with nightmares and sweats. To help reduce some of these effects, try drinking one glass of water for every alcoholic beverage consumed. You should stop all liquid consumption at least 2 hours before bedtime so that you are not waking up in the middle of the night to urinate.

4. Exercise at the Right Time – Regular exercise relieves stress and encourages good sleep. However, if a little exercise really gets your blood pumping, you'd be wise to avoid working out in the evening or just before bedtime.

5. Cut Down on Noise, Light and Extreme Temperatures – Try earplugs, a night light, an eye mask or drape clip. The best temperature for sleep is 65-69 degrees.

6. Eat Right and Sleep Tight – Avoid eating a large meal just before bedtime or going to bed hungry. It's about balance.

7. Respect the Purpose of the Bed – Avoid TV, eating and emotional discussions while in bed. The mind and body associate bedtime activities with being in bed. Don't let a bad habit keep you awake.

8. Nap Smart – A power nap early in the afternoon can really refresh you. Make it brief, no more than 20 minutes. Sleep too much and you may spend the night staring at the ceiling.

Be sure to invest in the best mattress you can afford. How you spend 1/3 of your life or eight hours a night you invest in bed will determine how you are able to invest the other 2/3 of your life that day. Invest in yourself. Invest in your rest and recovery.

AUGUST 14

WAR DOGS

Since ancient times, dogs have been trained as a valuable weapon for times of war.

A war dog is a dog trained specifically for the battlefield.

Their jobs have varied over the years - from attacking with the infantry and mauling the enemy in battle to sensing trouble nearby with their acute sense of hearing to sniffing out mines in the battlefield with their acute sense of smell.

Sometimes a war dog will even step on a mine or get in the way of enemy fire to save a soldier, giving its life for the betterment of the team.

When I work with a team, I use the term "War Dog" for those select few who give everything to the team and always place the team first and foremost.

For a person to be called a War Dog is emblematic of the highest of honors, bestowed only to those who are the greatest of teammates and who have truly earned it both in and out of the performance arena.

If you are reading this and think that you may not make the team, that you may be getting cut, ask yourself: Do I have what it takes to put my ego aside, be selfless and be a War Dog?

Can you choose the perspective of putting the team ahead of yourself and doing anything you can to help the team? That is truly the perspective of a champion.

If you have the right type of attitude, the right type of work ethic, and just don't have the physical skill yet to play the game at that level, you can still be a great teammate.

You can still be the War Dog on your team.

What can you do to be a War Dog today and help your teammates to get better?

AUGUST 15

ACE – ACTING CHANGES EVERYTHING

No matter what you do, think of yourself as an actor, not as an athlete, teacher or police officer. Commit to the belief that Acting Changes Everything. Acting changes your perception of your situation and the perception others have of you; and, remember, perception is reality.

Acting is a powerful art form, and the best in the business can produce emotional responses from an otherwise distant audience. This is due to the audience's belief in an actor's performance, thus changing the audience's perception of reality and producing an intimate connection through viewer empathy and identification with the character played by the actor.

Those who attain their full potential as peak performers are true actors. They have a true passion for their craft and have developed a commitment that transcends the difficult times when they are not feeling like they have their "A" game.

One of the single greatest examples of how acting changes everything is Game Five of the 1997 NBA Finals, more commonly known as simply The Flu Game.

In a series between the Chicago Bulls versus the Utah Jazz, Michael Jordan woke up in Utah before Game Five feeling nauseous and profusely sweating. He was diagnosed with a stomach virus/food poisoning and the Bulls trainers told Jordan there was no way he could play that night. As one of the greatest competitor's in the history of sports, Michael Jordan refused to accept a role on the sidelines, especially on the road with the series tied 2-2.

What transpired that evening was one of the most memorable games in the history of sports. In one of the greatest individual performances in NBA Finals history, Michael Jordan played 44 minutes of the 48-minute competition and led all scorers with 38 points in the Bulls' stunning victory over the Jazz. The series then went back to Chicago and the Bulls would go on to win the NBA Championship in Game Six.

Jordan's performance is the stuff of legend, but it also serves as a reminder of the power of mind over matter. Jordan didn't want to rest up to return home for Game Six. He didn't want to lie in bed and dream about the Bulls winning the championship. He didn't want to watch the competition; Jordan wanted to be a part of it and actively contribute the way he believed he could. Did he feel great? No chance. What he did was act differently than how he felt, and how you act dictates performance more than how you feel.

Jordan's performance is symbolic of those who are so passionate and committed to their craft that they can act themselves into the role they need to succeed, and in the process make believers out of those around them. What Jordan understood was that acting motivates both oneself and others, while simultaneously changing perceptions of possibility.

Today, act the way you need to be to succeed, because Acting Changes Everything. This is your ACE in the hole – the ACE up your sleeve and a technique used by performers in all arenas. Fake it till you make it and fake it till you find it today. Be an ACE!

ACTING CHANGES EVERYTHING!

AUGUST 16

COMPARED TO WHAT

During the course of cultivating a championship perspective, three of the most powerful words to be conscious of are "Compared to what?"

This three-word question has enormous significance for transforming daunting undertakings into reasonable tasks. Peak performers know how to utilize this question to shift their perspective on the work at hand. They learn, when faced with the prospect of a challenge, to take a moment to reflect and ask themselves, "Compared to what?"

Peak performers realize that the world is full of people who are less fortunate than others. The importance of perspective is premised on the fact that no matter how difficult a situation you are in, someone out there is in a more difficult one. If you're a college student and you don't want to go to class or do the reading because it's laborious, ask yourself, "Compared to what?" Compared to manual labor performed by the person who never had an opportunity to receive a college education.

If you're an athlete and you wake up for an early-morning team practice and you feel tired, ask yourself, "Compared to what?" Compared to the exhaustion felt by the soldier stationed in a hostile area who has to wake up for an early-morning lookout shift, knowing his comrades' lives are in his hands. I hope you get the picture.

You see, adversity is inevitable. Everyone deals with it. But the people who are most effective in dealing with adversity do so by maintaining a positive perspective. When faced with adversity, they use the three magic words to regain their positive perspective: "Compared to what?" This phrase places all adverse tasks into a realm of possibility.

Perspective is about appreciating what you have and the opportunities before you. We are all privileged in our own unique ways, so focusing on what makes a task difficult is a waste of time when you have the ability to focus on what makes the task easier for yourself.

My mother always told me that if 10 people stood in a circle and all threw their issues into the center, you would be happy to take yours back.

Someone somewhere always has more challenges to overcome than you do. So stop making excuses and change your perspective to one of encouragement by developing an attitude of gratitude.

Identify a constructive process you can follow to help bolster your psyche as you continue on your journey to excellence. Where in your life can you start using a comparison to help shift your attitude and energy to a more productive place?

____

____

____

____

THE COMPARED TO WHAT MENTALITY: THE EXCUSED EXTERMINATOR

AUGUST 17

THE STORY OF ROGER BANNISTER

On May 6th, 1954, a British medical student and world-class runner by the name of Roger Bannister made the impossible possible.

Since the archiving of world records and modern timekeeping in track events, no one had been able to break the seemingly impassable barrier of the 4-minute mile. His story is reflective of the prophecy of thought and the power of positive belief.

At the age of 25, the spotlight of the British sports media had already discovered Bannister, who had become one of the most scrutinized track athletes in the United Kingdom. His speed in the mile and 1500- meter events drew initial attention to his talent, while his decline to attend the 1948 Olympics in London, in order to concentrate on his training and his medical studies, drew the consternation of British track enthusiasts.

In 1951 Bannister won the British title in the mile; but his fourth-place finish in the 1500-meter race at the 1952 Olympics in Helsinki, the possible result of a last-minute schedule change that compromised Bannister's preparation routines, fueled further scrutiny from the track community for his unconventional training regimen.

After the media publicized his Olympic performance as a failure, Bannister resolved to redeem himself by breaking the seemingly unbreakable 4-minute mile barrier. He increased the intensity of his training, but not the duration, and saw steady improvements in his times - all while he continued to be a full-time medical student. In fact, the duration of his training was less than an hour per day, because he wanted to focus on the study of neurology. Bannister, however, was committed to his new goal and loyal to the process he felt would get him there. He was convinced that as long as he continued to see gradual improvements in his times he would maintain his own training regimen.

The opportunity Bannister had been training for arrived on May 6, 1954, in a meet between the British Amateur Athletic Association and Oxford University at the Iffley Road Track in Oxford. Running mates Chris Chataway and Chris Brasher exchanged setting the pace for Bannister's first three laps while completing the race. Bannister unleashed his kick in the last lap, finishing it in less than a minute, before he broke the tape and collapsed in the arms of the gathered crowd at the finish line. The announcer affirmed what the crowd of roughly 3000 spectators already knew, and to thunderous applause it was announced that Bannister ran 3:59.4. The unbreakable record had been broken and Roger Bannister had made history!

This story, however, is not simply about the historic moment of a broken world record. The story of Roger Bannister is about breaking mental barriers and the defeat of limiting beliefs. At the time, the world of track and field believed the 4-minute mile was an insurmountable human barrier, an impassable obstacle that could not be breached. The critics said it couldn't be done and that it was physically impossible to run a mile under four minutes. It was thought that the heart would stop, the brain would explode, and the lungs would collapse.

As the world scoffed at what it saw as an amateur athlete's hubris, Bannister hardened his resolve to the pursuit of excellence. What makes his feat even more remarkable was that he was dedicated to attain excellence not solely on the track, but also in his academic ambitions of becoming a doctor. Bannister believed in himself and he believed in the process to which he had committed himself. As long as steady improvements accrued, he knew the outcome he desired would take care of itself.

The most remarkable part of the story is that after the myth of the 4-minute mile had been debunked by Bannister, other runners around the world began breaking the 4-minute mile barrier. The week after his historic performance, Bannister and two other runners ran a sub-four-minute mile. Over the course of the following year, thirteen more runners broke the barrier. Within the next two years exactly 134 runners ran a mile in under 4 minutes and today over 20,000 have been recorded to achieve the feat. On July 7, 1999, Hicham El Guerrouj of Berkane, Morocco ran the current world record in 3:43:13. In 1997 Daniel Roman of Kenya ran two miles for the first time ever under 8 minutes in a time of 7:58:61.

This is evidence that there are no physical barriers, only self-limiting barriers. We are the ones who place these barriers within our own psyche as a result of the beliefs of those around us. You need to unlearn these limitations, and realize that once mental barriers are lifted, anything is possible. The world is perceived differently, and as perspectives change, the realm of possibility expands.

Today, set your goal to have no mental barriers, to believe you are capable of anything you desire. Bannister proved all the naysayers wrong with his positive mentality and self-belief; today, your goal is to do the same.

THERE ARE NO PHYSICAL BARRIERS SOMEONE WILL DO IT EVENTUALLY. WHY NOT YOU, WHY NOT NOW?

AUGUST 18

THERE ARE NO PINK ELEPHANTS

Champions know the importance of focusing on what it is they want over what it is they want to avoid.

Has anyone ever performed the mind tease on you where they instruct you to focus on something and then say, "Whatever you do for the next 10 seconds, don't think about a pink elephant"?

Naturally, the image of a pink elephant pops into your head and you have difficulty focusing on whatever it was you were told to focus on.

This little mental tease reflects the importance of an individual's ability to keep a focus on what you want vs. want to avoid - because the brain does not recognize the negative connotation of "don't" and only sees the image of that sentence, the pink elephant.

The key to ignoring the pink elephants is developing the ability to focus on what you are trying to accomplish, not what you are trying to avoid.

If you are a baseball pitcher, think about pounding the strike zone instead of trying not to give up a hit. If you are a hitter, think about driving the ball back up the middle instead of trying to not roll over it.

Academically, when you're taking a test, you want to focus on solving the problem or answering the question at hand, not worrying about what your grade will be or the amount of questions on the test. These general scenarios represent the present-moment focus that makes the difference between good and great.

By channeling your self-talk and focus onto what you want vs. what you want to avoid, you will be competing with a positive mentality that will keep you locked into the present moment and will give you the best chance for successful results.

FOCUS ON WHAT YOU WANT NOT WHAT YOU WANT TO AVOID

AUGUST 19

DO YOU HAVE A BIG ENOUGH WHY?

I was in Dallas, Texas at a fair and on a stage was a big, muscular strongman. He was performing some amazing feats of strength, ripping phone books in half and bending crowbars with his hands, to the thunderous applause of his audience.

In one of his acts, he pulled out a lemon and squeezed all the juice out of that lemon and said: "Ladies and gentlemen, I am a strongman. I've squeezed all the juice out of this lemon. I will give $1,000 to anyone who can come up and extract one more drop."

In response to the call, these two giant Dallas Cowboy-looking guys went up onstage to give it a try. The first guy grabbed the lemon and gave it a good hard squeeze. No drop fell. The crowd laughed in amusement as he stepped back to let his friend give the lemon a squeeze. The crowd becomes silent and watched the second guy give the lemon a squeeze, contorting his face in a grimaced concentration. He suddenly released his grip with a gasp for air, but no still no drop of lemon juice.

The crowd laughed and applauded as the two men exited the stage. The strongman was left on stage holding his arms in the air with the lemon in his hand when he saw an old lady, who looked to be in her seventies, walking up the stairs onto the stage.

The strongman said: "Ma'am, for the sake of time, can we move on? You're not going to squeeze any juice out of it. I mean, c'mon. The guys who just tried couldn't do it and they looked like professional football players."

"Sir, just give me a chance," the old lady said politely. "I have a big reason WHY."

"Okay. Here you go. One chance," said the strongman, who handed her the lemon as the crowd cheered in support.

The old lady took the lemon within her hands and began to squeeze. Her face became contorted. Her jaw set. Her veins began popping out of her forehead. Her glasses fell off her face. Her entire body shook back and forth from her intense struggle with the lemon as she squeezed it with all her might.

Out popped one drop of lemon juice.

The audience erupted! The sounds of clapping, whistles and cheers rang throughout the fair. The strongman was blown away as he was compelled to show the audience the plate on which the drop of lemon juice had fallen. The old lady stood there onstage with her hands on her knees as she recollected her breath. It was a scene to behold.

Then the strongman walked over with a check he had just written out for $1,000 and handed it to the lady as he said: "Ma'am, you've got to tell us. I've never had anyone be able to squeeze an extra drop of juice out of that lemon. How did you do it?"

She replied: "Sir, I have to tell you. I'm 74 years old. I just lost my husband. I've got three grandchildren that we're raising and I just lost my job. I needed that money."

The old lady was inspired. She was motivated. She had a reason WHY she needed to squeeze that juice out of the lemon and with a big enough reason why, you will always find a way how.

The reason why is the fuel that burns the fire of inspiration and motivation inside of you.

So what is your "why"? Why do you do what you do? Why are you reading this right now? What do you want to accomplish in your life, this season, this week, today? What is your process for making those dreams a reality?

What is your why?

____

____

____

____

____

____

____

SQUEEZE THE JUICE OUT OF LIFE!

AUGUST 20

MOTIVATION IS LIKE BATHING

Imagine if you only took a shower once a week? Your body odor would be impressive and you would probably break out in acne all over your body. You can't just bathe once a week and expect your hygiene to look good.

Inspiration and motivation work the same way as bathing, except they're not for your physical health, but your mental health. You should mentally absorb some form of inspiration daily to motivate you in your preparation and performance.

Don't read something inspiring once a week. Don't motivate yourself or your team once or even a couple times a week. Inspiration and motivation must be performed every single day and I am glad to see you using this book to do so.

AUGUST 21

THE MILLION DOLLAR QUESTION

One of the best ways for you to gain inexpensive experience is to ask the million dollar question of those who have gone ahead of you on the same journey:

What do you know now that you wish you had known when you were in my position that would have helped you on your way?

Asking this question can help you to uncover inexpensive experience that is invaluable to your personal education and will help you on your journey. Their expensive experience will help you to perform more intelligently because you will be more mentally equipped for the challenges that lie ahead.

I encourage you to ask your elders the million dollar question. If you are a freshman athlete, ask your successful senior teammates for advice. If you're a senior, ask your successful alumni. Ask your coaches or trainers for their advice.

Ask the question, and learn from others' experience.

Who will you ask the million dollar question of today?____

What did they say?

____

____

____

____

AUGUST 22

LIVE ONE PITCH/DAY AT A TIME

What do baseball and life have in common? A lot. One of the biggest lessons to take from the game and apply to your life is that you give yourself the best chance for success if you have an end-result goal and, more importantly, an action-oriented process to get you there.

The action-oriented process of playing championship baseball is to play one pitch at a time and in life it is to live one day at a time. Treat today with the importance of Game 7 of the World Series and get the most out of the 86,400 seconds you have been given to play the game called life.

AUGUST 23

DANCE LIKE NOBODY IS WATCHING

When you were alone at home and your favorite song came on, have you ever gotten caught in the moment and started cutting a rug and getting after it on the makeshift dance floor you call your kitchen or wherever you were when you heard that song?

When you were dancing by yourself, you did not care what you did; you did not care what other people were going to say or think because they were not around. You just got after it because you knew there was no result to your dance. You got lost in the process and were probably putting out some of the best dance moves of your career.

Your challenge today is to dance like nobody is watching. To go all out in what you do and get lost in the process of performance. Eliminate the self-doubt, fear and insecurities and bring a relentless positive energy to what you do today.

DANCE LIKE NOBODY IS WATCHING

AUGUST 24

LEARNING A WIZARD-LIKE TACTIC

When I teach the mental game, I try to use as much magic, aka wizardry, as possible to keep my audiences energized as they get educated.

I first saw wizard-like tactics being used on stage by Lou Holtz, the highly successful college football coach, and made the commitment to learn some tactics of the trade.

Where in your life might having a more visual or energizing message help you to get your point across? You are in a leadership position; can you find a new way to get your team energized and educated about the importance of and commitment to the execution of the fundamentals?

AUGUST 25

THE RIGHT WAY TO SHAKE HANDS

A handshake is more than just a sign of friendship; your handshake speaks volumes about who you are as a person. A soft handshake can indicate insecurity. A quick-to-let-go handshake can convey arrogance.

For some people a handshake is just a useless formality but to others it is a massive indication of a person's depth of character, trustworthiness and strength.

When you shake hands with a person, you are doing much more than saying "Hello." You are saying, "This is who I am." First impressions last - and it is often your handshake that makes the first impression.

Research has found that the most effective handshake is the "double handshake" where the left hand is placed under the right hand to "cup" the clasped hands. Positioning the left hand in this way adds an extra dimension of enthusiasm and trust to the shake and conveys a great sense of friendship and trust in the other person.

However, the actual shaking of the hands is, in reality, only a small part of the business of shaking hands. Here are a few tips on how you can make the perfect handshake:

1. Look the person in the eyes

The position of your eyes is almost as important as the hands themselves. In fact, many leading business men and women will tell you that it is your eyes that convey the most about you during that initial point of contact. If you look down to the ground, you are telling the person that you are shy, nervous and even untrustworthy. Avoiding eye contact is behavior typically seen in someone who has done something wrong and feels ashamed or guilty.

Looking the person in the eyes shows that you are engaging them. It shows that you are interested in this meeting and you are glad to see them. Always make sure you look a person in the eyes when you shake hands, no matter how busy or brief the handshake might be.

2. Use a firm grip

The key element of a good handshake is a firm grip. A soft grip doesn't speak very good things and sometimes people will take it to mean that you are weak of character or not really interested in the person with whom you are shaking hands.

A firm grip, on the other hand, shows confidence, strength and enthusiasm. It shows you are keen to get involved with the person and you are firmly committed to being there. Be careful not to go overboard, though, as a bone-crushing grip can appear extremely arrogant.

3. Don't be too quick to let go

A handshake should be inviting but not rushed. When you rush a handshake, you inevitably get caught in that embarrassingly halfhearted position where neither person is really gripping properly. When you go in for a handshake, offer your hand with your fingers straight and your thumb high and make sure you do not grip until the person's thumb is firmly locked next to yours.

You should also not be too quick in letting go. Germ freaks often let go quickly and it is seen by many people as a big insult: If you can't even shake my hand, how can we develop a trusting relationship? Make sure you hold on long enough to show the person that you are excited to meet them.

4. Don't shake too much

I know it is called a handshake but the term is a little bit misleading. One of the worst handshakes you can get is the one where the person shakes your arm like they are trying to tear it off. Not a good idea. Perhaps think of it more as a handgrip instead of a handshake. It is fine to do two or three small shakes but that is enough.

Too much shaking can convey over-excitement and in some cases it gives the impression that you are desperate. You never want to be portraying yourself as desperate, even if you are. Make sure you don't overdo the shaking.

5. Make correct use of the left hand

Cupping under the shaking hands is a safe place to go with the left hand but this may not always be appropriate. The cupped left hand is really quite an intimate grip. It is something you would do to someone you really admire or an old business friend that you haven't seen in years.

Humans are intimate beings and (with a few rare exceptions) love physical interaction. When I meet a new client, I give a firm shake with my right hand and use the left hand to touch them on the shoulder or elbow region.

If you are shaking hands to say goodbye to someone, you can use your left hand to pat them on the upper back as they walk away. These physical details of the handshake and what to do with the left hand are very important. Remember, first impressions are critical and little streams become big rivers.

But sometimes the "correct" use of the left hand is not to use it at all. You will find yourself in certain situations where it might not be appropriate to do anything other than give a quick shake with your right hand. Make sure you use your own emotional intelligence radar to determine the best use of the left hand.

6. Use your speech in conjunction with the handshake

Remember, the act of shaking hands is more than just the two hands meeting. It involves eye contact, shoulder touching, a firm grip, and many other factors. One thing you should never forget to do when shaking someone's hand is to use your speech in conjunction with the handshake.

The most important speech to remember when shaking hands is the person's name. ALWAYS call them by name and never use lazy substitutes like "mate," "brother" or "dude."

People love to hear their own name. When you shake a person's hand and greet them by name, you are effectively saying, "You are important enough to me that I bothered to remember your name." Using a word like "man" shows you don't really care.

When you use your speech and recall something unique about that individual in conjunction with the handshake, you are interacting with the person physically, verbally and emotionally. A triple-header handshake like this leaves an impression.

7. Remind people of your name right away

> Nobody likes to forget a name. If you have met a person before, try to give them a little reminder as you shake their hand. You could say something like, "Brian Cain, great to see you again, Coach Wooden." This will help to put them at ease and hopefully make the meeting a little more streamlined.

The handshake is extremely important to our society. Peace treaties have been promised over a handshake. Wars have been ended by a handshake. Great business deals have begun because of a good handshake and blue chip athletes have made commitments to schools via a handshake.

Make sure you follow the tips above whenever you shake someone's hand. A good handshake is a first impression that will last a long time in person's mind.

**THE HANDSHAKE IS OFTEN
THE FIRST IMPRESSION
AND THE MOST IMPORTANT ONE**

AUGUST 26

WATERED-DOWN SOUP

Patricia Skinner owned the greatest diner in all of Burlington. Skinner's Diner was known for its amazing soups and friendly, fast customer service. Skinner's had a following of generations of families that came to taste the "greatest soup in Vermont, and in the world."

Skinner's soup was the talk of the town. If you were visiting, it was on your "to DOMINATE" list, and it had been called the city's main culinary attraction.

When Patricia sold her diner to Matthew Simonds, he kept the Skinner's name, but he made one costly mistake that caused the diner to go from top attraction to closed in less than three years.

After Simonds took over, he noticed how much each crock of soup was costing the diner to produce. He tried to cut costs by watering down the soup. Over time, this one mistake caused the diner to go from first to worst, and it finally closed.

You must learn from Simonds' mistake. You cannot cut corners and expect to make it to the top. There are no shortcuts on the path to success. You cannot water down the soup and expect it to taste the same as it did when you put everything you could into making it. Where in your life are you watering down the soup? How can you change before you are forced to close?

AUGUST 27

THE THOUGHT POLICE

Who do you call when your thoughts are speeding or are being driven under the influence of others? You should call the thought police.

The thought police are there to serve and protect you from the dangers of negative thinking. And help increase your awareness to the thinking under the influence of others.

You are your own thought police. Today, police the thoughts you choose to carry and be sure that you accept responsibility for the thoughts that run through your mind.

AUGUST 28

YOUR BOY SCOUT AND BOUNTY HUNTER

Who you are or who you need to be to be successful? Which is more important? In the athletic arena I teach that you must be who you need to be to be successful.

If you need to be more aggressive but that is not your nature, then you better change your nature and act more aggressive or you will be replaced by someone who will.

Understanding who you really are is a journey that you never stop. Understanding who you need to be to perform at your best is a journey that has a much closer finish line. You won't be a competitive athlete forever and must ask yourself, "Who do I need to be to be successful?"

The boy scout is your white collar, polite and caring person who puts others first and does whatever they can to help the team.

The bounty hunter is your do whatever it takes, grind it out, blue collar, put your life on the line butt-kicker who can be selfish and does not care about what other people say or think. Bounty hunters are too busy fighting for their lives and competing to care what others say or think.

The bounty hunter can never show fear; he knows that if he does, he gives the opposition the edge.

In life and in social settings you are often well served bringing your boy scout self. In competition the bounty hunter and his confident, aggressive, dirt bag, grind you out, never quit mentality serves you well.

Ask yourself who you need to be to be successful throughout your day, and then be who you need to be when you need to be there.

WHO DO YOU NEED TO BE TO HAVE SUCCESS?
DO YOU NEED TO BE MORE BOUNTY HUNTER?
DO YOU NEED TO BE MORE BOY SCOUT?
DO YOU NEED TO BE MORE OF BOTH?

AUGUST 29

BE YOUR OWN CHEERLEADER

We as competitors and pursuers of excellence are often first to be our biggest critics and last to be our own biggest fans.

I want you to make the commitment to start celebrating your own successes and being your biggest fan by doing two things.

1. At a consistent time each day, write down at least three wins you have had in the last 24 hours and give yourself a pat on the back for each.

   Becoming more aware of your wins will help you to strengthen your confidence.

2. Focus more on what you did well and less on what you did poorly. I recently worked with one of the top college baseball programs in the country in a double-header and had a player go 7-8 with 9 RBI's.

That was an amazing day at any level. His last at-bat was a strikeout with the bases loaded to end the second game.

Almost four hours later at a team meeting I asked him if he was thinking more about the seven quality at-bats he had or the one strikeout, and what do you think he said?

Yes, he was focused on the one strikeout and had virtually forgotten about the 7 quality at-bats.

Today, work to write down your three wins and replay the successful events of the day in your mind more than the negative ones.

WHAT ARE THREE WINS YOU HAVE HAD THIS WEEK?

1. ____

2. ____

3. ____

AUGUST 30

BEFORE AND AFTER PHOTOS

The best strength coaches in the college programs I work with all take before and after photos of their athletes at the beginning and end of their strength and conditioning seasons.

They do this so that the athletes can see their physical development and progress. What the human eye does not notice by looking in the mirror on a daily basis is picked up beautifully by before and after photos and serves as a motivational tool and a validation of the work you have or have not been putting in during the season.

Today, commit to a strength and conditioning program where you do a little a lot, not a lot a little, and take your before and after photos every 30 days to visually see your progress.

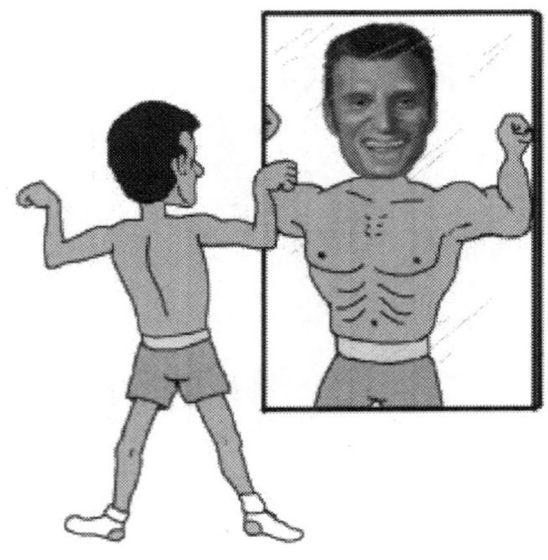

AUGUST 31

THOUGHTS BECOME THINGS

What you think about you bring about. Many baseball players will thus write mental game reminders in their hats so that before an inning starts or any time they pick up their hats they are reminded of the mentality they need to have to be successful.

1. Today, advertise the mentality you want to yourself by hanging a Post-it® note or piece of paper with a motivational reminder.

You can also set a reoccurring appointment or reminder on your phone with the same message.

What message will you remind yourself of today?

____

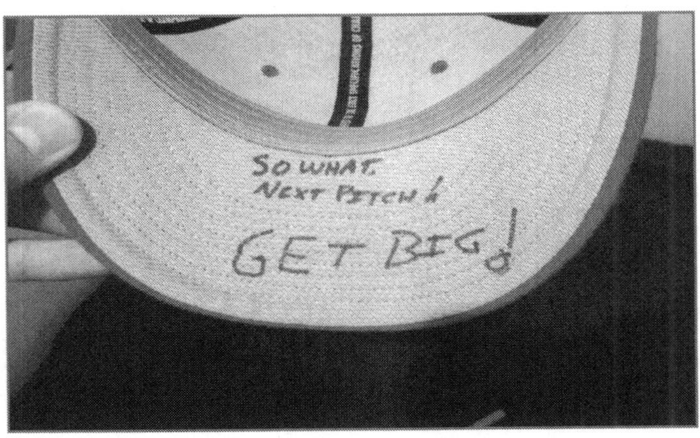

SEPTEMBER

September is the month for me to dominate...

SEPTEMBER 1

DON'T GO TO IT, GO THROUGH IT

In my live seminars and private work with teams, I have live board-breaking demonstrations with the participants to show the importance of not just going to your challenges, but going through them.

You want to be the type of person that addresses the elephant in the room and does not shy from confrontation.

You don't have to love confrontation, but you must be willing to address what needs to be addressed and be willing to not just go to, but go through, the adversity that lies ahead of you each day.

What must you address today that you have been putting off?

____

SEPTEMBER 2

PEOPLE REACH THE BAR YOU SET

Sam was the student who through elementary and middle school was always told by his teachers that he was not smart and always met their low expectations for his performance.

In 9th grade, when he took the national standards test with his classmates, he received a notice in the mail saying that he scored the best in the nation and that there would be an assembly at his school in his honor.

Everyone - Sam's teachers, family and friends, even Sam himself - was shocked and amazed at his performance. Everyone started to call him a boy genius, and immediately his bar had been raised higher than anyone else's in the school district's history.

From that moment forward, Sam was placed in all advanced courses, sat in the front and middle of each class and was called upon by his teachers more than ever. Sam's self-image had completely changed because of one test score.

Sam went on to an Ivy League school and graduated from both high school and college #1 in his class.

The amazing part of his story is that the day he returned home after graduation from college Sam received a letter in the mail from the national standards testing company. The letter explained that they had mixed up his score with someone else's; he had not finished first in the nation but had finished last in his school.

Your environment shapes you at a subconscious level and you will often meet the standards that those who have influence over you - teachers, coaches, parents - have set.

Be careful of the standards other set for you and, more importantly, the standards you set for yourself.

You will meet your standards so set them high: your goal is the moon, and your failure is still a star.

RAISE YOUR BAR

SEPTEMBER 3

GLADIATOR ROUTINES

We have invested much text in this book to the importance of routines.

The mixed martial arts gladiators I work with are very consistent in their daily routines and how they come in and out of training sessions and how they walk to the cage and enter the battle field.

Russell Crowe in the movie *Gladiator* bends over and picks up dirt before his battles to help him get into the present.

What are your routines to help you get present during the day for each battle you face?

WHAT ROUTINES DO YOU HAVE?

SEPTEMBER 4

ARE YOU HYPNOTIZED?

Have you ever been to a hypnotist show where they get people on stage to answer a shoe as if it were a telephone or act as if their bodies are covered in poison ivy?

I have been to a few of them and find them to be hilarious. What I don't find funny is how many of us go through life hypnotized and oblivious to how we beat ourselves.

What limiting beliefs, negative self-talk or other performance crushers have you allowed to be hypnotized into you by others?

Today, start to become more aware of what you say to yourself when you are faced with adversity or struggle. Let go of the mental bricks that weigh you down and keep you from being at your best. Dehypnotize yourself.

SEPTEMBER 5

YOU ARE ALLOWED TO FIRE YOURSELF

You are the CEO of (write your name here) ____________________________, inc.

You are responsible for managing your most important personnel, yourself.

If your old self was negative, lazy, out of shape and lacked the motivation and drive to be the best possible you that you are capable of being, take a line from Donald Trump and tell your old self that "You're FIRED."

Today, be the best version of you that you have ever been.

Not great or honest in relationships - that was your old self.

Cut corners in workouts - again that was your old self and you FIRED his butt.

What traits were responsible for the firing of your old self and what are you going to bring to today with your new self?

FIRED TRAITS:

____

____

NEW SELF TRAITS FOR TODAY:

____

____

YOU CAN FIRE YOUR OLD SELF AND BUILD YOUR NEW SELF ANY TIME YOU WANT

SEPTEMBER 6

LOCK IT IN FOR TODAY

What do you need to lock in on today? What is the number one thing that will make you feel successful if, when your head hits the pillow, you can look back at your day and say you did this?

____

____

This is the mission you are locking in on and locking down today. Lock in your focus and eliminate the distractions by implementing some of the strategies you have learned in this book. Put yourself in a metaphorical lockup and lock in on your task at hand and lock it down. No excuses.

Success in life is about your ability to focus, get distracted and quickly refocus. Take your focus to the next level today.

**LOCK IN YOUR FOCUS
TO LOCK DOWN THE GOAL**

SEPTEMBER 7

AND DO THE HARLEM SHAKE

I think you would agree with me that there is tremendous value in humor. One of the more humorous team building activities you can do with your team or at your office is the Harlem Shake. This short dance is sweeping the nation and is a You Tube sensation.

Two of my favorites are the UGA Swimming and Diving underwater Harlem Shake and the Saint Leo University Baseball Harlem Shake.

This dance may or may not be appropriate for you and your team; that is your decision and responsibility to decide. I just wanted to make you aware of this little piece of humorous team building excellence.

SEPTEMBER 8

ADVERTISE TO YOURSELF

The image below shows the bedroom of an athlete at Stony Point High School in Texas. This athlete is a doer.

He went home after one of our seminars and typed up the mental game signs of success that meant the most to him and posted them where he could see them every day.

I did the same thing when learning from Ken Ravizza in graduate school at Cal State Fullerton. Today I want you to hang a sign of success where you can see it every day.

What will the sign of success be?

____

____

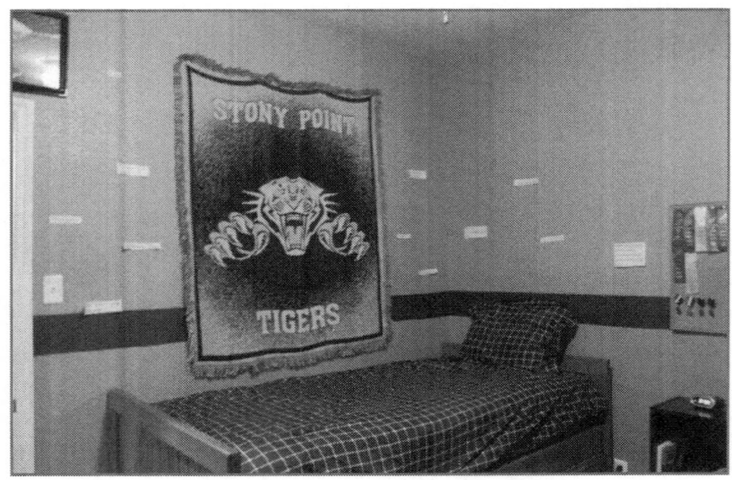

SEPTEMBER 9

MENTAL CONDITIONING MIRRORS

The same master of the mental game you read about yesterday took his mental conditioning to the next level by writing messages on his mirror with a dry erase marker.

Today, go get a dry erase marker and start writing your goals and mental conditioning signs of success and reminders on your mirror. This will only work if you act on it. Go get that dry erase marker and start using your mental conditioning mirror.

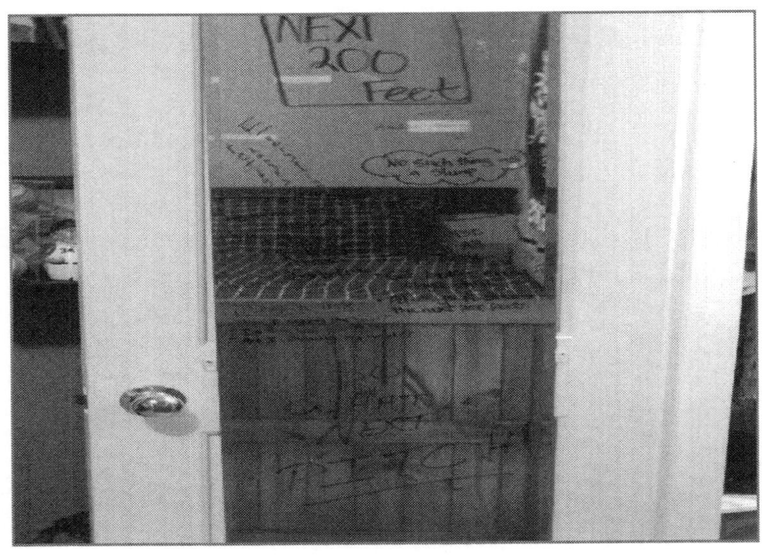

ADVERTISE TO YOURSELF
THOUGHTS BECOME THINGS

SEPTEMBER 10

10 SUGGESTIONS FOR SUCCEEDING

1. Fear no opponent. Respect every opponent.

2. Remember, it's the execution of the smallest details that makes big things happen.

3. Keep in mind that hustle, effort and energy make up for many a mistake.

4. Be more interested in character than reputation.

5. Be quick, but don't hurry.

6. Understand that the harder you work the more luck you will have.

7. Know that valid self-analysis is crucial for improvement. Don't lie to yourself.

8. Remember that there is no substitute for hard work and careful planning. Failing to prepare is preparing to fail.

9. Commit to the team, team policies, team coaches and teammates.

10. Make your best effort every minute of every day. Everything counts.

I am not what I ought to be, not what I want to be and not what I am going to be, but I am thankful that I am better than I used to be.

"Success is a peace of mind which is a direct result of self-satisfaction in knowing that you did your best to become the best you are capable of becoming."

John Wooden

Will you take this advice?

Do you really want to succeed?

Which of the 10 suggestions for succeeding will you work on today?

____

____

____

____

____

SEPTEMBER 11

ALWAYS REMEMBER THE HEROES

I can remember 9/11/2001 like it was yesterday. I was driving from my apartment in Costa Mesa, California to the campus of Cal State Fullerton when the program I was listening to on the radio was interrupted with a special news announcement.

I remember thinking that the first plane that hit the World Trade Center must have been a small two-person plane and had no idea of the terror taking place.

I recall parking and walking past people in an eerie silence on my way to get the key to unlock the weight room so I could teach a class - and then seeing the TV. It was just after 6:00am PST.

Due to the events that took place that day, I have always stopped in grocery stores, airports and other public places to thank police, fire fighters, emergency medical service and the armed service men and women of our country, those heroes who risk their lives to protect our freedom.

It was initially uncomfortable for me to approach them and simply thank them for their service. It always made me feel more uncomfortable afterwards when I didn't.

I challenge you to make this part of your life routine. Give thanks to those willing to risk their lives to save those they don't even know. True American Heroes.

SEPTEMBER 12

ARE YOU A WINNER OR A LOSER?

When winners make a mistake, they say, "I was wrong." When losers make mistakes, they say, "It wasn't my fault."

A winner works harder than a loser and has more time. A loser is always "too busy" to do what is necessary.

A winner goes through a problem. A loser goes around it and never gets past it.

A winner makes commitments. A loser makes promises.

A winner says, "I'm good, but not as good as I ought to be." A loser says, "I'm not as bad as a lot of other people."

A winner listens. A loser just waits until it's his turn to talk.

A winner explains. A loser explains away.

A winner respects those who are superior to him and tries to learn something from them. A loser resents those who are superior to him and tries to find chinks in their armor.

A winner says, "Let's find out." A loser says, "Nobody knows."

A winner feels responsible for more than his job. A loser says, "I only work here."

A winner shows he is sorry by taking corrective action and not making the same mistake again. A loser says, "I'm sorry," but does the same thing the next time.

A winner says, "There ought to be a better way to do it." A loser says, "That's always the way it has been done here."

Your team needs to have a winner's attitude if you are going to be successful this season. Winners are fountains, energy givers and eagles who soar above. Losers are drains, energy takers and ducks that complain about the challenges they face.

Today, be a winner, not a loser. Help others to see the difference between a winner's and a loser's mentality.

Which of these makes the most sense to you?

SEPTEMBER 13

FOUNTAINS AND DRAINS

The Fountain is always part of the answer.

The Drain is always part of the problem.

The Fountain always has a program.

The Drain always has an excuse.

The Fountain says, "Let me do it for you."

The Drain says, "That's not my job."

The Fountain sees an answer for every problem.

The Drain sees a problem for every answer.

The Fountain sees a green near every sand trap.

The Drain sees two or three sand traps near every green.

The Fountain says, "It may be difficult, but it's possible." The Drain says, "It may be possible, but it's too difficult."

If you are a going to be a great teammate, you MUST be a Fountain. Drains only clog thing up.

Today, be a Fountain.

SEPTEMBER 14

ATTITUDE

The following poem by Charles Swindoll is one of my all-time favorites and shows the power of choosing one's own way. His books are necessities in your peak performance library.

The longer I live, the more I realize the impact of attitude on life. Attitude to me is more important than facts. It is more important than the past, than education, than money, than circumstances, than failures, than successes, than what other people think, say, or do. It is more important than appearance, giftedness, or skill. It will make or break a company... a team... a home. The remarkable thing is we have a choice every day regarding the attitude we will embrace for that day. We cannot change our past... We cannot change the fact that people will act in a certain way. We cannot change the inevitable. The one thing we can do is play on the one string we have, and that is our attitude... I am convinced that life is 10% what happens to me and 90% how I react to it. And so it is with you... we are in charge of our attitudes.

The attitude you take is a decision you make. What kind of attitude will you choose to take today?

Attitudes are contagious; is yours worth catching?

SEPTEMBER 15

WHAT IS EXCELLENCE?

Excellence is preparing more than others care to or expect; practicing more often than the average person believes is necessary; and believing in the quality of every moment, every day and every person. This is what excellence is all about.

Excellence comes from striving for and maintaining the highest standards and the highest beliefs, looking after the smallest detail and executing the fundamentals while going the extra mile.

Excellence means caring - caring enough about making a difference.

It means making a special effort to do more than is asked and to expect more of oneself.

Today, check your ego at the door and accept the responsibility you have to make a difference within your team and put we over me.

SEPTEMBER 16

EXCUSES

Excuses are for average people. Forget them.

There are thousands of excuses available to all losers. To have a good excuse is to have what every other loser in the history of the world has had.

Don't make the ridiculous mistake of thinking that your particular brand of excuse is somewhat more valid than the last twenty million that have been uttered.

Hopefully your mother will believe you and maybe your significant other, or at least they may sympathize and keep their mouths shut if they don't, but everyone else knows an excuse when they hear it.

Your particular excuse is just as terrible as everyone else's.

There. Now you know it.

Now you are free to accomplish things and to work and to concentrate, excuse free.

Forget about excuses. They are an enormous waste of time and words.

Get the most out of today by living excuse free.

SEPTEMBER 17

MORE EXCUSES

How did you do yesterday at living an excuse-free life?

Regardless of how you did, live an excuse free-life today.

Excuses are like feet and rear ends.

Everyone usually has them and they typically stink.

We all make excuses at one point or another. However, nobody cares to hear our excuses.

If we don't have a good game or a good day at work, nobody cares. They want to see the results of our process and efforts.

When you pick up a newspaper tomorrow, it will not say: "Cain was 0-4 at the plate today and had a very unproductive day at work, but feel sorry for him. He was not feeling well, and he couldn't get to sleep last night," etc.

Today, exterminate all excuses and DOMINATE The Day excuse free.

Have an accountability partner help you and hold you accountable.

Who could be your accountability partner?

____

____

____

SEPTEMBER 18

MENTAL TOUGHNESS

Nobody ever said it would be easy, so don't expect it to be. No one is immune from everyday problems.

Sometimes you have to perform at your best when you're feeling at your worst.

Block the hurt, the pain and the sickness out of your head for the short time you must perform by locking into what it is you want to do.

Shape up and get it together because excuses don't count! Nobody cares if you are hurt or sick: You either get the job done or you don't.

There might be times when you would rather be somewhere else, but face up to the challenges at hand.

No matter what has happened, you must always give yourself the best chance for success and win the mental battle royal that is taking place in your head between the red and green assassins.

You must force yourself to act confident, enthusiastic and positive.

You must force yourself to work even harder when you are sick, hurt, sad or troubled. That is mental toughness.

Life is easy when the going is good.

Mental toughness comes into play when the going gets bad.

Never let your opponents see your weakness, because then they can take advantage of it.

The fighter automatically goes for the cut eye, the bloody nose.

Mental toughness is also the ability to keep after a goal, to look one or two years ahead and keep going full throttle after that goal today, even in the face of adversity.

You don't accomplish much in life if you only work on the days that you feel good.

You need to be in the best physical and mental condition of your life in order to be truly successful this season.

If you cheat yourself in your workout today, you are going to lack confidence when the going gets tough because you know you have cut corners.

Today, attack everything you do with an enthusiasm and relentless positive energy unknown to mankind.

How will you show mental toughness today?

____

____

____

____

____

____

____

SEPTEMBER 19

THE TREASURY OF TIME

What would you do if you had a bank that credited your account each morning with $86,400 that carried over no balance from day to day, allowed you to keep no cash in your account, and every evening cancelled whatever part of the amount you had failed to use during the day?

You would draw out every cent, of course, and use it to your advantage.

Did you know you have such a bank? Its name is TIME TO ______________________. (Insert your game here: time to play college baseball, time to be a high school teacher, etc.)

Every morning it credits you with 86,400 seconds. Every night it rules off as lost whatever of this you have failed to invest in preparing yourself for success.

It carries over no balances. It allows no overdrafts.

Each day it opens a new account with you. Each night it burns the record of the day. If you fail to use the day's deposits, the loss of preparation for your success is yours. There is no going back.

There is no drawing against the "tomorrow."

It is up to you to invest this precious fund of hours, minutes and seconds in order to get the utmost out of your physical talent, mental capabilities, knowledge of your career of choice and the confidence that comes with the blood, sweat and tears of preparation.

ONLY YOU AND TIME WILL DETERMINE YOUR DESTINATION AND THE DIFFERENCE YOU WILL MAKE.

What will you do today to get better?

Yesterday is history. Tomorrow is a mystery. Today is your gift; that is why we call it the present.

GET THE MOST OUT OF TODAY!!!

Today I will ____

____

____

____

____

____

____

____

____

____

____

____

____

SEPTEMBER 20

YOUR BIRTHDAY GIFT TO ME

Today is my birthday.

The greatest gift you can give me is to keep working at yourself, to keep reading this book and to keep implementing what you are learning on a daily basis.

Today, please write on my Facebook page **www.facebook.com/briancainpeak** or tweet me at @briancainpeak about the difference this book has made in your life.

I believe that the greatest gift anyone can receive is the one that can't be returned, re-gifted or refused.

The gift of experience.

Birthdays are the celebration of the day you were brought into this world.

I hope that when my days are done, people will remember me as a teacher, a giver and a person who helped others reach a level they may not have found on their own.

How do you want to be remembered?

____

____

____

____

SEPTEMBER 21

WHAT IS A CHAMPION?

At your level of competition, almost everyone has the physical tools to be the best.

It comes down to a few things: How badly you want it, what you do when things get hard and whether you are able to stay focused amid adversity, turmoil, challenge, chaos and demands.

It's all in your head and in your heart.

Being a champion is a lifestyle, not an event.

Champions are all they can be in every facet of their lives.

They prioritize what they need to get done.

A champion is someone who works every single day on being a better player and a better person.

A champion knows that it is what you do when no one is watching that counts.

Do you still get the job done when you have no one to work out with or when you don't feel well?

Today, live your life with the attitude of a champion.

SEPTEMBER 22

IT ALL STARTS WITH HOW YOU THINK

Watch your thoughts;

They become words.

Watch your words;

They become actions.

Watch your actions;

They become habits.

Watch your habits;

They become character.

Watch your character;

It becomes your destiny.

Author Unknown

Become more aware of what you think today and what you think about most often.

VISUALIZE YOUR SUCCESS TODAY

SEPTEMBER 23

SHAKE IT OFF AND STEP UP

One day a farmer's donkey fell down into a well.

The animal cried for hours as the farmer tried to figure out what to do. Finally, he decided the animal was old and the well needed to be covered up anyway; it just wasn't worth it to retrieve the donkey.

He invited all his neighbors to come over and help him. They all grabbed a shovel and began to shovel dirt into the well. At first, the donkey realized what was happening and cried horribly.

Then, to everyone's amazement, he quieted down. A few shovel loads later, the farmer finally looked down the well and was astonished at what he saw.

With every shovel of dirt that hit his back, the donkey was doing something amazing. He would shake it off and take a step up.

As the farmer's neighbors continued to shovel dirt on top of the animal, the donkey kept shaking it off and moving up a step.

Pretty soon everyone was amazed as the donkey stepped up over the edge of the well and trotted off!

Life is going to shovel dirt on you, all kinds of dirt. The trick to getting out of the well is to shake it off and take a step up.

Each of our troubles is a stepping stone. We can get out of the deepest wells just by not stopping, never giving up! Shake it off and take a step up!

Remember the five simple rules you need to follow to be happy:

1. Free your heart from hatred.

2. Free your mind from worries.

3. Live a simple life.

4. Give more to others than they expect.

5. Expect to get less from others.

The moral of this story is that when you think life has dealt you the most difficult hand, you need to stop feeling sorry for yourself, shake it off and step up. What do you need to shake off and step up on today?

SEPTEMBER 24

WHAT GREAT TEAMMATES WON'T ASK

1. They won't ask what kind of car you drive, but will ask how many people you drive who don't have transportation.

2. They won't ask the square footage of your house, but will ask how many people you welcome into your home.

3. They won't ask about the fancy clothes you have in your closet, but will ask how many of those clothes helped the needy at times of crisis.

4. They won't ask about your social status, but will ask what kind of class you display.

5. They won't ask how many material possessions you have, but will ask if they dictate your life.

6. They won't ask what your highest salary has been, but will ask if you compromised your character to obtain that salary.

7. They won't ask how much overtime you put in, but will ask if you worked overtime for your family and loved ones.

8. They won't ask how many promotions you have received, but will ask how you promoted others.

9. They won't ask what your job title is, but will ask if you perform your job to the best of your ability.

10. They won't ask what you do to help yourself, but will ask what you do to help others.

11. They won't ask what you do to protect your rights, but will ask what you do to protect the rights of others.

12. They won't ask in what neighborhood you live, but will ask how you treat your neighbors.

13. They won't ask how many times your deeds match your words, but will ask how many times they didn't.

How do you want to be remembered by your teammates today?

____

____

____

____

____

What have you been asked by a teammate that is something that a great teammate would not ask you?

____

____

____

____

____

SEPTEMBER 25

BUILDING A FIRE

A fire needs two things to live: fuel and oxygen. A fire cannot live and breathe if these two elements are not present.

Right now your goals might be a distant flame. In order for a flame to grow into a raging fire, it needs a constant supply of fuel and oxygen. Every time you run you give the fire oxygen. Every time you lift you put fuel on the fire. It is a daily commitment to keep building the fire stronger than it was the day before.

As that fire grows, it gains strength, speed and intensity. The fire starts to spread. It is an impressive sight to see a blazing fire demolish everything in sight. A strong, fast fire destroys everything in its path with no regrets. When the fire runs out of fuel and you sift through the ashes, you find that only the strongest elements survived: Elements that have been pushed to the limit and still kept their strength. Elements that will stand the test of time. Elements like gold and diamonds. Elements like those in championship rings.

What are you doing today to keep the fire burning inside of you and inside of your teammates? ______________________

____

Will you be made of the elements that are necessary to be a championship team this season? ____________________

____

SEPTEMBER 26

WHO THE IMPORTANT PEOPLE ARE

Take this quiz:

1. Name the five wealthiest people in the world.

____

____

____

____

2. Name the last five Heisman Trophy winners.

____

____

____

____

3. Name the last five winners of the Miss America contest.

____

____

____

____

4. Name ten people who have won the Nobel or Pulitzer prize.

____

____

____

5. Name the last half-dozen Academy Award winners for the best actor and actress.

____

____

____

6. Name the last decade's worth of World Series winners.

____

____

____

How did you do?

The point is, none of us remember the headliners of yesterday.

These are no second-rate achievers. They are the best in their fields. But applause dies. Awards tarnish. Achievements are forgotten.

Accolades and certificates are buried with their owners.

Here's another quiz. See how you do on this one:

1. List a few teachers who aided your journey through school.____

____

2. Name three friends who have helped you through a difficult time. ____________________________________

____

3. Name five people who have taught you something wonderful. _______________________________________

____

4. Think of a few people who have made you feel appreciated and special. ___________________________

____

5. Think of a few people you enjoy spending time with. ____

____

6. Name half a dozen heroes whose stories have inspired you.______________________________________

____

Was this test easier?______________________________________

The point here is that the people who make a difference in your life are not the ones with the most credentials, the most money or the most awards. They are the ones that care the most.

Do you care about your teammates or only yourself? What will you do today to demonstrate that you care for your teammates?

DOn't walT = DO IT

SEPTEMBER 27

ARE YOU MENTALLY TOUGH?

What does it really mean to be mentally tough?

____

Are you overly sensitive to criticism or really tough-skinned?

____

How are your attitude and your outlook on life?

____

What goes through your mind after you make an error?

____

In your "Self-Talk" are you overly critical of yourself? ____

Do you have a strong self-concept of who you are even when you may not be playing well or not playing at all?

____

Are you self-confident on the inside when things aren't going well on the outside?

____

Do you have the ability to recover quickly from a mistake or a bad call?

____

Are you a victim of outside circumstances or a fighter who battles back aggressively?

____

How well do you deal with adversity, unfairness, injury, failure? ____

Can you get back into a competitive frame of mind quickly?

____

Are you a pessimist or an optimist about your next competition? ___________________________________

Are you a competitor who does better under pressure or do you ever throw away an opportunity by getting consumed by the pressure?

____

How well do you keep things in perspective and look at all possible outcomes?

____

Consider whether you have the desire to get the most out of your ability.

____

How much of a commitment are you willing to make to become the best you can be, not compared to others, just to yourself?

____

Do you take pride in what you have accomplished in your career?

____

What are you especially good at?

____

How can you become even better?

____

How can you enjoy competing in the game even more than you do now?

____

How can you enjoy it when you are frustrated and not performing well?

____

Have you set any limits on what you can achieve?

____

Is it possible to have unlimited heights of achievement?

____

Do you have positive self-talk about yourself?

____

When can you expect to achieve a small part of your larger goal?

____

Do you have a backup plan in case?

____

What does life mean to you if you could never do what you are doing now again?

____

Today is the most important day of your career. Answering these questions will help you build the championship perspective you need to succeed. DOMINATE The Day!

PERSPECTIVE IS REALITY

SEPTEMBER 28

A FEW WRITTEN "UNWRITTEN" RULES

1. EFFORT AND ATTITUDE

There are only two things in this world that you can control: your effort and your attitude. Set your priorities and eliminate all other distractions. Come early or stay late when necessary. Be motivated by an inner desire to improve yourself. Give all-out effort and possess a positive attitude every day.

2. PATIENCE WITH YOUR PACE OF PROGRESS

Compete in the moment and live in the big picture. Be willing to put in the hours and be willing to overcome the obstacles and the tough days. Develop the ability to never quit and a "compared to what" perspective.

3. ACCOUNTABLE AND RESPONSIBLE

If you fall short in a task or requirement, have courage and admit your errors. Carry out your responsibilities for failure and move on. It is that simple.

4. POSITIVE OR POISONOUS

For every environment you experience you have a choice at how you look at it, how you talk about it, how you become successful within it. There are only two types of people in this world: Positive and poisonous. Which are you?

5. RESPECT FOR THE PROGRAM AND THE TEAM

Our ups and downs are ours to share. Think twice before you share your "funny or humiliating story" to an outsider who may "act" like they really care.

Possess the sincere ability to respect your teammates whether you can "relate" to them or not. Whether you socialize with them or not.

Every person has positives within, something that makes him or her special. It is your job to find those positives and focus on them. You have a choice.

Today, how will you show you are following the team's standards of excellence?

____

Today, how will you maximize your effort by having the right attitude?

____

Today, how will you demonstrate patience with the process and progress of your own and your team's development?

____

____

Today, how will you be more accountable and responsible?

____

____

If you can be more accountable and responsible today than you were yesterday, what are you waiting for?

____

____

Today, will you be a positive or a poisonous influence on the team?

____

How will you show this?

____

Do you have respect for the program and the team, and do the program and team respect you?

____

How do you show this?

____

How does your team?

____

SEPTEMBER 29

BE PERFECT

What is perfection? Is it attainable?

Has any team or any player ever played the perfect game?

Most people view perfection as doing something without making any mistakes or any errors. Perfection is a double-edged sword.

While it drives you to do better, at the same time it is a constant critic and you are never good enough.

If you have seen the movie *Friday Night Lights*, you will remember the speech that coach Gary Gaines gave to his Permian Panther team at half-time in the state championship game.

He talked to the team about being perfect.

Being perfect is not about the scoreboard. It's not about winning. Being perfect is about you and your relationship with yourself, your family, your friends and your teammates. It is about being able to look your teammates in the eye and know that you did everything you could and that there wasn't one more thing you could have done. Being perfect is to live in that moment as best you can with clear eyes, love and joy in your heart.

Gary Gaines, Head Football Coach
Permian Panthers, Friday Night Lights

The attainment of perfection is relative to your definition.

If you evaluate perfection on doing everything that is within your control to give you and your team the best chance for success today, that is perfection.

How do you define perfection as it relates to you and your current situation today?

____

____

____

____

____

What must you do today to have the perfect day?

____

____

____

____

____

____

SEPTEMBER 30

THE SUCCESSFUL ATTITUDE EQUATION

What makes up 100%?

What does it mean to give MORE than 100%?

Ever wonder about those people who say they are giving more than 100%?

We have all been to those meetings where someone wants you to give over 100%.

How about achieving 110%?

What makes up 100% in life?

Here's a little mathematical formula that might help you answer these questions:

If:

A B C D E F G H I J K L M N O P Q R S T U V W X Y Z

is represented as:

1 2 3 4 5 6 7 8 9 10 11 12 13 14 15 16 17 18 19 20 21 22 23 24 25 26,

Then: H-A-R-D-W-O-R-K

8+1+18+4+23+15+18+11 = 98%

and

K-N-O-W-L-E-D-G-E

11+14+15+23+12+5+4+7+5 = 96%

But,

A-T-T-I-T-U-D-E

1+20+20+9+20+21+4+5 = 100%

So, one can conclude with mathematical certainty that while hard work and knowledge will get you close it is your attitude that will get you there.

Remember, the attitude you take is a decision you make.

Today, you can control your attitude in every situation you face.

Your attitude is contagious and your attitude will determine your altitude.

What type of attitude will you bring with you today?

____

____

____

____

OCTOBER

October is the month for me to dominate...

OCTOBER 1

ATTITUDE AND ADVERSITY

Jonah is the kind of guy you love to be around. He is always in a good mood and always has something positive to say. When someone asked him how he was doing, he would reply,

"If I were any better, I would be twins!"

He was a natural motivator, a master of the mental game.

If a teammate was having a bad day, Jonah was there telling him how to look on the positive side of the situation.

Seeing this style really made his coach curious, so the coach went up to Jonah and said: "I don't get it! You can't be a positive person all of the time. How do you do it?"

Jonah replied:

Each morning I wake up and tell myself that I have two choices today. I can choose to be in a good mood or ... I can choose to be in a bad mood. I choose to be in a good mood.

Each time something bad happens, I can choose to be a loser or I can choose to be a learner. I choose to be a learner at all times.

Every time someone comes to me complaining, I can choose to accept their complaining or... I can point out the positive side of life. I choose the positive side of life.

"Yeah, right. It's not that easy," the coach protested.

"Yes, it is," Jonah said. "Life is all about choices. When you cut away all the garbage, every situation is a choice. You choose how you react to situations. You choose how people affect your mood. You choose to be in a good mood or bad mood. The bottom line: It's your choice how you live your life."

The coach reflected on what Jonah said. Soon thereafter, Jonah graduated and went on to college. The coach lost contact with Jonah but often thought about him when he made a choice about life instead of reacting to it.

Several years later, Jonah was involved in a serious accident, falling some 60 feet during a hike with his friends. After 18 hours of surgery and weeks of intensive care, Jonah was released from the hospital with rods placed in his back.

The coach saw Jonah at an alumni event about six months after the accident and six years after they had last seen each other. When he asked Jonah how he was holding up, Jonah replied: "If I were any better, I'd be twins. Want to see my scars?"

The coach declined to see his wounds, but did ask him what had gone through his mind as the accident took place.

"The first thing that went through my mind was the well-being of my family and how they were going to react," Jonah replied. "Then, as I lay on the ground, I remembered that I had two choices: I could choose to live or... I could choose to die. I chose to live."

"Weren't you scared? Did you lose consciousness?" his former coach asked.

Jonah continued: "...the paramedics were great. They kept telling me I was going to be fine. But when they wheeled me into the ER and I saw the expressions on the faces of the doctors and nurses, I got really scared. In their eyes, I read 'he's a dead man.' I knew I needed to take action."

"What did you do?" the coach asked. "Well, there was a big burly nurse shouting questions at me," said Jonah. "She asked if I was allergic to anything. "Yes," I answered. The doctors and nurses stopped working as they waited for my reply. I took a deep breath and yelled, 'Gravity.' Over their laughter, I told them that 'I am choosing to live. Operate on me as if I am alive, not dead.' "

Jonah lived, thanks to the skill of his doctors, but also because of his amazing attitude. His message: Every day we have the choice to live fully. Attitude, after all, is everything.

Do not worry about tomorrow, for tomorrow will take care of itself. Today has a life and history of its own. After all, today is the tomorrow you worried about yesterday. Dominate The Day!

OCTOBER 2

JOHN WOODEN'S TWO SETS OF THREE

John Wooden is one of the greatest coaches of all time. His father taught him two sets of three guiding principles while he was growing up that still hold true to your success today.

SET ONE

1. Never Lie.
2. Never Cheat.
3. Never Steal.

SET TWO

1. Don't Whine.
2. Don't Complain.
3. Don't Make Excuses.

Today, which of these six principles will you be more aware of and live?

____

____

____

____

OCTOBER 3

SIX QUESTIONS WHY?

1. Why is it easier to criticize than to compliment?

____

2. Why is it easier to give others blame than to give them credit?

____

3. Why is it that so many who are quick to make suggestions find it so difficult to make decisions?

____

4. Why can't we realize that it only weakens those we want to help when we do things for them that they should do for themselves?

____

5. Why is it so much easier to allow emotions rather than reason to control our decisions?

____

6. Why does the person with the least to say usually take the longest to say it? _________________________________

These questions come from a must-read book, *Wooden: A Lifetime of Observations and Reflections On and Off the Court* by Steve Jamison.

OCTOBER 4

RUNNING IN THE RAIN

A young girl had just finished shopping with her mother when it started to rain very hard, the kind of downpour that hurts when it hits you.

Most people stood under cover, some patiently and others irritated because Mother Nature messed up their hurried day.

The young girl looked at her mother and said, "Mom, let's run through the rain."

"We'll get soaked if we do," the mother said.

"No, we won't, Mom. That's not what you said this morning," the young girl said as she tugged at her Mom's arm.

"This morning? When did I say we could run through the rain and not get wet?" the mother asked

"Don't you remember? When you were talking to Daddy about his cancer, you said, 'If we can get through this, we can get through anything!' "

The entire crowd stopped dead silent. You couldn't hear anything but the rain.

Everyone stood silently. The mom looked into the little girl's face, paused and thought for a moment about what she would say.

Some may have laughed it off or scolded her for being silly. Some might have even ignored what was said.

“Honey, you are absolutely right. Let’s run through the rain. If we get wet, well, maybe we just needed washing,” the mom said.

Off they ran, smiling and laughing as they darted past the cars and through the puddles.

They held their shopping bags over their heads just in case.

They got soaked. But they were followed by a few who screamed and laughed like children all the way to their cars.

Life’s circumstances can take away your material possessions, your money, your health - but no one can ever take away your precious memories.

Today bring a heightened awareness to making memories.

Enjoy this day, every day, because you never know when you might not have any left.

DOMINATE THE DAY!

OCTOBER 5

10 THINGS I WON'T DO FOR MY TEAMMATES

1. I won't steal for my teammates.
2. I won't cheat for my teammates.
3. I won't act dumb for my teammates.
4. I won't do drugs for my teammates.
5. I won't disrupt the class for my teammates.
6. I won't disrespect, laugh or ridicule others for my teammates.
7. I won't intentionally fail for my teammates.
8. I won't behave irresponsibly for my teammates.
9. I won't knowingly hurt others for my teammates.
10. I won't destroy my life or anyone else's for my teammates.

What are you willing to not do for your teammates?

____

What are you willing to do?

____

____

OCTOBER 6

THERE AIN'T NO FREE LUNCH

Many years ago, an old king called his wise men together and gave them a task:

"I want you to compile for me the 'wisdom of the ages.' I want you to put it in book form so that we may leave it for future generations."

The wise men left their king and began working day and night on their task.

They finally returned with twelve volumes and proudly proclaimed that this truly was the "wisdom of the ages."

The king looked at the twelve volumes and said:

"Gentlemen, I'm certain this is the wisdom of the ages and contains the knowledge we should leave to mankind. However, it is so long that I fear the people won't read it. Condense it."

Again, the wise men worked long and hard before they returned with only one volume.

The king, however, knew that it was still too lengthy so he ordered them to further condense their work. The wise men reduced the volume to a chapter, then to a page, then to a paragraph, and finally, to a sentence.

When the wise old king saw the sentence, he was absolutely elated. "Gentlemen," he said, "this is truly the 'wisdom of the ages.' And as soon as all men everywhere learn this truth, then most of their problems will be solved."

The sentence simply said,

"There ain't no free lunch."

There is a price to pay for anything worthwhile. In this world, you get nothing of value for free.

If you want to be a great athlete, a great student, a great friend, a great lover, there is an investment that must be made

An investment of time, energy, effort and attention to detail. Today, what investments are you going to make?

OCTOBER 7

THE BOTTOM LINE

Face it. Nobody owes you a damn thing.

What you achieve or fail to achieve in your lifetime is directly related to what you do or fail to do.

No one chooses his or her parents or childhood, but you can choose your own direction.

Everyone has problems and obstacles to overcome, but they too are relative to each individual.

Nothing is carved in stone. You can change anything in your life if you want to badly enough.

Excuses are for losers. Refuse to make them. Those who take responsibility for their actions are the real winners in life.

Winners meet life's challenges head-on knowing there are no guarantees. The only guarantee they know is that if they give it all they've got they give themselves the best chance for success in any endeavor.

It's never too late or too early to begin. Time plays no favorites and will pass whether you act or not. Take control of yourself and your life. Dare to dream and take risks. With risk comes reward. If you aren't willing to work day and night for your goals, don't expect others to work for you.

Enthusiasm and work ethic are contagious. Today, make sure that yours are worth catching!

OCTOBER 8

A JAR OF ROCKS

A sport psychology professor stood before his class and had several items in front of him on a table.

When class began, he picked up a large empty mayonnaise jar and proceeded to fill it with rocks, then asked the students if the jar was full.

They agreed that it was.

The professor then picked up a box of pebbles and poured them into the jar. He shook the jar lightly. The pebbles, of course, rolled into the open areas between the rocks. He asked the students again if the jar was full.

They again agreed that it was.

The professor then picked up a box of sand and poured it into the jar. Of course, the sand filled up everything else.

He continued:

Now, I want you to recognize that this is your life.

The rocks are the important things - your family, your significant other, your health, your teammates, and anything that is so important to you that if it were lost you would be nearly destroyed.

The pebbles are the other things that matter like your grades, your house, your car, playing time. The sand is everything else. The small stuff.

If you put the sand into the jar first, there is no room for the pebbles or the rocks.

The same goes for your life. If you spend all your energy and time on the small stuff, you will never have room for the things that are important to you.

Pay attention to the things that are critical to your happiness.

Take care of the rocks first, the things that really matter. Then take care of your pebbles. Set your priorities appropriately. The rest is just sand.

Are you making your practice, preparation and your teammates the big rocks, or is your social life more important? Do you want to drink beer and party or play your best and win?

What are your big rocks?

____

What are your pebbles?

____

What is your sand?

____

OCTOBER 9

GOOD OR GREAT?

Today you have to make a choice. Are you going to be good or great?

Good has a fine shapely figure along with a pleasant personality, and everyone loves good's persona. Great is a more serious individual who gets along with some, but always manages to mentally keep on top of the competition.

Many think that good and great are very much alike. A qualifying example of this, though, would be: "Is it good to you, or is it great for you?"

In reality, there is no comparison of good and great.

To be good is to simply wake up in the morning, plow along with your life and give an honest day's work ethic. As long as you keep your nose clean, everyone will be happy with you and love you because you are good.

To be good you can fail often, but if you secure that one big win every ten tries, you will still be good.

We are born to be great, but it is a quality that we so easily relinquish. To be born, you beat over two billion other sperm cells. You were the best and you didn't even know it.

Then your life starts. People sell you on how awesome it is to be good and you are suckered into their game.

Muhammad Ali's war cry was never that "I am good"; it was always "I am the greatest."

To be great, the best, you must possess a persona of conceit without being conceited. You must learn to be intense without being tense and be comfortable with being uncomfortable. In reality, very few people like those who are great.

The great ones are never satisfied with an honest day's work, only with an excellent, efficient and effective day's work. The one big win is of no value to the greatest because they want to win everything they do and fully expect to win every time they compete.

The great do not accept failure; they learn from their mistakes and losses and use that adversity as a springboard to get to the next level.

The great might not succeed all the time; but by studying their failures and faults, they turn negatives into positives, failure into success. The great never want to be known as good. Only one can wear the championship belt or hoist the trophy after their last game. Only one team gets to go to the White House, but many (the good) can walk in the parade.

Starting today, what will your choice be: to be good or to be great? What are you going to do today differently than yesterday to show yourself you are committed to being great?

____

____

____

____

____

____

OCTOBER 10

THE BRIDGE BUILDER

Will Allen Dromgoole wrote one of the greatest poems of all time about the importance of leaving your program better for the next person or your teammates of the future who you don't know yet.

An old man going down a lone highway came in the evening cold and gray, on a chasm vast and deep and wide, through which was flowing a sullen tide.

The old man crossed in the twilight dim; That swollen stream held no fears for him; But he turned when safe on the other side, and built a bridge to span the tide.

"Old Man," said a fellow pilgrim near, "You are wasting your strength with building here; Your journey will end with the ending day; You never again must pass this way; You have crossed the chasm deep and wide. Why build you this bridge at the eventide?"

The builder lifted his old gray head.

"Good friend, in the path I have come," he said, "There followeth after me today a youth whose feet must pass this way. This swollen stream which was naught to me, to that fair-haired youth may a pitfall be; He, too, must cross in the twilight dim; Good friend, I am building the bridge for him."

What kind of bridge are you building for the future players in your program and the teammates you don't know yet?

Erik Bakich, head baseball coach at The University of Michigan, assigns a team number to each team to help remind them that they are a part of something much bigger than themselves.

He asks them what the legacy of their team will be.

I ask you, what is the legacy you are leaving today?

____

____

____

____

____

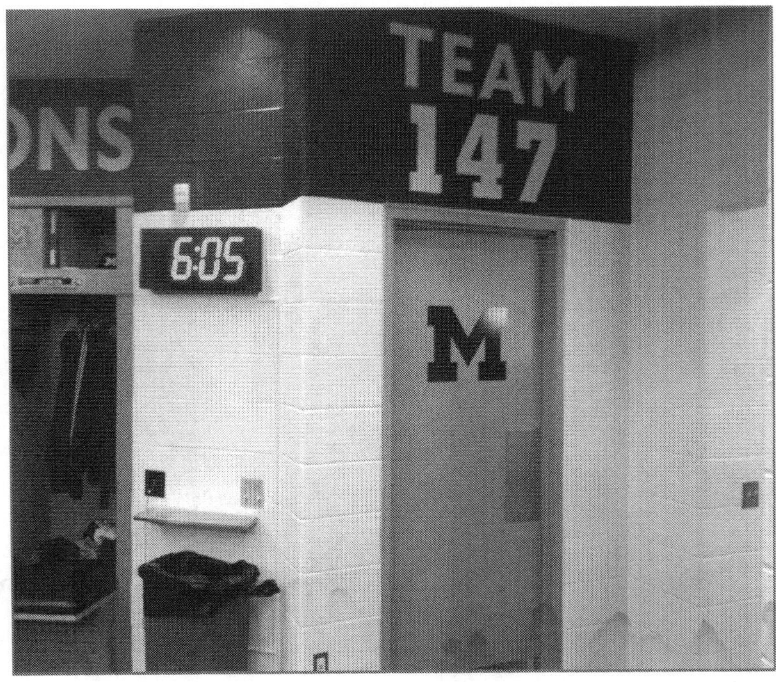

OCTOBER 11

BUILT TOGETHER

There are parts of a ship which taken by themselves would sink. The engine would sink. The propeller would sink. The captain would sink.

But when the parts of a ship work together as a team, they not only float, they sail.

In life there will be failure and success; when they are put together, they form the person and the team that you are today.

Is your team built together?

Are all your parts working together?

Is your ship going to sail successfully when the waters get choppy, or will it sink when you hit tough waters?

What can you do today to help strengthen your ship and keep your parts working together?

____

____

____

____

MAKE SURE YOUR SHIP SAILS TOGETHER!

OCTOBER 12

WHAT IT MEANS TO BE HEADS-UP

The most influential book in my life is without a doubt *Heads-Up Baseball* by Ken Ravizza and Tom Hanson. The list below was modified from this great book. I suggest that your mission for today is to order it if you don't have it already in your library and break it out if you do.

1. Take responsibility for your thoughts and actions.

2. Commit to a mission: Know why you do what you do and what character traits you want to possess and what you want to accomplish in your life.

3. Make your daily actions consistent with your mission.

4. Play the game one pitch at a time and play life one day at a time. Be confident and focused on each play and compete with disregard for past or future days.

5. Focus on the process of playing the game rather than the outcome of your performance. Understand that you do not have control of the outcome; you only have control of the process.

6. Realize that you can't control what goes on around you but that you have total control of how you choose to respond and that you must be in control of yourself before you can control your performance.

7. Develop your mental skills so you can consistently perform near the best of your ability and have "something to go to" when faced with adversity.

8. Practice what you will do in a game at game speed with a game-like mindset.

9. Learn and get better each and every day.

10. Keep it super simple.

Which of these ten characteristics of the heads-up competitor do you need to develop the most and are committing to today?

____

____

____

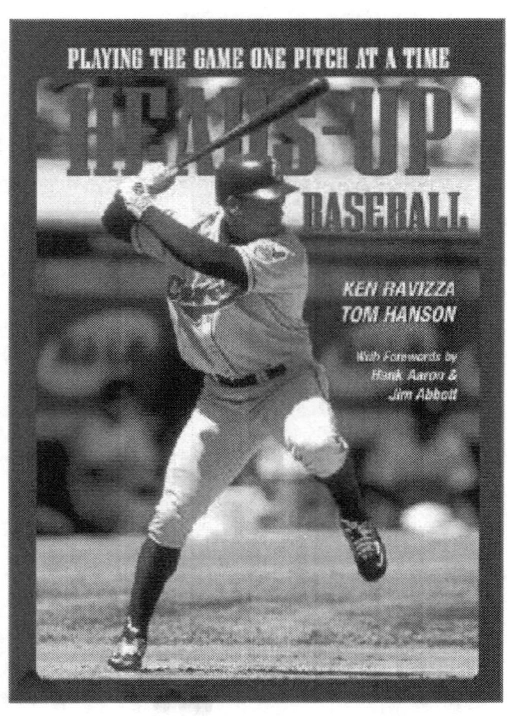

OCTOBER 13

ELEMENTS OF EXCELLENCE

What is it that those who achieve excellence do that others do not? Here are ten strategies for achieving excellence.

1. Increase your commitment: For those who achieve excellence in their profession, excellence is often the top priority in their life and everything revolves around their training and competition schedules.

2. Increase your quality of training: Top performers train and prepare with the highest degree of quality and competition on a daily basis.

3. Set daily, weekly, monthly and yearly goals: Top performers have very clearly defined goals and their actions on a daily basis are in line with their plan for accomplishing those goals.

4. Using mental imagery: Top performers use mental imagery on a daily basis for a variety of purposes and often are unaware that they are doing mental imagery. Before they train they will imagine themselves executing what they are to do that day. They will imagine themselves making skill improvement, physical corrections, having success and dominating the competition.

5. Have more detailed practice plans: The best coaches I have encountered have very detailed and individualized training goals and practice plans for each day and are committed to following their plans.

6. Have pre-practice and pre-competition routines: The best coaches and athletes I have been around have very specific routines they carry out pre-practice and pre-game to get themselves in the right frame of mind and body to compete and train at a high level. They know exactly what they need to do to get ready to go and they do it.

7. Develop your ability to control distractions: There will always be distractions. The higher you go in performance, the more distractions there will be. The great ones develop effective ways of dealing with distractions and if they get derailed, they have release and refocus routines to get back on track quickly. The most consistent performers I have worked with have the best refocusing skills.

8. Accurate self-evaluation: The ability to accurately evaluate yourself and to draw out important lessons from each day is a critical part of the peak performance toolbox. Failure is positive feedback. What are the lessons learned from today's performance?

Which of the elements of excellence do you need to develop the most? ____

What will you do today to develop this element of excellence? ____________________________________

Remember, you don't have to be excellent to get started, but you do have to get started to be excellent.

GET STARTED TODAY!

OCTOBER 14

IF YOU THINK... YOU CAN

Walter D. Wintle wrote one of the most powerful poems of all time about the importance of how you think in competition.

If you think you are beaten, you are.
If you think you dare not, you don't.
If you'd like to win, but think you can't,
It's almost for sure you won't!

If you think you are losing, you've lost.
For out in the world we find
Success begins with a person's will.
It's all in the state of mind.

If you think you're outclassed, you are.
You've got to think high to rise.
You have to stay with it,
In order to win the prize.

Life's battles don't always go
To the one with the better plan.
For more often than not, you will win,
If only you think you can.

Today, believe you can do anything. If you think you can, you are right; if you think you can't, you are right. Confidence is a choice.

OCTOBER 15

EQUIPMENT

Edgar A. Guest is one of the greatest poets of all time. His poem *Equipment* has been an inspiration in my life to remind me that I have everything I need to succeed.

Figure it out for yourself, my lad.
You've all that the greatest of men have had:
Two arms, two hands, two legs, two eyes;
And a brain to use if you would be wise.
With this equipment they all began.
So start from the top and say "I can."

Look them over, the wise and great.
They took their food from the common plate
And with similar knives and forks they use,
With similar laces they tie their shoes.
The world considers them brave and smart,
But you've all they had when they made their start.

You can triumph and come to skill,
You can be great if you only will.
You're well equipped for what fight you choose;
You have legs and arms and a brain to use,
And the man who has risen great deeds to do
Began his life with no more than you.

You are the handicap you must face,
You are the one who must choose your place,
You must say where you want to go,
How much you will study, the truth to know;
God has equipped you for life, but He

Lets you decide what you want to be.

Courage must come from the soul within,
The man must furnish the will to win.
So figure it out for yourself, my lad.
You were born with all that the great have had,
With your equipment they all began.
Get hold of yourself and say: "I CAN."

Today, understand that you have everything you need to be successful.

Life's great wins don't always go to the bigger, faster or strongest man. The wins go to the person who thinks they can.

TBT – Thoughts Become Things.

Watch what you think today; it will become your destiny.

OCTOBER 16

PRIDE

Great competitors never quit! Why? In a word, Pride! They believe in themselves very strongly and feel they're the best in their sport – bar none.

Such feelings drive champions to success. They want to be No. 1 – pure and simple. It's their pride that makes them No. 1 and keeps them there.

Proud competitors have confidence in themselves. They aren't necessarily arrogant, but they can be. They've worked long and hard, made sacrifices and have paid the price of success.

They've earned the right to be proud.

Losing is very difficult when you have pride.

The more of it you have, the harder it is on you when you lose.

That's why they hurt so much when they lose. Winning, on the other hand, increases your pride. And the prouder you are, the harder you'll work to deserve your sense of pride.

Pride is not a skill you are born with or given. It is developed.

You won't gain it by a half-hearted effort. You have to give all you have all of the time.

When you do, your pride will increase dramatically. Why? Because the more intense your effort is, the more intense your pride will be.

The more intense your pride is, the more you'll want to win.

Eliminate the negative elements in your life and stress the positive.

Set specific goals for yourself.

Whatever your goal, strive to become the best person, best student or best competitor you can become.

If you don't like what you're doing, don't do it anymore.

If you don't feel you're working hard enough to be proud of yourself, work harder. Success isn't a complex process.

If you really don't like what you see in the mirror, change it by taking responsibility for your own life. If you want to be successful, then think, act and look successful.

Take risks and go beyond the ordinary.

When two competitors have equal natural ability, preparation, conditioning, concentration and reaction to pressure, who will have the edge? The one with the most pride.

Today, live your life with pride.

OCTOBER 17

SLOW DANCE

David L. Weatherford wrote *Slow Dance* and I think, more now than ever, this poem is a necessary read to remind us that the journey is more important than the destination, that the process is more important than the outcome.

Don't count the days; make the days count. None of us are getting out of this place alive, so make the most of the time you do have by investing into your relationship with others.

Have you ever watched kids on a merry-go-round, or listened to rain slapping the ground? Ever followed a butterfly's erratic flight, or gazed at the sun fading into the night? You better slow down, don't dance so fast, time is short, the music won't last.

Do you run through each day on the fly? When you ask, "How are you?" do you hear the reply? When the day is done, do you lie in your bed, with the next hundred chores running through your head? You better slow down, don't dance so fast, time is short, the music won't last.

Ever told your child, we'll do it tomorrow, and in your haste not see his sorrow? Ever lost touch, let a good friendship die, 'cause you never had time to call and say "hi"? You better slow down, don't dance so fast, time is short, the music won't last. When you run so fast to get somewhere, you miss half the fun of getting there. When you worry and hurry through your day, it's like an unopened gift thrown away. Life is not a race, so take it slower, hear the music before the song is over.

Today, invest in others.

Stop, take a breath and dial down your life speed.

What will you do to help slow down your life speed and slow dance today?

____

____

____

____

____

OCTOBER 18

WINNERS AND LOSERS

Peter J. Bush wrote *Winners and Losers,* a poem about the importance of making good decisions and reminding yourself that you are not invincible. Many of the coaches and athletes I work with think they are invincible; and while this confidence helps them on the field, it unfortunately can kill them in life.

"Winners" was the name that described them best. They'd survived each trial, each challenge, each test. But after the night of the last exciting game, The team of "winners" was just a name.

They had worked all year to achieve this place. It was a kind of honor... a "social grace." Now that the last and final game was here, man, what a way to end the year.

They used the same game plan that night. To be possessed with confidence and to endure the fight; To try like hell to win the final game; To give the team a glorified name.

Once again, the team fought hard and they prevailed, and for the win, they were praised, honored, and hailed. So the team decided to try something new---To celebrate the victory the way some "winners" do.

They left from the bus with one thing in mind, to drink those six cases, and have a good time.

Laughing and remembering the game that they had played, reminiscing on how these "winners" had been made.

Then all of a sudden, the road made a curve. They all gripped their seats as they started to swerve. A loud "crash" pierced the night air, and a great blaze of fire was visible there.

The following morn, not one of them walked. Cries filled the air where once they had talked. Neither man nor beast could smile that day, when they heard the "winners" had gone away.

Now it's only the names that will survive---The "celebration" of victory had cost them their lives. The booze, the drugs; they had never been users, yet this is the reason that they were turned into losers.

And even though they will never play again, a lesson was delivered by these great men. The lesson we got from the price that they paid? "This is not the stuff of which 'winners' are made!"

How do you celebrate a big win?

Are you naive enough to think that you are invincible?

Have you ever had too much to drink and gotten behind the wheel to drive? If you have, be reminded that you are putting your life and the life of everyone else in danger.

Next time you or a teammate has had too much to drink and get behind the wheel to drive, know that you are making one of the biggest mistakes of your life, a mistake that will haunt you forever. If you care about yourself and your teammates, NEVER let yourself or them drink and drive.

By signing my name on the line below I commit to never allowing myself or my teammate to drink and drive.

The cost of a cab is much less than the risk of costing a life because of a terrible decision.

____

YOUR NAME DATE

OCTOBER 19

HOW DO YOU JUDGE YOURSELF?

The world judges you by what you have done, not by what you have started out to do; by what you have completed, not by what you have begun.

The bulldog wins the battle by holding on to the finish.

Excellence is a lifestyle, not an event.

Excellence is not a sometime thing; it's an all-the-time thing.

You are not excellent once in a while. You don't do things right once in a while. You do them right all the time.

Winning is a habit. Unfortunately, so is losing.

It is not a question of how well each person on a team works; the question is how well they work together.

The price of success is hard work, dedication to the job at hand, and the determination that whether we win or lose, we have applied the best of ourselves to the task at hand.

Today, be dedicated to a cause greater than yourself. Put the team ahead of yourself.

OCTOBER 20

TEAM FIRST, TEAM LAST

Jim Schlossnagle is the head baseball coach at Texas Christian University in Ft. Worth, Texas and is one of the top coaches in all of college athletics.

A Master of the Mental Game, Schlossnagle has been able to effectively get the best college baseball players in the nation to put team success ahead of their own personal achievement.

One of the ways he reinforces his messages to his team is by posting those messages where they will see them every day.

One of the prominent signs you see as you exit their locker room to the field is "Team First, Team Last."

Today, prioritize TEAM in all of your actions.

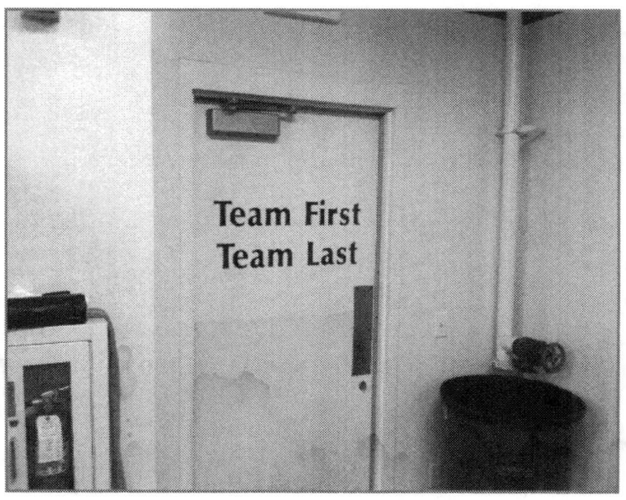

OCTOBER 21

TOMORROW

Edgar A. Guest is one of my all-time favorite poets and a man who has had tremendous impact on my life. In his poem *Tomorrow,* he teaches us the importance of the day.

He said he was going to be all that a mortal could be, tomorrow.

None would be braver and stronger than he, tomorrow.

A friend who was weary had trouble he knew, needed a lift and wanted one too; give him a call to see what he could do, tomorrow.

He stacked up the letters he would read, tomorrow.

He thought of the friends he would write, tomorrow.

It was too bad indeed he was busy today, but hadn't a moment to stop on the way; more time I'll give to others he would say, tomorrow.

The greatest of workers this man would have been, tomorrow.

And the world would have known him had he ever seen tomorrow.

But the fact is that he died and faded from view, and all that he left when his living was through, was a mountain of things to do.

Tomorrow.

Do not wait for tomorrow to start preparing for this season.

Tomorrow never comes.

Start today.

Your career and, more importantly, your life are the sum of your todays.

OCTOBER 22

YOUR WORK PERCEPTION

A newly hired coach went out in the field to determine how people who worked on the campus felt about their work. She went to a building site on the edge of campus.

She approached the first worker and asked, "What are you doing?"

"What? Are you blind?" the worker snapped back. "I am cutting these bricks with primitive tools and putting them together the way the boss tells me. I'm sweating under this blazing sun, it's backbreaking work, and it's boring me to death!"

The coach quickly backed off and retreated to a second worker.

She asked the same question:

"What are you doing?"

The worker replied: "I am shaping these bricks into useable forms, which are then assembled according to the boss's plans. It's a job. It could be worse."

Somewhat encouraged, she went to a third worker.

"And what are you doing?" she asked.

"Why, can't you see?" beamed the worker as he lifted his arms to the sky. "I'm on a team that is building the greatest library in the school's history. This building is going to change the lives of the students who pass through its doors, and I am honored to be a part of the process."

Perspective is reality.

The attitude you take is a decision you make.

What attitude will you bring to the team today?

Are you part of a team, willing to do what is best for the group, or are you just doing it because someone else wants you to or because you are on a scholarship?

You are responsible for your attitude, thoughts and actions.

Nothing can take away that responsibility and the control you have over yourself as a human being.

BE A PART OF THE SOLUTION, NOT PART OF THE PROBLEM

OCTOBER 23

DON'T YOU QUIT

Edgar A. Guest reminds us that when times are tough you must lock in and never quit.

When things go wrong, as they sometimes will, when the road you're trudging seems all uphill, when the funds are low and the debts are high, when you want to smile, but you have to sigh, when care is pressing you down a bit - rest if you must, but don't you quit.

Life is queer with its twists and turns, as every one of us sometimes learns. And many a fellow turns about when he might have won had he stuck it out. Don't give up though the pace seems slow; you may succeed with another blow.

Often the goal is nearer than it seems to a faint and faltering man; often the struggler has given up when he might have captured the victor's cup; and he learned too late when the night came down, how close he was to the golden crown.

Success is failure turned inside out, the silver tint of the clouds of doubt; and while you never can tell how close you are, it may be near when it seems far. So stick to the fight when you're hardest hit; it's when things seem worst, you must not quit.

When the tough get going, are you going to fold your hands or are you going to go all in?

What do you do when times are tough? Hold on till you catch on; you are closer than you think.

OCTOBER 24

HAVE YOU HAD A CHANCE TO HIT YET?

Having spent much of my life around the game of baseball at all levels, I was at a game for children between 6 and 8 years old and was reminded of the power of perspective.

My friend's son was playing in the game. When I got there, my friend's wife was keeping score and said it was 11-0.

On my way to the concession to get a hot dog with mustard and onion, as I try to do at every baseball game, I stopped by the bench to see my friend, who was coaching his 7-year-old son.

As I checked in to say hello, one of the kids came up and said, "Coach Bayliss, we need just one more out and then we get to hit, right?" My friend told him that was true and the kid skipped away.

I did not realize it was only the top of the first inning. When I asked my friend if his team was having an off day and what the deal was, why they were down 11-0, he said: "It's no big deal. We have not had a chance to hit yet."

What a great perspective! Always the optimist, my friend reminded me of the importance of not giving up before you get started.

In life it is the start that stops most people. What is the decision or action that you have been putting off and are going to do today?

OCTOBER 25

I COULD HAVE CHANGED THE WORLD

The following poem reminds us of the importance of working at yourself first. If you work at your career, you will have a job; if you work at yourself, you will have everything.

When I was a young man, I wanted to change the world.

I found it difficult to change the world, so I tried to change my nation.

When I found I couldn't change the nation, I began to focus on my town.

I couldn't change the town; and as an older man, I tried to change my family.

Now, as an old man, I realize the only thing that I can change is myself; and suddenly I realize that if long ago I had changed myself, I would have made an impact on my family. My family and I could have made an impact on our town. The impact of the town could have changed the state and the state could have changed the nation and the nation could have made the world a better place.

Indeed, I could have changed the world if I had only started with myself.

You need to think big and act small. Know where you want to go and get immersed in the journey of getting there.

Work at yourself first.

Be the change you want to see in others.

As a leader, those whom you lead may need a motto to say, but they need a model to see more.

Invest most of your time where you have the most control - yourself, your attitudes and your actions. Everything begins with you.

Remember that these seven small words make up the strongest sentence in the English Language.

IF IT IS TO BE, IT IS UP TO ME

OCTOBER 26

A WISH FOR LEADERS

Dr. Earl Reum was a magician, educator and speaker. He delivered one of the most moving leadership seminars I have ever been to and challenged us with his wish for leaders.

I sincerely wish that you will have the experience of thinking up a new idea, planning it, organizing it and following it to completion, and then have it be magnificently successful. I hope you'll go through the same process and have something "bomb-out."

I wish you could know how it feels "to run" with all your heart and lose - horribly!

I wish that you could find something so worthwhile that you deem it worthy of investigating your life within it.

I hope that you become frustrated and challenged enough to begin to push back the very barriers of your own personal limitations.

I hope that you make a stupid mistake and get caught red-handed and are big enough to say those magic words: "I was wrong."

I hope that you give so much of yourself that some days you wonder if it is worth the effort.

I wish you had a magnificent obsession that will give you a reason for living and a purpose and direction in life.

I wish for you the worst kind of criticism for everything you do, because that makes you fight to achieve beyond what you normally would.

I wish for you the experience of leadership.

Reum taught that leadership was never easy.

If it were, everyone would be a leader on the team or in your school.

Can you handle the adversity and responsibility that come with being a leader?

Who are the best leaders that you know personally?

____

____

What makes you say that about them?

____

____

____

____

____

____

____

____

OCTOBER 27

INVISIBLE WAYS TO WIN

As a mental conditioning coach who is privileged to work with some of the top programs in the country, I enjoy taking photos of all the various motivational material I come across in the different facilities.

The quote below hung in the locker room at The University of Tennessee and reminds us that all things that matter cannot be measured and all things that can be measured do not matter.

What will you do today to help your team win? Know the difference between what is important and what is visible to others.

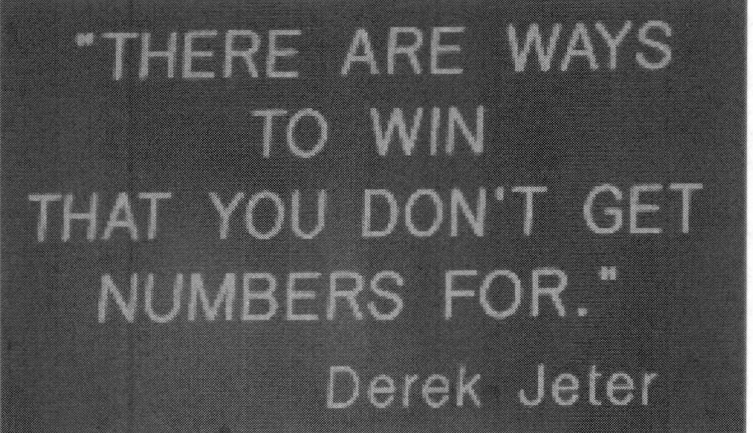

"THERE ARE WAYS
TO WIN
THAT YOU DON'T GET
NUMBERS FOR."
Derek Jeter

OCTOBER 28

TODAY IS A NEW DAY

William Heartsill Wilson was one of the world's greatest sales professionals and motivators. In his poem *A New Day,* he reminds us of the importance of a day.

This is the beginning of a new day.

I have been given this day to use as I will.

I can waste it or use it for good.

What I do today is important, because I'm exchanging a day of my life for it.

When tomorrow comes, this day will be gone forever, leaving it its place whatever I may have traded for it. I pledge to myself that it shall be gain, not loss; good, not evil; success, not failure; in order that I shall not regret the price I paid for this day.

What price are you willing to pay today to get what you want tomorrow?

____

What is it that you want?

____

____

____

____

OCTOBER 29

LITTLE EYES UPON YOU

Kimberly Sedlacek's poem *Little Eyes Upon You* reminds us that no matter how old or young we are we have a responsibility to the youth of our communities to act as role models. The more visible your work, the more responsibility you have. Responsibility is the price of greatness. Use your gifts to make the world a better place and inspire others with your actions and attitudes.

There are little eyes upon you,
and they're watching night and day.

There are little ears that quickly
take in every word that you say.

There are little hands all eager
to do anything you do,

And a little boy who's dreaming,
of the day he'll be like you.

You're the little fellow's idol,
you're the wisest of the wise.

In his little mind about you
no suspicions ever rise.

He believes in you devotedly,
holds all that you say and do;

He will say and do, in your way,
when he's grown up like you.

There's a wide-eyed little fellow
who believes you're always right.

And his eyes are always opened,
and he watches day and night.

You are setting an example,
Every day in all you do,

For the little boy who's waiting
To grow up to be just like you.

We all have an inherent responsibility to those who are watching us to carry ourselves in a mature and responsible manner.

We are all idolized by youth in our community.

Carry yourself in a way that you would want your child or your younger sibling to emulate.

Would you be proud to see yourself act the way you do on national TV??

____

How would you want to be seen?

____

____

____

____

____

OCTOBER 30

THE GPS MENTALITY

When you use the GPS in your car, does it ever swear at you or tell you that you are stupid or terrible at driving?

NO!

It tells you to reroute or recalculate.

We can all learn a very important lesson from the GPS. When you make mistakes or take wrong turns in life - and everyone has, does and will - simply find a way to reroute yourself back onto the highway to excellence and get back on the path you have created for yourself.

You can reroute or recalculate by asking yourself what you must start, stop and continue doing to help take your performance to where you want to be.

To reroute yourself back to excellence, what must you:

Start? ______________________________________

Stop? ______________________________________

Continue? ___________________________________

OCTOBER 31

THE IMPORTANCE OF HALLOWEEN

Halloween is my favorite day of the year.

This is the day you dress up and act like anyone you want.

The importance of Halloween is that it proves you can act differently than how you feel.

If you can do it on Halloween, you can do it any day you want - and acting differently than how you feel is the foundation of long-term, consistent success.

NOVEMBER

November is the month for me to dominate...

NOVEMBER 1

A CALL FOR GOOD CHARACTER

Good character is very hard to find these days. Schools don't teach it, we want more of it in our children and in all the adults who interact with them, and most of us believe we have plenty of it.

Character is the sum total of your moral qualities: Are you a person worthy of trust and admiration or not?

Someone who has good character is described as having worthy traits like integrity, courage and compassion.

They are guided by ethical principles even when the right decision may wrongfully impact their health, wealth, career or social status.

They do the right thing even when it costs more than they want to pay.

No one is born with good character; it's not a hereditary trait.

It isn't determined by a single noble act.

Character is established by sticking to and living your moral values.

How can you demonstrate good character today?

____

____

____

NOVEMBER 2

PERSPECTIVE

Would you think differently if you knew that...

The jerk who cut you off in traffic last night is a single mother who worked nine hours that day and was rushing home to cook dinner, help with homework, do the laundry and spend a few precious moments with her children?

The pierced, tattooed, disinterested young man who can't make change correctly is a worried 19-year-old college student, balancing his apprehension over final exams with his fear of not getting his student loans for next semester?

The scary-looking bum, begging for money in the same spot every day (who really ought to get a job!), is a slave to addictions that we can only imagine in our worst nightmares?

The old couple walking annoyingly slowly through the aisles and blocking our shopping progress are savoring this moment, knowing that, based on the biopsy report she got back last week, this will be the last year that they go shopping together?

The greatest gift you could give is the gift of your love?

It was not enough to only share that love with those you hold dear, but that you would have a bigger impact on the world if you opened your heart not just to those who you are close with, but to all of humanity?

Today, be slow to judge and quick to forgive. Seek out those who have no connection to a group and are searching for a way, searching to be a part of something bigger than themselves.

Today, be a hunter who takes a shot at helping others instead of walking by and later thinking what if you had only...

At the end of the day, come back here and write down what difference you made in the life of someone else and how you had a different perspective today.

____

____

____

____

____

____

____

____

____

____

____

**YOU ARE GOING TO
MAKE A DIFFERENCE TODAY
BE SURE THAT IT IS A POSITIVE ONE!**

NOVEMBER 3

MAKE YOUR GREATEST WEAKNESS YOUR GREATEST STRENGTH

I was at a judo tournament with one of my mixed martial arts fighters who was there to support one of his training partners. A young boy was competing with only one arm.

As the young boy battled his way through the tournament, I noticed that he finished all of his matches with the same move.

In the finals he was pitted against the defending champion in his weight class, a beast of an adolescent.

The young boy was nervous and scared but knew that he could never show weakness on the mat, so he acted differently than how he felt. He went out and competed and won.

Come to find out, the boy only knew one move. His instructor had only been preparing him for a few weeks, not nearly enough time for someone to enter, let alone win a tournament of this stature.

The instructor had taught him only one move. It was the only move he needed to know because the only counter to that one move was to grab the boy's other arm.

My friend Georges St. Pierre says that the best thing that ever happened to him was getting knocked out by Matt Serra at UFC 69 on April 7, 2007 as the UFC's Welterweight Champion.

St. Pierre knows the value of turning the worst thing that has ever happened to you into the best thing.

What do you need to do to turn your greatest weaknesses into your greatest strengths?

____

____

____

____

____

WORK TO STRENGTHEN YOUR WEAKEST LINK TILL THERE ARE NO MORE WEAK LINKS

NOVEMBER 4

NO PRECONCEIVED NOTIONS

Major League Baseball Hall of Fame pitcher Satchel Paige started his career with the Chattanooga Black Lookouts of the Negro Southern League in 1926 and played his last professional game in 1966 for the Peninsula Grays of the Carolina League.

Paige is the oldest rookie to ever debut in Major League Baseball when he broke through with the Cleveland Indians in 1948.

One day, Paige was asked by reporters how old he was and he replied,

"If you didn't know how old you were, how old would you be?"

If you did not know what your past had been, how would you act differently today than you did yesterday?

The past is history; learn from it and leave it.

Attack today with no preconceived notions about yourself or your upcoming day.

Attack today with an energy and attitude that you can do anything.

NOVEMBER 5

8 COMMON TRAITS OF CHAMPIONS

I have been blessed to work with World, Olympic, NCAA National and High School state champions. I want to share 8 common traits of these champions with you.

1. Champions are positive thinkers and although not always confident (nobody is confident 100% of the time), they always think confident and act big.

2. Champions visualize their successes and know that thoughts become things so they bathe themselves with positive images.

3. Champions know they are the average of the five people they hang out with most so they surround themselves with positive people.

4. Champions set daily, weekly, monthly, yearly and five-year goals. They know where they want to go and have a plan to get there.

5. Champions are disciplined and consistent in their daily decisions and habits. They apply the compound effect to all aspects of life.

6. Champions are learners before they are winners and see each competition as a test and an opportunity to learn and get better.

7. Champions have developed their ability to live in the present and are able to focus and concentrate intensely for extended periods of time.

8. Champions view hard work as a privilege and know that extra effort is expected effort.

Remember, the only difference where people will call you CHAMP or CHUMP is U (you).

Which one of the eight common traits of champions are you going to lock in on today and commit to developing?

What will this look like today when you are doing this?

NOVEMBER 6

THE TOUR de DEFENSE

What you measure gets done and Rewarded behavior is repeated behavior.

Ole Miss baseball coach and Master of The Mental Game, Mike Bianco, created a yellow jersey to be given to the defensive leader of the day.

Much like the Tour de France leader wears the yellow jersey, the best defensive player of the day is rewarded with the yellow jersey the next day at Ole Miss.

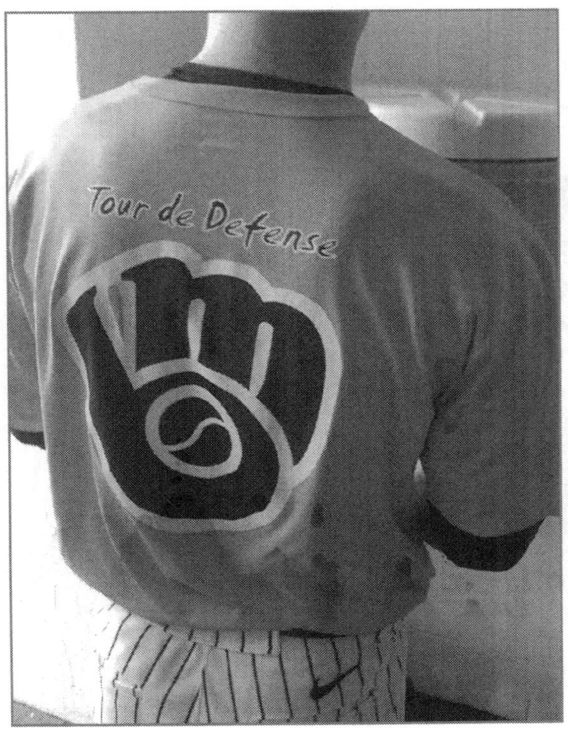

NOVEMBER 7

WILL BEATS SKILL EVERY TIME

What do you have more control over, your will or your skill?

Although you have a significant amount of control over your physical skill, you have total control over your will. Think of will to the mental game what skill is to your physical game.

Will is a muscle that must be trained and conditioned by acting differently than how you feel and by being comfortable with being uncomfortable.

Western Kentucky baseball assistant coach Brendan Dougherty hangs this sign in the Toppers dugout.

NOVEMBER 8

HOLD THE ROPE

If you were hanging off of a cliff and the only thing keeping you from falling to your sheer death was the person on the opposite side of the rope you were holding, who would you want on the other end of that rope?

Write your answer here: ______________________________

At Ole Miss, the answer is simple.

Anyone who has Ole Miss Baseball written across his chest.

Do you have this type of faith in your teammates?

What can you do to build this trust today?

NOVEMBER 9

EATING FIRE, FOLLOWING THE FUNDAMENTALS

Champions in any field are relentless in their execution of the fundamentals.

When eating fire, you must follow the fundamentals or you can get burned.

In competition, you must follow the fundamentals or, worse than getting burned, you will beat yourself.

NOVEMBER 10

BEND, NEVER BREAK

Why do I have participants at my seminars put a metal rod between their throats and run towards each other?

I want them to physically experience the importance of committing to their teammates and continuing to move forward in the face of adversity.

When the activity is done, we are also reminded that the metal rod will bend under pressure but will never break, a lesson in resiliency that we can all learn from.

Who do you know that has bent, but never broken?

____

____

NOVEMBER 11

WHAT DO YOU WORK FOR?

Two garbage men were working the truck when the president of the company drove by and stopped to say hello to one of the men.

After the president drove off, the other garbage man told his co-worker that he was impressed that he knew the president of the company.

"We used to work together on this truck about ten years ago," the garbage man said, "I came to work for the money; he came to clean up the city."

You must always ask yourself, "Why do I do what I do?"

What are you working for?

With a big enough reason why, you will find the motivation to do the dirty work and find the gift in the grind of doing what you do every day.

Why do you do what you do?

____

____

____

____

____

NOVEMBER 12

WALK THE PLANK, FOCUS ON WHAT IS

Why do I have participants in my live seminars and on the teams I work with walk across a beam held up by two step ladders?

I want them to experience the difference between walking the plank on the ground and suspended in the air.

If you approach the plank with a "what is" attitude, you realize it is no different.

The "what if" attitude makes you focus on all the things that could go wrong in the Walk the Plank activity, as in competition.

What is a "what if" that you will release today?

NOVEMBER 13

PLANT GRASS, PULL WEEDS

When I bought my first house, my lawn was in disarray. I called a friend of mine who owns a lawn care company and he told he that the only thing I needed to do was plant grass.

I asked him if I needed to pull the weeds and he said: "Just plant grass and be patient. Plant grass every day and trust that your process and consistent execution will get you the lawn you desire."

This was great advice for life. Keep planting grass, keep bringing relentless positive energy with you wherever you go, and your consistency will kill off the weeds in your life and in your head. If you don't keep planting grass every day and if you give **your mental weeds an inch, they will take a yard.**

NOVEMBER 14

TRAFFIC JAMS IN YOUR HEAD?

When you are at your best, you are thinking so clearly and presently that it appears you are not thinking at all. When you are at your worst, you have the metaphorical traffic jam going on in your head. You don't know if you should start, stop, speed up, slow down, etc.

Great competitors are clear in their thinking and actions.

Today, breathe and clear your mind of the mental traffic jams in your life.

NOVEMBER 15

TRUST

There was a man so daring that he rode his bike over a high wire spanning Niagara Falls. When he crossed the falls face first, he then rode back over the wire backwards.

For his next feat, he wanted to have someone ride over on the pegs on the back of his bike. Nobody raised a hand except for one young boy who jumped on and, amid the disbelief and shock of the crowd, made it safely to the other side with the daredevil.

Reporters asked the man how he could be so crazy as to risk a child's life like that and asked the boy how he was so brave.

The boy replied that the man was his father and that he had complete trust in him.

Are you working today with a purpose and at a pace that will develop such a trust in your teammates that they will get on your bike?

NOVEMBER 16

CAN YOU WALK ON WATER?

Why do I have participants in my live seminars and on the teams I work with step into a chest full of water?

I want them to experience the fact that they cannot walk on water and should not demand perfection of themselves.

If they were perfect, they could walk on water.

Strive for excellence, not perfection.

NOVEMBER 17

FLUSH IT!

One of the only guarantees in life and in competition is that there will be challenge and struggle.

What do you do when you are in the middle of competition and adversity hits?

Go to your release routine and "flush it!"

Rick Lynch, head baseball coach at Tomball High School in Texas, has a toilet bank that he puts on the bench every day to remind his players of this life skill.

What do you do physically to help flush the mental?

NOVEMBER 18

CHANGE YOUR PERSPECTIVE, CHANGE YOUR LIFE

Perspective is reality. Perspective is similar to attitude in that it is a choice. If you change your perspective and change your attitude, you change your reality.

When you look at the image above, you most likely see an older woman.

When you flip this page upside down, you will experience a perspective change, also known as a paradigm shift. BOOM! Just like that you change your perspective/attitude and reality.

What perspective/attitude will you choose today?

NOVEMBER 19

THE THANKSGIVING TABLE TEST

My good friend Tom Murphy, who fought at UFC 58 and was on the Ultimate Fighter Season Two Reality Show, challenged me to anticipate and think about what I will say at the Thanksgiving table this year.

He challenged me to look at my character and morality.

He challenged me to think about me and my family sitting around the Thanksgiving dinner table and having open discussion and dialogue about all of the things we do and the choices we make, fully exposing our inner characters at the table.

He encouraged me to assess my choices and character around the Thanksgiving Table Test.

He said that if you would not speak openly and honestly about what you do and who you are, you should probably not do them or be that kind of person.

Would you be willing to let your family read an open book about your life at the Thanksgiving dinner table?

How you live today will come out on turkey day. Are you living with character and morality?

A common technique I use to get people to think about the future is what I call "Fast Forward." I want you to "Fast Forward" to Thanksgiving of this year.

Get the experience of you and your family sitting around the table.

See what that will look like, feel what that will feel like, hear what that will sound like, smell what that will smell like, and taste what that will taste like. Make it as real as you possibly can.

As you sit at the table, would you talk about "everything" you do, the choices you make, your character?

You should assess your choices and character, and you should probably not do them or be that kind of person if you would not talk about it at the Thanksgiving Day table.

What do you want to say about yourself at the Thanksgiving Day dinner table?

____

____

____

____

____

____

____

____

____

LIVE YOUR LIFE SO YOU CAN SPEAK OPENLY AND HONESTLY ABOUT YOUR TRUE SELF

NOVEMBER 20

FIVE ESSENTIAL QUESTIONS

Five questions from Og Mandino's book *The Choice* to help you identify your present location on the journey to the summit of the Mountain of Excellence:

1. Are you in control of your life?

____

____

2. Are you at peace with yourself and those around you?

____

____

3. Are you proud of your life's accomplishments?

____

____

4. Are you and your family enjoying the fruits of your work?

____

____

5. Are you happy and contented?

____

____

NOVEMBER 21

THE CENTURY PLANT

The Century Plant received its name as it was believed to only flower once every hundred years and then die after flowering.

Research has shown that the flowering usually takes place on average after 28 years and the Century Plant is unlikely to live more than 50 years.

The Century Plant, however, has unlimited potential to blossom at any point, just like you.

You have unlimited potential to blossom at any point. You never know when your opportunity to bloom will come so you must always prepare and be ready.

When you are selected as a captain of a team or put in a position of leadership, that is not the time to prepare to lead.

At that point it is too late.

You must prepare now for your opportunity to lead in the future so that when your opportunity to lead arises you are prepared

PREPARE TODAY
FOR YOUR TIME TOMORROW

NOVEMBER 22

HAVE AN ATTITUDE OF GRATITUDE

There is strength in the written word. You never know when something that you write will have a life-changing effect on the person who reads what you have written.

I still have letters written to me by my middle school football coach Mark Shaw. He was the first coach I had who made me feel as if I could accomplish anything and that I was destined for greatness.

Reading Coach Shaw's words made me feel as if he believed in me and thus, so should I.

Today you are to write a letter, not a text message or an e-mail, to someone who has had a huge impact on your life.

Thank that person for what they have given you and let them know how you have continued to pass the gift on to others that they have given you:

The gift of self-belief and the gift of being grateful for what you have - the gift of an attitude of gratitude.

LOOK FOR WAYS YOU CAN MAKE A DIFFERENCE FOR OTHERS TODAY

NOVEMBER 23

BE THANKFUL

When you show thanks it improves the heart's rhythmic functioning, which reduces stress, promotes clarity of thought, and aids the healing process.

It is physiologically impossible to feel stressful and grateful at the same time that you feel grateful and demonstrate an attitude of gratitude.

Coaches and athletes trying to find their ideal performance state certainly should consider an attitude of gratitude as one of their significant "green" light indicators.

Instead of focusing on the "what ifs" and the pressure of the situation, focus on "what is" and the pleasure of the situation.

An attitude of gratitude promotes a focus on playing the game in the moment and on playing to win and honor the game vs. playing not to lose and to avoid the pressure, pain and stress of poor performance.

PLAY TO WIN vs. PLAY NOT TO LOSE.
TURN PRESSURE INTO PLEASURE

NOVEMBER 24

DON'T WAIT – DO IT

Why wait? It is the start that stops most people. If you are planning to set New Year's resolutions, why wait till January 1 to get started?

Start NOW!

Don't Wait, drop the (n't and wa) and DO IT!

Remember when you were a kid and you would get together with your friends and sit in the merry-go-round?

The hardest part about getting that bad boy in motion was breaking inertia and getting started.

Once that disc was spinning, you could keep it going with the push of a finger, but to get it started you needed to drive it like an NFL lineman hitting the seven-man sled.

Get a jump start on your resolutions.

Get started now by doing a little a lot vs. waiting till a month from now and trying to do a lot a little.

You can do ANYTHING if you just get started, build up uncle mo(mentum) and keep going.

**INCH BY INCH IT'S A CINCH,
YARD BY YARD IT'S HARD**

NOVEMBER 25

BEGIN WITH THE END IN MIND

The journey of a thousand miles begins with a single step. Sir Edmund Hillary first climbed Mount Everest by taking a step at the bottom of the mountain.

What is the mountain you wish you start climbing? What were you going to set as your New Year's Resolution that you can start working on today?

Begin with the end in mind: What is it that you really want?

By beginning your journey with your target in place and with your end in mind, you increase your motivation and chance for success because you will know where you want to end up.

Write down your end-result goal and then write down one small thing you can do in the next 24 hours to help you take a baby step towards your target. Nothing succeeds like success - and small wins compound over time and turn into BIG wins.

YOUR BIG GOAL:

____

YOUR SMALL STEP TODAY TO HELP GET THERE:

____

____

____

____

NOVEMBER 26

DOES WHAT YOU LIVE = WHAT YOU LIVE TO DO?

When you die, how do you want to be remembered?

It may be a morbid thought for some, but the bottom line is that none of us are making it out of this world alive and we must KNOW how we want to be remembered if we are going to live in a way that will leave a legacy that we desire.

Nothing happens by chance.

When you have been successful in life, it has most often been when you had a clear goal and mapped out a process and a plan to get there.

Ask yourself this question.

Does the way you live equal what you live to do and how you live to be remembered?

____

Is the way you have been treating others and going about your daily routine leaving the legacy behind that you want to leave?

____

If so, what are you doing?

____

If not, what can you do to start taking steps towards this most important goal?________________________________

NOVEMBER 27

WHO DO YOU WANT TO BECOME?

If you had three days left to live, what would you do?

Getting clear on what you would do if you had three days left to live helps to provide a focus for your life.

This week can you do more of what you would do in your three days left on this earth?

If you had to answer that question now, what would you say?

1. ______________________________

____

2. ______________________________

____

3. ______________________________

____

CAN YOU LIVE PART OF YOUR LAST THREE DAYS TODAY?

NOVEMBER 28

ADMIT WHEN YOU ARE WRONG

To admit when you are wrong is a sign of strength, a sign of maturity and a sign of leadership.

When you admit that you were wrong, you show that you are logical, human and are governed by what is right, not by a need to be right.

The best coaches and leaders on the planet have a burning desire to find out what is right, what is the best way.

Those who fall short get stuck on it being "their way." Your way may have gotten you here, but what got you here will not always get you there.

Getting to the next level is about working with others to find the best way possible.

Admit when you are wrong, pass praise to others as often as you can, and take more accountability and responsibility when things go south.

IF YOU LEAD AND NOBODY FOLLOWS, YOU ARE SIMPLY OUT FOR A WALK

NOVEMBER 29

SHORT-TERM PAIN, LONG-TERM GAIN

Have you ever had a decision to make that you knew was going to bring you short-term pain and long-term gain?

Maybe it was a relationship breakup, moving, starting an exercise program or writing that first book.

Knowing what you want most is one of the key factors in living a successful life.

Having the ability to put off what you want in the moment for what you want most is a sign of a determined and disciplined person.

What is the decision that you must act on now to be better off a week or two from now?

____

Remember, it is the start that stops most people.

What steps are you going to take today to help you be in a better place tomorrow?

____

____

____

____

PAIN IS TEMPORARY - JUST DO IT!

NOVEMBER 30

ATTITUDE IS A DECISION

The attitude you take is a decision you make.

The attitude and perspective you bring to everyday situations determines the magnitude of those situations.

It is by choice that you make the mountain out of the molehill or the molehill out of the mountain.

Famed motivational speaker Zig Ziglar said, *"It is your attitude [will] more so than your aptitude [skill]) that will determine your altitude in life."*

Famed poet Maya Angelou said: *"If you don't like something change it. If you can't change it, change your attitude."*

Joel Osteen, author of *Your Best Life Now*, says that *"Choosing to have a positive attitude and an attitude of gratitude will determine how you live your life."*

I suggest you choose wisely.

What attitude are you choosing to take today? How would you describe what it looks like?

____

____

ATTITUDES ARE CONTAGIOUS

DECEMBER

December is the month for me to dominate...

DECEMBER 1

THE LAW OF THE PALM TREE

Palm trees will bend but never break.

They will roll with the wind and adversity, staying flexible under pressure in their strategy to survive the storm.

The palm tree knows that it must adapt to the challenge and that when the challenge has passed it can POP RIGHT BACK UP and continue to grow.

Unlike the oak tree that is rigid, inflexible and has to get its way or it will buckle under pressure, the palm tree is flexible, chooses a path that works for the situation and then pops back up ready to fight another round.

BEND BUT NEVER BREAK

DECEMBER 2

THE FOUR ESSENTIALS OF ADVERSITY

Challenge yourself to take on the adversity you face today, this week, this month as a person committed to excellence and by using the four essentials of adversity.

1. Adversity is an unavoidable part of the PURSUIT OF EXCELLENCE.

2. COMPARED TO WHAT others are dealing with, your situation is not that bad. Get over the drama and break down your situation into a process that can be managed vs. an outcome that is inevitable.

3. The problem is not the problem. HOW YOU HANDLE THE PROBLEM IS THE PROBLEM.

4. Remember what you read yesterday, The Law of The Palm Tree - weather the storm, be flexible and POP RIGHT BACK UP and continue to grow every day.

ADVERSITY IS AN UNAVOIDABLE PART OF SUCCESS

DECEMBER 3

THE ANT PHILOSOPHY

Like great coaches and athletes, ants never quit. If you try to stop them, they go around, over or under and always find a way.

They try forever, and either they'll get there alive or they'll die trying. They are relentless and just keep coming.

While we don't use the life-and-death situation in trying, the ant philosophy is what we need to get the most out of our potential and DOMINATE The Day.

Ants accept their role and never stop doing their job. They are the supreme competitors. Some ants mate with the Queen and die after just three weeks of life. But they did their job. They are the ideal bench players who go in, do their job and give of themselves to make the team better. Others will protect the Queen until they die, totally committed to the big picture. Others will hunt, carrying objects 10 to 50 times their weight.

Ants are masters of the fundamentals and they know that a breakdown in fundamentals eliminates a breakthrough in performance.

Their thinking is excellent and their philosophy is great. Ants think winter during the summer. They are always thinking about what will happen if they don't get it done now.

They always think that winter is around the corner and DOMINATE every day because they know they can't survive in the winter if they don't produce in the summer.

If you are ahead, you must think more production because winter is coming. If you are behind, you have to work harder and the momentum will come. You can't give up - every second, every hour, every day you must keep working, keep grinding and keep the ant philosophy of exceptional living.

THINK SUMMER IN THE WINTER AND WINTER IN THE SUMMER

DECEMBER 4

YOU MUST RUN TO ROAR

Every morning in Africa the lions and gazelles wake up and the game begins. The slowest gazelle must outrun the fastest lion or it will be eaten, and the fastest lion must outrun the slowest gazelle or it will starve.

The lions figured out that if they work together and surround the gazelle with young lions on one side and adult lions on the other, the gazelle goes into a frenzy when the adult lions roar and runs away from the roar - right into the waiting jaws and paws of the young lions.

The moral of the story is that when we are faced with adversity and challenge, we are doomed if we run away from roar. Face your obstacles head-on and run to roar today!

DECEMBER 5

DO OR DO NOT - THERE IS NO TRY

Excuses are a sign of weakness. Using the word "try" is an excuse for failure before an attempt is made.

Yoda, the great green master of the mental game, said that you must either do or do not, there is no try. What Yoda was trying to say was that you either get it done or you don't.

If you set up a meeting with someone and they say they will try to make it, they will never show.

The person who commits to trying commits to nothing. You don't try to get your workout in first thing in the morning when you wake up; you either do or you don't - there is no try.

TRYING IS LYING

DECEMBER 6

PAIN AND PLEASURE ARE NEIGHBORS

Every morning when you wake up you must decide which is greater, the pain of not doing something or the pleasure of doing?

Average people think that pain and pleasure are opposites. That could not be further from the truth. Pain and pleasure are neighbors separated by only a few inches.

Often the difference between a "try" and a success is holding on just a little longer, working just a little bit harder, giving just a little extra effort.

There are no traffic jams on the extra mile.

Can you hold on just a bit longer so that the pain you feel provides a reward?

When you are in pain, you are already suffering; you might as well get a reward from it.

PAIN IS A PART OF THE SUCCESS PROCESS

DECEMBER 7

CHANGE IS INEVITABLE, GROWTH IS OPTIONAL

Change is inevitable, growth is optional. The most successful people I know live with a growth mindset and perspective.

If you are reading this, my guess is that you are already very successful at what you do.

You are probably at the top of your field and looking to go higher.

You understand that there is always something you can learn from others.

Sometimes we learn what to do and sometimes we learn what not to do to help us get to the next level.

If you find that you are learning more of what not to do, I suggest that you investigate finding others to associate with.

You become the average of the five people you hang out with most. Are they propelling you forward, or holding you back from your goals and dreams?

Who are the five people you hang out with most?

____

____

____

____

____

DECEMBER 8

PAINT THE PICTURE YOU WANT TO SEE

Great leaders can paint the picture that others want to see.

You are a leader, and the most important person you will lead today is YOU!

Your brain works in pictures.

You must paint the picture of yourself performing at your highest level and hold onto that image so strongly that it ultimately becomes not an image of who you are but rather simply who you are.

The mistake a lot of people make is that they paint the picture they don't want to see.

Today, be sure that you are painting the picture of you that will go in into your mind's museum of excellence.

DECEMBER 9

MAYBE SHOULD ALWAYS BE A NO

Many people feel the pressure to please others and have a difficult time saying NO!

Early in our careers and lives we say yes to everything because we don't want to miss an opportunity to learn, to grow, to find some excitement.

There does come a time when you reach a level of success where NO must become a part of your vocabulary or you will not be able to get to the next level.

What got you here won't get you there; and saying YES or even worse, MAYBE, to things that don't get you FIRED UP will not only suck your time away like a vampire, but will also keep you from investing the time into places in your life that really need it.

Been at work too much and not with the family as much as you want?

Time to start saying NO and trust your world will be okay.

What do you need to say NO to?

____

____

CHECK IN ON HOW YOU INVEST YOUR TIME

DECEMBER 10

PERFECTION IS A DOUBLE-EDGED SWORD

Top performers in any field often display some sort of perfectionist tendencies. You have to have a desire for perfection to do the work necessary to be successful. Being a perfectionist can provide motivation as long as you are having success.

When you get to a certain level, that perfectionism becomes a double-edged sword.

While it drives you to be your best and provides motivation, perfectionism will become a constant critic that screams you are never good enough and zaps you of your confidence.

As the competition gets stiffer, you must move from a place of perfection to a place of excellence. Excellence is being able to take the necessary risk where you might make a mistake but get back up off the ground and continue to fight, while the perfectionist tries not to make any mistakes.

Excellence is playing to win. Perfection is playing not to lose.

PLAY TO WIN!

Where in your life can you move from a place of perfection into excellence, and learn to forgive yourself for not being perfect and get up off the mat and keep fighting?

____

____

____

FOCUS ON EXCELLENCE, NOT PERFECTION

DECEMBER 11

DO YOU KNOW YOUR BOGEYMAN?

Statistics show that pro golfers putt more accurately when putting for par than when putting for birdie. Birdie is one stroke lower or better than par and bogey is one stroke over par.

Golfers fear the bogey more than they desire the birdie.

In 2009, Pope and Schweitzer, professors at the University of Pennsylvania Wharton School of Business, gathered data from 239 tournaments between 2004 and 2009. They concentrated on 2.5 million putts attempted by 421 professional golfers who each made at least 1,000 putts.

The Bogeyman, fear of missing the putt, costs the average professional golfer about one stroke during a 72-hole tournament.

For the top 20 professional golfers, that translates to a combined loss of approximately $1.2 million in prize money a year.

What are the metaphorical putts in your life that you must make to give yourself the best chance for success?

____

____

A PUTT IS A PUTT - KEEP IT SIMPLE

DECEMBER 12

TAKE ACTION

My high school football coach always told us that it is better to have one player take action than to have 99 standing around talking about taking action.

He also would say that knowledge without action is useless.

There are many people who know what to do, but do not do what they know; thus, they are no better off than the people who don't know what to do.

Taking action is not always easy, but it is always necessary. You don't have to be great to get started, but you do have to get started to be great.

What are you waiting for?

____

What are the excuses you are making that are keeping you from getting started?

____

Knowledge minus Action equals Nothing.

K-A=O

DECEMBER 13

THREE A DAY KEEPS FAILURE AWAY

One of the best ways to assure your long-term success is to recognize and celebrate your daily wins.

Each night before you go to bed, or at a specific time of the day, take out your iPhone notes page or an index card and write down three wins you had today.

Your thoughts determine your actions, your actions determine your performance, and your performance determines your destiny and what you will or will not accomplish.

By celebrating your wins each day, you build off of your previous success and can see your progress on a daily basis, which adds up over time to great success.

THREE WINS IN THE LAST 24 HOURS:

1. ____

____

2. ____

____

3. ____

____

DECEMBER 14

THE LAW OF ACCUMULATION

Small things turn into big things. Mosquitos do more damage to human beings than elephants each year. The small crack in the foundation of your home will cause it to crumble if not addressed early on.

John Brubaker, my friend and author of *The Coach Approach: Success Strategies From The Locker Room To The Board Room,* says:

Great accomplishments in any individual's career are the result of cumulative effects of hundreds of thousands of smaller activities, sacrifices and achievements behind the scenes that combine to create the finished product.

Yesterday you were to write down three wins; did you do it? If not, what are you waiting for? If yes, do it again.

1. ____

____

2. ____

____

3. ____

____

DECEMBER 15

FAILURE IS A NECESSARY PART OF SUCCESS

The greatest performers of all time don't see failure as a negative; they see it as an essential part of the success process.

Georges St. Pierre, The Ultimate Fighting Championship Welterweight World Champion, says the best thing that ever happened to him was getting knocked out in the first round as an 11-1 favorite over Matt Serra at UFC 69 because it made him respect and value the preparation process more than ever before in his career.

John Wooden, who won 10-12 NCAA Basketball titles from 1963-1975, did not win a title in his first 15 years at UCLA.

In life, there are winners and learners.

Those that win the most see failure as positive feedback, learn from their losses and use those losses to make themselves stronger.

You are only a loser when you quit or when you stop learning.

What lessons did you learn from a loss today?

____

____

____

____

DECEMBER 16

THE COMPOUND EFFECT OF TAKING A DAY OFF

Doing a little a lot is one of the secrets of success that is intertwined throughout this book.

Successful people realize the value of a single day and have made it part of their routine to do a little a lot vs. a lot a little.

Motivation is not permanent; neither is bathing. In both cases you must do a little each day or you physically and mentally start to stink.

One workday is 20% of your work week. Two workdays a month are 10% of your month.

If you lose two workdays a month, that is the equivalent of losing a month of production each year.

Think about the importance of a day the next time you want to stay home from school or work and just don't "feel" like going.

What can you do today to act differently than how you feel?

____

____

____

TODAY + TODAY = YOUR CAREER

DECEMBER 17

NO EXCUSES

If there is one sign of success that can summarize what it takes to make it to the summit of the Mountain of Excellence, the Montreal Canadians of the National Hockey League have it figured out.

This sign hangs above the door they use to go from the locker room to the ice where, as in life, you must make no excuses if you are going to be the best you can be.

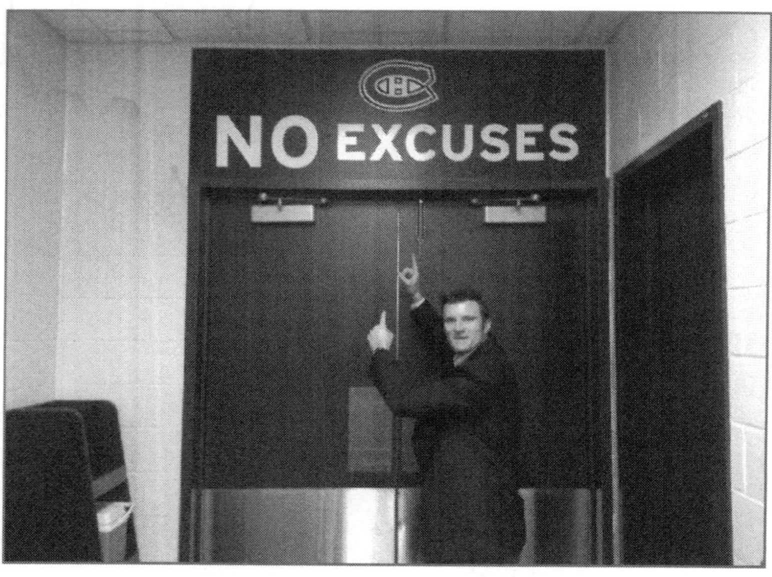

YOU CAN MAKE EXCUSES OR MAKE IT HAPPEN BUT YOU CAN NEVER DO BOTH

DECEMBER 18

PULL FOR EACH OTHER

One of the top coaches in all of college athletics is Mike Bianco, the head baseball coach at The University of Mississippi.

Bianco had his players compete in a series of tug-of-war competitions to see who made the best 8-man team.

When a team won, they hooted and hollered with the energy you would expect from a group of competitive college athletes.

After a "winner" was declared by defeating all other challengers, Bianco asked, "Who was the winner today?"

When they pointed to the "winning" team, he stated, "You are wrong."

"We all lost today," he said. "The only time we win is when we all pull for each other, not pull against each other."

His point was made.

YOU ARE EITHER PULLING FOR OR AGAINST EACH OTHER

DECEMBER 19

PROCESS OVER OUTCOME

To focus on the process is to focus on the aspects of your performance and your life that you can control and that will contribute to your performing the tasks ahead of you in the present moment.

Nick Saban, the head football coach at The University of Alabama, says:

Focus on the process of what it takes to be successful.

It's not the end result. Don't think about winning the SEC Championship.

Don't think about the national championship.

Think about what you needed to do in this drill, on this play, in this moment.

That's the process: Let's think about what we can do today, the task at hand.

Thank you, Coach Saban, for providing us with the process map for success.

WIN THIS PLAY, WIN THIS DAY

DECEMBER 20

WIN THE NEXT PITCH

Dave Serrano is one of eleven coaches to ever lead two programs to the College World Series.

In 2007 he led the University of California, Irvine and then Cal State Fullerton in 2009. Serrano was the head coach for the Team USA Collegiate National Team in 2012 and is respected as one of the best in the business.

When he took over at Tennessee in 2009, one of his first missions was to put a focus on the process and on winning the next pitch.

Learn from the message on the sign that was posted at a local gas station upon his hiring.

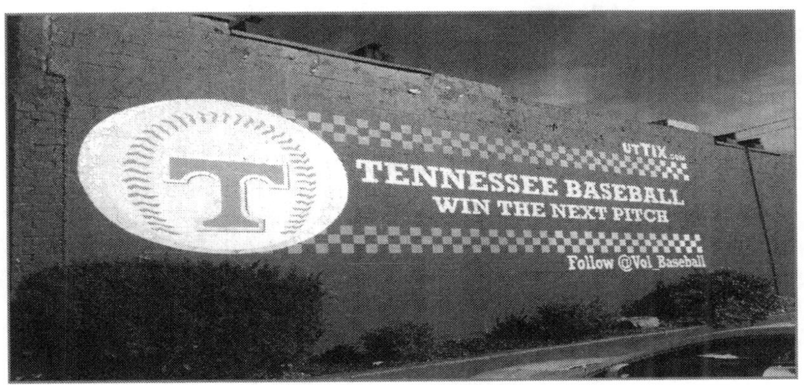

TENNESSEE BASEBALL
WIN THE NEXT PITCH

DECEMBER 21

THE GOLDILOCKS THEORY

Goldilocks knew one thing: that you have got to get it "just right."

What we must learn from Goldilocks is that if you want to lead people and you want to be a person of influence that can motivate others, you must learn to ask the "just right" questions.

If you ask questions that are too hard, those who you lead get frustrated and quit. If you ask too easy of a question, those who you lead become less motivated because they know the answer without much effort.

To lead and motivate you must ask just the right questions. The best coaches I have been around are the best question askers. They ask and get those who they lead to think for themselves and come up with the answer, thus empowering them to self-coach - a key step on the path to the summit of the Mountain of Excellence.

DECEMBER 22

CONSISTENCY WINS

Consistency is the name of the game when looking at the difference between good and great.

To be great you must perform at your best on a consistent basis. Day in and day out you produce with the same level of effectiveness and proficiency.

Anyone can be a flash in the pan and have a great day. The great ones have great days all the time.

You must give of yourself and give your best self to everything you do every day.

99% is never good enough. If it were, 22,000 checks would be deducted from the wrong accounts in the next hour and 12 babies would go home with the wrong parents today.

Routines help you to establish consistency.

Do you start and end your day with the same "bookend" routines?

This is the foundation of consistency.

ROUTINES LEAD TO CONSISTENCY

DECEMBER 23

GROWING OR DYING

You are either growing or you are dying; there can never be time when you are maintaining.

When you try to maintain, you are dying. You must always be growing and taking steps towards the summit of the Mountain of Excellence.

Growing does not always mean you are working. Sometimes we must stop work and remove ourselves from the day-to-day grind and routine to see life from a different perspective.

That is growth.

Taking a vacation with the family is growth if you are able to stay present.

Investing time with loved ones and giving them your presence is growth; spending time with them while you are on your cell phone is dying.

You must always be growing and sharpening your knives in your drawers at the office and at home. If you have sharp blades at work and dull blades at home, you are dying.

DO YOU HAVE A MAINTENANCE MENTALITY OR A GROWTH MINDSET?

DECEMBER 24

HARD WORK

Alabama football coach Nick Saban is one of the best coaches of all time.

He knows that the secret to success is sustained, hard work on the process. Saban said:

I'm tired of hearing all this talk from people who don't understand the process of hard work—like little kids in the back seat asking "Are we there yet?" Get where you're going 1 mile-marker at a time.

Whether it is one mile at a time or 200 feet at a time, what are you doing today to help you get to where you want to be tomorrow?

Steve Jobs, the late CEO of Apple said, *"The journey is the reward, the destination is the disease."*

What mountain are you climbing today?

____

What is the destination that most often distracts you from the journey and the day-to-day commitment to excellence necessary to get there?

____

____

THE JOURNEY IS THE REWARD

DECEMBER 25

THE GREATEST GIFT YOU CAN GIVE

The greatest gift anyone can give you is their time. Time is more valuable than any monetary or material gift that can be given. If you disagree with that statement, just try not having any more time to give and you will quickly realize the importance of this moment, of this day.

In your life, there are places where you can invest more time and get a greater return on your investment. Where will you invest that time?

DECEMBER 26

FAILURE IS POSITIVE FEEDBACK

Any time you fail, you can do one of a few things:

1. Get encouraged or discouraged.
2. Get turned on or turned off.
3. Get frustrated or fascinated.
4. Think that you have to or that you want to.
5. Get bitter or get better.

Failure is never final and failure is never fatal. Failure is a necessary step on the road to the summit of the Mountain of Excellence.

In life there are winners and learners, and the only time you are a loser is when you quit.

Having worked with some of the best athletes on the planet, I can tell you that they are not superhuman - but they are super in their human commitment to excellence.

To be super, you must accept failure as positive feedback.

FEEDBACK IS THE BREAKFAST OF CHAMPIONS

DECEMBER 27

ONE STEP AT A TIME

To arrive at your final destination, you must go one step at a time. You cannot get from A to Z by passing up B.

The best coaches I have worked with don't mention winning titles or championships.

They know that the way to win a championship is to concentrate on what you're doing today and try to build on that tomorrow.

End-result thinking is a trap. Resist the sexy temptation to think about winning the conference or national championship.

Instead, think about what you need to do in this drill, on this play, in this moment.

That's the process, a focus on what we can do today, the task at hand.

Great coaches motivate players and help them be successful not by talking about results, but by setting the goal to DOMINATE The Day!

What is your DOMINATE The Day goal for today?

____

____

____

____

____

DECEMBER 28

IT IS THE START THAT STOPS MOST PEOPLE

You don't have to be great to start, but to be great you have to get started.

It is often the start that stops most people from getting going.

I have known a lot of people that never got started because they looked at the top of the mountain or the end of the project and said, "NO WAY - that mountain is too big."

Little did they realize that all they had to do to get started was take the first step.

Success is a lot like a merry-go-round.

Breaking inertia and getting going can be the hardest part.

Once you get going and you have momentum, it gets easier and easier.

Remember when you were a kid and you had to have someone really push hard to get you going on the merry-go-round? Once you got going, it was smooth sailing and you could push that merry-go-round with a finger.

Success is the same way.

Get going and get that merry-go-round spinning. Surround yourself with energy givers who have the same goals you do and watch what a little momentum on your side will do for you.

What will you do today to get the momentum you need going in your direction?

____

____

____

____

____

____

____

____

____

DECEMBER 29

PREDICT YOUR SUCCESS

Predicting your success by creating a vision in your mind of what it is you want to accomplish and who you want to become is a critical part of setting yourself on that path to success.

Visualizing your success well in advance and creating your future in your mind is a fundamental of greatness.

Colin Kaepernick, quarterback for the San Francisco 49ers, came off the bench to earn the starting position during the 2012 season.

During a game in which Kaepernick led the 49ers to a 41-34 win over the New England Patriots, NBC flashed a letter that he wrote to himself when he was in the fourth grade.

Kaepernick is achieving and living his career aspirations.

His path to excellence started the day he set his mind on his goal.

Your mind is like a goal-seeking missile. Are you focusing on what you DO want or what you DON'T want?

You will never outperform your self-image.

All great accomplishments happen in the mind before they ever happen with the body.

Thoughts become things.

What you visualize with all of your mind, heart and soul you are destined to become.

Your opportunity is going to come. It may be today, it may be tomorrow, it may be next month. The question is this: Are you waiting for your opportunity to visualize and prepare for success, or are you going to visualize and prepare for your success so that when the opportunity arises you are ready?

GREATNESS STARTS IN THE MIND
VISUALIZE AND PREPARE FOR YOUR FUTURE

I'm 5ft 2inches 91 pounds. Good athelet.
I think in 7 years I will be between
6ft - to 6ft 4inches 140 pounds. I hope
I go to a good college in [illegible]
Then go to the pros and play
on the niners or the packers even if
they aren't good in seven years.
My Friend are Jason, Kyler, Leo,
Spencer, Mark and Jacob

Sincerly
Colin

DECEMBER 30

SEE TOMORROW'S HEADLINES TODAY

One of the best ways to assure that you live your life with integrity is to constantly ask yourself this question: If what I am about to do were going to be on the headlines of tomorrow's paper, would I do that today?

With all of the pressure and temptation in today's society, especially around college athletes, to think about the ramifications of your decision before you act is critical.

Successful people face temptation and pressure just like you and I.

What they are able to do that unsuccessful people are not able to do is put off what they want in the moment for what they want most.

By being able to say no and walk away, you live to fight another day.

Putting off the temptation of the moment for what you want most is a true sign of integrity and mental toughness.

What do you need to put off in this moment to get what you want most?

____

____

PUT OFF WHAT YOU WANT IN THE MOMENT FOR WHAT YOU WANT MOST

DECEMBER 31

SUCCESS IS CAUGHT, NOT TAUGHT

John C. Maxwell is one of the foremost authorities on leadership in the world. In his great book *The 21 Irrefutable Laws of Leadership,* he states that the most valuable gift you can give is being a good example.

Setting the example that you want for others is a foundation of success.

Baylor baseball coach Steve Smith says people need a model to see more than they need a motto to say.

A motto is only as strong as the character of the person saying it.

Norman Vincent Peale, author of *The Power of Positive Thinking,* says, *"Nothing is more confusing than people who give good advice but set a bad example."*

Nothing is more powerful than being a person who gives great advice and sets a great example.

TODAY - DWYSYWD
DO WHAT YOU SAID YOU WOULD DO
START READING THIS BOOK AGAIN TOMORROW
REPETITION IS THE MOTHER OF ACQUISITION
THANK YOU FOR JOINING ME ON
THE JOURNEY TO EXCELLENCE
PERFORM YOUR BEST TODAY, EVERY DAY!

WHO IS BRIAN CAIN?

About The Master of The Mental Game

Brian M. Cain, MS, CMAA, is the #1 best-selling author of *Toilets, Bricks, Fish Hooks and PRIDE: The Peak Performance Toolbox EXPOSED* and *So What, Next Pitch! How To Play Your Best When It Means The Most* and *The Mental Conditioning Manual: Your Blueprint For Excellence.*

An expert in the areas of Mental Conditioning, Peak Performance Coaching, and Applied Sport Psychology, Cain has worked with coaches, athletes, and teams in the Olympics, the National Football League (NFL), National Basketball Association (NBA), National Hockey League (NHL), Ultimate Fighting Championship (UFC), and Major League Baseball

(MLB) on using mental conditioning to perform at their best when it means the most.

Cain has also worked with programs in some of the top college athletic departments around the country, including Vanderbilt University, the University of Alabama, Auburn University, the University of Tennessee, the University of Mississippi, Mississippi State University, Florida State University, the University of Iowa, the University of Michigan, the University of Maryland, Oregon State University, the University of Southern California, Washington State University, Texas Christian University, Texas A & M University, Baylor University, The University of Houston, Coastal Carolina University, Yale University, and many others.

Cain has worked as a mental conditioning consultant with numerous high school state, NCAA national, and professional world championship winning teams and programs. He has delivered his award-winning seminars and presentations at coaches' clinics, leadership summits, and conventions all over the globe. As a former director of athletics, he is one of the youngest ever to receive the designation of Certified Master Athletic Administrator from the National Interscholastic Athletic Administrators Association.

A highly sought-after coach, clinician, and speaker, Cain delivers his message with passion, enthusiasm, and in an engaging style that keeps his audiences energized while being educated. Someone who lives what he teaches, Cain will inspire you and give you the tools necessary to get the most out of your career.

Find out when Cain will be coming to your area by visiting his calendar at www.briancain.com.

HOW YOU CAN BECOME A MASTER OF THE MENTAL GAME

Cain offers a range of training materials to get you or your team to the top of your game. Available at www.BrianCain.com

MASTERS OF THE MENTAL GAME SERIES BOOKS

Champions Tell All: Inexpensive Experience From The Worlds Best

Cain provides you with all access to some of the World's greatest performers. Learn from mixed martial arts world champions and college All-Americans about mental toughness.

The Daily Dominator: Perform Your Best Today. Every Day!

You get 366 Daily Mental Conditioning lessons to help you start your day down the path to excellence. Investing time each day with Cain is your best way to become your best self.

The Mental Conditioning Manual: Your Blueprint For Excellence

This is the exact system Cain uses to build champions and masters of the mental game and has helped produce NCAA and High School, champions, MMA world champions, and more.

So What, Next Pitch: How To Play Your Best When It Means The Most

A compilation of interviews with top coaches and players where Cain teaches you their systems and tricks. Learn from the insights of these masters of the mental game.

Toilets Bricks Fish Hooks and PRIDE: The Peak Performance Toolbox EXPOSED

Go inside the most successful programs in the country that use Cain's Peak Performance System. Use this book to unlock your potential and learn to play your best when it means the most.

PEAK PERFORMANCE TRAINING TOOLS

The Peak Performance System: (P.R.I.D.E.) Personal Responsibility In Daily Excellence

This big, video-based training program is Cain's signature training program for coaches, athletes and teams. It will take you step by step to the top of the performance mountain.

Diamond Domination Training : The New 4RIP3 System for Baseball and Softball

This training program is being used by 11 teams in the NCAA top 25 in college baseball and 8 of the top 25 in college softball. It will help you and your team to unlock your potential and play the best baseball and softball of your life.

4RIP3 MMA Mental Conditioning System

Get the techniques used by the best fighters in the world to and start bringing the fighter you are in the gym into the cage. It will help you unlock your potential, teach you drills to sharpen your focus and give you the confidence of a champion

The Peak Performance Boot Camp

This introductory program will give you the tools, power, and mental toughness you need to be prepared for every game, every play, and every minute. Learn techniques to get the absolute best chance of maximizing your potential and getting the most out of your ability.

And more at www.BrianCain.com/products

"Cain has tapped into the mental side of performance like no one ever has."

Tom Murphy
President, The Fitness Zone Gym

"This is your blueprint for making excellence a lifestyle not an event."

Jim Schlossnagle

2010 National College Baseball Coach of The Year

"Cain's books, DVDs and audio programs will give you a formula for success between the ears."

Bob Tewksbury
Sport Psychology Consultant, Boston Red Sox

"If you make one investment in coaching excellence and impacting the lives of the youth you lead, this is the program you want to follow."

Clay Chournous
High School Football and Baseball Coach, Bear River H.S.

"This will not only help you on the field, it will help you in life."

Nate Yeskie
Assistant Baseball Coach, Oregon State University

"Brian Cain will give you and your team a system for playing at your best when it means the most."

Todd Whitting
Head Baseball Coach, Univ. of Houston

"This was the best presentation I have seen in all of my clinics/ conventions I have attended over the years. OUTSTANDING!!!"

Michelle Daddona
Riverside Community College

"The information you get from Brian is the highest quality and can benefit a team, an athletic department and coaches of all experience levels."

Bill Gray
Missouri Southern State University

CONNECT WITH CAIN

Your link to doing a little a lot, not a lot a little

twitter.com/briancainpeak
facebook.com/briancainpeak
linkedin.com/in/briancainpeak
youtube.com/wwwbriancaincom
briancain.com/podcast

SIGN UP FOR THE PEAK PERFORMANCE NEWSLETTER

Cain's newsletter is full of information to help you unlock your potential and perform at your best when it means the most. Subscribe for free and get a bonus audio training.
www.BrianCain.com/newsletter

VISIT CAIN ON THE WEB

www.BrianCain.com

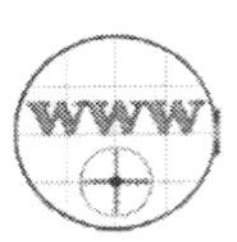

Remember to go to www.BrianCain.com/experience for all the BONUS Mental Conditioning material mentioned in this book.

NOTES:

NOTES:

NOTES:

NOTES:

NOTES:

Made in the USA
San Bernardino, CA
05 July 2016